# Up Close *and* Personal

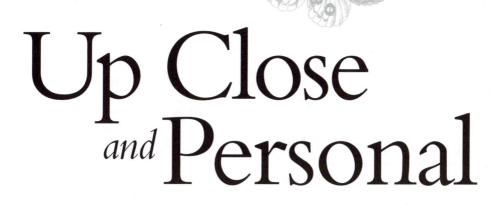

# Up Close
## *and* Personal

### The Teaching and Learning of Narrative Research

*Edited by*
**Ruthellen Josselson, Amia Lieblich,
and Dan P. McAdams**

American Psychological Association
*Washington, DC*

Published by
American Psychological Association
750 First Street, NE
Washington, DC 20002
www.apa.org

To order
APA Order Department
P.O. Box 92984
Washington, DC 20090-2984
Tel: (800) 374-2721
Direct: (202) 336-5510
Fax: (202) 336-5502
TDD/TTY: (202) 336-6123
Online: www.apa.org/books/
Email: order@apa.org

In the U.K., Europe, Africa, and the Middle East, copies may be ordered from
American Psychological Association
3 Henrietta Street
Covent Garden, London
WC2E 8LU England

Typeset in Goudy by World Composition Services, Inc., Sterling, VA

Printer: Data Reproductions, Auburn Hills, MI
Cover designer: Naylor Design, Washington, DC
Project Manager: Debbie Hardin, Carlsbad, CA

The opinions and statements are the responsibility of the authors, and such opinions and statements do not necessarily represent the policies of the American Psychological Association.

**Library of Congress Cataloging-in-Publication Data**

Up close and personal : the teaching and learning of narrative research / edited by
  Ruthellen Josselson, Amia Lieblich, Dan P. McAdams.
      p. cm. — (The narrative study of lives)
    Includes bibliographical references and index.
    ISBN 1-55798-940-0 (alk. paper)
    1. Narration (Rhetoric)  2. Autobiography.  I. Josselson, Ruthellen.  II. Lieblich,
  Amia, 1939–     III. McAdams, Dan P.  IV. Series.
  PN212.U68 2002
  808–dc21                                                              2002067565

**British Library Cataloguing-in-Publication Data**
A CIP record is available from the British Library.

*Printed in the United States of America*
*First Edition*

# CONTENTS

# ACKNOWLEDGMENTS

The editors would like to thank the many people who reviewed manuscripts and provided substantive input for this volume. In particular, we offer our thanks to Marla Arvay, Norman Denzin, Alan Elms, Gelya Frank, Hubert Hermans, Vince Hevern, Catherine Kohler-Riessman, James Marcia, Michael Pratt, June Price, Gabriele Rosenthal, Mac Runyan, and Judith Schoenholtz-Read for their hard work in reviewing manuscripts. We also extend a special thanks to Chris Rector, who served as our editorial assistant for this second volume in the American Psychological Association series *The Narrative Study of Lives*. Finally, we wish to thank Jeanne M. Foley and the Foley Center for the Study of Lives for their generous support of our book series and for establishing the Foley Center for the Study of Lives at Northwestern University.

## THE NARRATIVE STUDY OF LIVES ADVISORY BOARD

Gil Herdt, Anthropology, *San Francisco State University*
Hubert Hermans, Psychology, *University of Nijmegen, The Netherlands*
James E. Marcia, Psychology, *Simon Fraser University*
Jean Baker Miller, Psychoanalysis, *Stone Center, Wellesley College*
Elliot Mishler, Psychiatry, *Cambridge Hospital*
Richard L. Ochberg, *Boston, Massachusetts*
June H. Price, Nursing, *Farleigh Dickinson University*
Gabriele Rosenthal, Sociology, *Gesamthochschule Kassel, Germany*
George C. Rosenwald, Psychology, *University of Michigan*
William McKinley Runyan, School of Social Service, *University of California at Berkeley*
Abigail J. Stewart, Psychology and Women's Studies, *University of Michigan*
George E. Vaillant, Psychiatry, *Dartmouth Medical Center*
Guy Widdershoven, Philosophy, *University of Limburg, The Netherlands*

# CONTRIBUTORS

**James William Anderson**, Northwestern University, Chicago, IL
**Susan E. Chase**, University of Tulsa, Tulsa, OK
**Blythe McVicker Clinchy**, Wellesley College, Wellesley, MA
**Colette Daiute**, City University of New York, New York
**Sara N. Davis**, Rosemont College, Rosemont, PA
**Margot Ely**, New York University, New York
**Michelle Fine**, City University of New York, New York
**Mary Gergen**, Pennsylvania State University, Media
**Henry Greenspan**, University of Michigan, Ann Arbor
**Ruthellen Josselson**, Fielding Institute, Baltimore, MD, and
　　　Hebrew University of Jerusalem, Israel
**Amia Lieblich**, Hebrew University of Jerusalem, Israel
**Richard Ochberg**, Boston, MA
**Suzanne C. Ouellette**, City University of New York, New York
**Annie G. Rogers**, Harvard University, Cambridge, MA
**George C. Rosenwald**, University of Michigan, Ann Arbor
**William Todd Schultz**, Pacific University, Forest Grove, OR
**Steven Weiland**, Michigan State University, East Lansing

# Up Close *and* Personal

# INTRODUCTION

Research based on studying whole persons in context and in time through the narratives of their experience is enjoying a renaissance across the social sciences. In considering people as constuctors of their experience, such research takes a giant step away from parsing human experience into predefined "variables" and requires of the researcher an equally major shift in perspective and approach. Rather than forming hypotheses, the researcher frames questions for exploration; in place of measurement are the challenges of deeply listening to others; and instead of statistics are the ambiguities of thoughtful analysis of texts. These shifts in task and epistemological foundation require a new set of skills of the researcher and raise important questions about how such skills are learned and taught.

Similar to the Moliere character who discovered that he had been speaking prose for the past 40 years, I discovered several years ago that I had been doing a form of "grounded theory" (Strauss & Corbin, 1990) for 30. I learned to do narrative research by adapting the skills I had acquired as a clinical psychologist to the interpretive study of normal populations and was much influenced by the personologists of the mid-twentieth century who seemed to me in their writings to be doing much the same thing.

None of us now teaching narrative research were ever ourselves "taught" how to do it—and this "us" includes we who have edited this volume and those who have written for it and, we suspect, most of those who are today offering narrative or qualitative research[1] courses in psychology and the social sciences. We all learned it "on the road," learned it while doing it—and we are still learning it. Yet we are teaching it, with no internalized teacher models from our experience to guide us. Each of us, on

---

[1] Throughout this book, we are using the terms *qualitative* and *narrative* research somewhat interchangeably, as tends to be the current mode in the social sciences. Narrative research is a subcategory of qualitative research. By qualitative research we mean research that is inherently inductive and rooted in phenomenological or hermeneutic forms of inquiry.

our own, has grappled with the dilemmas of initiating students into an approach to research that seems often heretical to those reared in a positivistic, scientistic atmosphere. Students come to narrative and qualitative research courses because they are intrigued by the possibility of studying lives in a closer and more personal way, of trying to wrestle with the mysteries of whole lives, lives in progress, including, either overtly or covertly, their own lives and the lives of people close to them. Often, it is student demand that accounts for the proliferation of narrative research courses in our institutions of higher learning. But generally students are surprised by what this approach involves and worry that what actually occurs is not quite kosher by the orthodoxy they have learned elsewhere.

This second volume of the American Psychological Association *Narrative Study of Lives* series is intended for those who teach and learn narrative research (or might wish to do so). This volume is "up close and personal" in a number of ways. First of all, narrative research is up close and personal in that it involves in-depth study of particular individuals in social context and in time. Second, teaching this work is similarly intensive and person-centered; the mode of inquiry requires a highly sensitized and self-reflective inquirer rather than a set of objective, impersonal skills—and the usual technique-based pedagogy is not useful here. Third, we asked the contributors to this volume to let readers come in close, in a personal way, to what they do and think, which for many has involved telling as well about their own biography and path to doing and teaching narrative research.

While the study of lives was a major force in the early period of psychology, led by such giants as Henry Murray, Gordon Allport, Robert White, and Erik Erikson, this form of research was largely swept aside by the tidal wave of behaviorism. But it has been revived recently, in psychology as well as sociology, education, nursing, and other human science fields. Courses in life history and narrative research are proliferating and many departments are hard-pressed to find people experienced enough to teach them.

There are many books that purport to detail how to *do* qualitative/ narrative research, but none that tell us how to teach it. (One way not to teach it effectively is to try to follow a "methods" text telling students how to do it.) Neither the doing nor the teaching of narrative research is linear. It is inherently an inductive process that involves shaping the instrument of research, the researcher, as a medium for the discovery and interpretation of meanings. In talking about how to teach narrative research, we find that we end up discussing the essential principles of what constitutes the work itself.

This volume represents an effort to gather the collective wisdom of those who have been feeling their way through the dilemmas of teaching narrative research at both the graduate and undergraduate levels. We have invited senior professors who are well-known for their published narrative research to reflect on what they have learned about teaching these matters—what dilemmas they have encountered, how they have understood them, and what they have undertaken to resolve them. The result is a fascinating set of reflections that shed as much light on the doing of narrative research as on the teaching of it. Therefore, we believe that students will find these papers illuminating about, paradoxically, how to *do* narrative research.

This is not a book about method—that is, in any case, a word I have recently banned from my narrative research vocabulary. The word "method" suggests to me (and, I fear, to my students) something much too formulaic and procedural for something as inductive and creative as narrative approaches to inquiry. And this may indicate one of the first dilemmas of teaching about narrative research. Students come hoping to be told what to do; we, as teachers, however, are (or ought to be) bent on teaching them a new way to think. Narrative research is, in Clifford Geertz's phrase, a "mixed genre," marrying science and the humanities, integrating systematic study of phenomena with literary deconstruction of texts and hermeneutic analyses of meaning.

It is thinking and approach that are critical matters in narrative research. Our task as researchers is to raise questions about the phenomena and ever more probing questions about what it is we are doing—questions about standpoint, about the role of the researcher, about how we know something about another person and what it may mean. These are unsettling questions—and, for seasoned researchers, the more unsettling the better. But for students, raising these questions raises intense anxiety (in teachers as well as students), especially when the questions have no straightforward answers. Our task as teachers is to empower our students as knowers, to support inquiry, to suggest conceptual frames and penetrating analytic lenses—and this, of course, parallels the process of narrative inquiry itself. But we can only do so if we, as teachers, are supported by a community of others who share our viewpoints and purposes.

Those of us who teach narrative research are aware of the radical nature of what we are attempting. Our students have previously been rewarded for objectivity and distance, but we urge them to immerse themselves in a phenomenon and to reflect on how who they are influences what they are able to see. Our students have previously learned that those who can interpret and theorize quickly are regarded as the smart ones; we, on the other hand, want them to hold off on the rush to theory until they can get the phenomena more clearly and deeply in view. In addition, we ask our students to interpret the lives of others when we acknowledge that they will never get an undistorted view or even a view that someone else would necessarily obtain. We also urge our students to learn to imagine and think inductively when they have previously sworn allegiance to airtight planning in research design.

Then, most heretical of all, we ask our students to write up their work the way they really did it, owning their role as knowers in an "I" voice, when they may have been cautioned by publication outlets and gatekeepers to stick to traditional formats normed on quantitative or deductive designs.[2]

In response to my efforts to open my students to new ways of approaching and analyzing narrative forms of human experience (and most of human experience *is* constructed narratively), one of my students, in some frustration, demanded to know, "But what do you think is *bad* narrative research?" I found this question no easier to answer simply than it was to define once and for all what is good narrative research. Underlying the question, of course, is the question, How do I know when what I am doing is right? We find ourselves, as teachers, often in the quagmire of guiding students through territory that is, and must to some extent remain, uncharted. Narrative research at its best is always a voyage of discovery.

All of the contributors to this volume have created personal roadmaps that they use to mentor their students. We have asked master narrative researchers who also teach narrative research courses to write in a personal, even autobiographical voice—to do in print what narrative research professors talk about when they come together and compare notes with one another. What does it mean to learn/study/teach this work? is the question we wanted to explore together and to share the reflections with our readers.

To be sure, postmodernism is often taken for granted as an epistemological framework in narrative research, but our authors are at various points along the modernist–postmodern continuum. Although we do not reflect directly on epistemological disputes (see Denzin & Lincoln, 2001, for a fuller discussion), these are always beneath the surface as we discuss our work and implicit in everything we teach.

We have ordered these papers in a quasi-narrative fashion so they tell an unfolding story. But it is a postmodern story in that many of the issues double back on one another as the authors discuss related concerns, differently contextualized. The organization of the book moves roughly from the general to the specific and back to the more general. Many authors in reflecting on the essence of teaching narrative research find that this is best communicated by metaphor or example.

As most of the contributions are personal, evocative pieces, they are no more easily "summarized" than a poem—or a life. We can say what we found particularly meaningful in them, and why we chose them for this volume, but undoubtedly readers will find their own, different nodes of illumination within and among these essays.

---

[2] I am indebted to Mark Chessler and Judith Lynch-Sauer for conceptualizing some of these oppositions.

Suzanne C. Ouellette details in an inspiring way how lessons from her painting classes helped her understand the processes of teaching narrative research. She draws illuminating parallels between learning to paint and learning to do narrative research—and I have been struck by how meaningful her paper has been to my students who have read it in draft form. Unlike the linearity of hypothesis-testing research, narrative research involves what Ouellette describes as working simultaneously on all four quadrants of a blocked-out painting. The actual doing of narrative research requires recursive exploration until a whole image emerges—procedure, theory, results, and conceptualization forming a meaningful Gestalt. Similar to painting, it also requires inspiration, passion, and conviction—and we, as teachers, must nurture these in our students.

Blythe McVicker Clinchy describes her intellectual path to narrative research and draws on the developmental theory she and others presented in *Women's Ways of Knowing* (Belenky, Clinchy, Goldberger, & Tarule, 1986/1997) to understand the differing capacities students bring to learning narrative research. The processes of understanding others' meanings and seeing the world from another's perspective are different for the separate, the subjective and the connected knower and require different responses from the teacher. She details how this framework might inform pedagogy and practice in classes about narrative research and shares her experiences in creating a course based on connected knowing.

Annie G. Rogers also begins with stories of her intellectual journey as a way of portraying the particularities of a narrative point of view. She ends by considering the issues of teaching qualitative research within traditional research environments. In contrast to quantitative approaches that value researcher facelessness and distance, in qualitative research, "One aspires to be influenced and changed by the process, and to grapple actively with the intersubjective nature of understandings gleaned from complicated social relationships." Rogers details the pitfalls inherent in all aspects of mentoring this process, from the genesis of the research idea to the writing of the research report, and offers both students and teachers lucid and detailed ideas about approaching and evaluating such research.

Colette Daiute and Michelle Fine, who together teach a course in qualitative methods, detail how they use narrative theory to develop in their students what they term "a qualitative stance." This involves operating from a highly particular critical epistemological position in relation to the questions asked, materials collected, practices of analysis and interpretation, and process of writing. These authors recognize the balance between courage and anxiety that students must employ in order to arrive at this stance. In their approach to teaching, narrative research is construed as an opportunity to learn, not prove oneself correct, and the elusive nature of "truths" is offered as a pleasure rather than a frustration. In their chapter, Daiute and

Fine present the thorny questions students ask and how they, as teachers, approach their exploration.

In narrative research, interviewing, listening, and interpretation do not occur separately but interact with and merge into each other, as many of the authors of these chapters point out. Still, all successful interview-based research is grounded in good listening, which is rarely taught with enough depth and care. And listening is a first step in the process of interpretation, which itself involves artistry, both in its practice and in teaching. The next two chapters focus on specific approaches to teaching and thinking about issues of listening, drawing on the authors' own research for examples.

In her contribution, Susan E. Chase stresses the need for listening well in interview-based research and discusses the ways in which knowledge of the processes of narrative analysis recursively shapes the capacity to listen. "When we listen carefully to the stories people tell, we learn how people as individuals and as groups make sense of their experiences and construct meanings and selves," writes Chase. Thus, people's narratives reflect not only their own meaning-making but the themes of the society or culture in which they live. In a manner that will be highly useful to both students and teachers, Chase offers lively details about how her course teaches students to use the principles of narrative analysis to ground their interviewing practice.

Henry Greenspan is also concerned with issues of listening. Years of listening to Holocaust survivors recount their experiences has taught him how intricate this process can be. An example interview fragment he presents to his class serves as a way of demonstrating how he raises and addresses questions about the process and meanings of memory, retelling, and the role of narrative in an individual life. This model also serves to highlight the enigmas of critical listening and the fragility of human communication in general.

As narrative researchers, once we think we have obtained the "raw data" of human experience, the next formidable hurdle is that of interpretation. As many of these authors stress, though, moving from "the story" to a compelling and intellectually satisfying analysis of it requires finesse, imagination, and discipline on the part of the student as well as experienced researchers. Teaching others about interpretation is, however, itself an art.

Richard Ochberg takes a microscopic look at teaching interpretation. Beginning with his discovery of the impossibility of writing a "rulebook" for this process, he describes how he uses Thematic Apperception Test (TAT) stories to arrive at clusters of meanings. What he aims to teach his students is that meaning comes from *how* a narrative is constructed, not just its content. In addition, Ochberg reflects on the nature of interpretation itself and how it is shaped by the standpoint and goals of the interpreter. Throughout, Ochberg engages us in the conversations he has with his students and offers a close reading of a text that students could use as a model.

George C. Rosenwald explores the pedagogical strategies necessary for the project of trying to make psychobiographical sense of an individual life. Although students often approach this task with great enthusiasm, the actual analysis of a life presents rather daunting challenges. Cultural values that highlight adaptation as a source of motivation often blind students to the subjectivities that shape a life. Why, for example, was Emily Dickinson shy—and what would constitute a satisfactory explanation? Rosenwald offers a thoughtful analysis of culturally based resistances that students must overcome when trying to analyze a life, and he demonstrates how students can be helped to view lives in complex, internal, and multidetermined ways.

Trying to understand life experiences of others with regard to individually specific meanings is also a concern of William Todd Schultz. His approach to teaching this material is through the process of identifying "prototypical scenes" in a life. Schultz has found, in his teaching, that these scenes provide an anchoring device and that this approach assists students in orienting themselves to a life history. Schultz offers analyses of such prototypical scenes in the lives of Kathryn Harrison, Jack Kerouac, Franz Kafka, and Sylvia Plath as a way of demonstrating how he and his students identify and analyze a scene that epitomizes and illuminates a life.

Writing about what one has learned through narrative research is a central part of the whole endeavor. Rarely, however, is this activity the focus of active teaching, which means that it is often a formidable hurdle for students.

James William Anderson, in his chapter, details his thinking and decision making as he writes, demonstrating how a psychobiographer actually operates. He approaches the problem of teaching about psychobiography by offering an annotated version of a paper he is writing about the relationship between the brothers Henry and William James. Accompanying this illustrious psychobiographer as he works offers both teachers and students a focused look at the thinking and choices that underlie writing life history.

Steven Weiland offers his ideas about guiding novice scholars toward recognition of the role of writing in their research. He believes that it is their experiences as readers that can inspire and inform their work as authors of narrative. Thus, the art of writing in narrative research rests in wide reading of other scholarship, especially works in which authors have made their narrative strategies relatively transparent. Weiland discusses the innovations found in a number of texts in life history writing as a means of encouraging students to reflect on their own expository and narrative choices.

In her writing, Margot Ely takes seriously what narrative researchers often stress as making the form follow the content. Rather than being a linear piece in academic style, Ely's chapter tries to capture process by interweaving themes to bring interrelationships among experiences into view. Herself open to learning through experience, she gains insight into the similarities between teaching a fifth-grade public school group and teaching her graduate students. Both groups of students thrive when they can be prodded to shake off the fetters they have acquired in their education and to trust their own capacity to know and discover. In her evocatively written article that renders the emotional aspects of teaching this work, Ely gives us a very close-up look at how she teaches (and learns) and offers much detail for others to learn from as well.

Mary Gergen and Sara N. Davis take us behind the scenes of a collaborative research project they carried out and offer a retrospective of their conversations as research collaborators. The questions they asked themselves and each other at each stage of their research and the highlights of their discussions form a template of how investigators develop knowledge in narrative research. Writing from a social constructionist viewpoint, these authors trace the chronicle of their own learning over an extended period of time. In the form of a kind of annotated drama, Gergen and Davis enact what classroom collaboration, stressed by many of our other contributors as a key aspect of learning to do narrative research, might look like. The heart of narrative research, these authors stress, is in how one asks questions—at many levels and throughout the process.

The matter of the evolving nature of narrative research questions, though, can be a thorny one, and never more anxiety-provoking for students than when they must submit a dissertation proposal, especially in more traditional social science departments. Amia Lieblich and I address the ubiquitous problem of students in most graduate departments of psychology trying, like Procrustes, to wrench their narrative research projects into proposal models that are designed for quantitative research. Students contort themselves to address in their dissertation proposals what hypotheses they are testing—when narrative research does not test hypotheses, or they find themselves writing long exegeses on the philosophical foundations of narrative research in hopes of persuading their academic committees that their approach is valid. At their committee meetings, they often have to defend themselves for not knowing at the outset what they will learn from their research or exactly how many participants they will study. In our chapter, we offer a model for proposals for qualitative/narrative research that is based on compatible principles of approach and organization—a model that has already been adopted at a number of universities.

Taken together, then, these papers represent a tour through the emotional and intellectual nitty-gritty of *doing* as well as teaching narrative research. Being pioneers in the teaching of narrative research has clearly been an exhilarating and creative experience for all who have so generously shared here the secrets of their work. We are deeply thankful to them for offering the wisdom of their experience, and we come out of the editorial work on this volume full of new ideas and replenished energy to teach our courses with insight and passion.

We believe that both teachers and students—and those who are considering being teachers or students—of narrative research will be inspired and enlightened by the depth and diversity of the approaches these authors have taken and that the teaching and learning of research that is up close and personal will be strengthened and expanded.

Ruthellen Josselson
In collaboration with Amia Lieblich and Dan P. McAdams

## REFERENCES

Belenky, M., Clinchy, B., Goldberger, N., & Tarule, J. (1986/1997). *Women's ways of knowing: The development of self, voice, and mind.* New York: Basic Books.

Denzin, N. K., & Lincoln, Y. S. (2000). *Handbook of qualitative research* (2nd ed). Thousand Oaks, CA: Sage.

Strauss, A., & Corbin, J. (1990). *Basics of qualitative research: Grounded theory procedures and techniques.* Newbury Park, CA: Sage.

# 1

## PAINTING LESSONS

### SUZANNE C. OUELLETTE

"One trade helps another," says Elijah Tilley about his creation of a farm on land with skills he learned at sea. Although working with graduate students at a university in New York City lacks the rigors of lobstering and plowing in Maine depicted in Jewitt's (1886/1989) classic American story, I identify with the old fisherman's appreciation that knowledge and practices gained in one line of work can be applied in another. For me, it is the trade of painting that helps my trade of teaching. With brush in hand, I gather lessons about psychology. This chapter shares what I learn as a painting student[1] and apply in my advising and collaborative work with graduate students in narrative and other qualitative research projects.

Four lessons depict something of what goes on in the painting studio, experiences that lead me to rethink what I do as a teacher of psychology, and specific practices that I bring from the studio to the classroom and research office. But first, comments on painting clarify what makes it a powerful source of ideas, and comments on qualitative work present why I think there is a special need for lessons among students seeking to do such work. Although most of the points I have drawn from my experiences as a painting student have relevance for all kinds of research, I see a need for special concern about qualitative training.

---

[1] After a very long absence, drawing and painting came back into my life about 10 years ago; it began with drawing classes once a week and has now progressed to painting sessions in the studio at least three times a week. I have studied at the Parsons School of Design and more recently and to more serious ends, the National Academy of Design School of Fine Arts, both in New York City. Watching, listening to, and working with wonderful artists who teach have influenced my teaching, research, and writing practices. Listed in the order in which I met them, my teachers have included Jean Feinberg, Keith Long, Mark LaRiviere, Stephanie DeManuelle, John Silver, Dan Gheno, Anthony Antonios, Sharon Sprung, and Sam Adoquei. There is also a more personal basis for the lessons. Although life's demands prevented him from doing more than an occasional art project at home, my late father, Wildor Ouellette, cleared the way for my brother, Bob, and me to find inspiration, passion, and conviction when we picked up the brush. And when I paint, I know the caring, kind, and sensitive man who was my father paints with me.

# WHY PAINTING?

Every time I paint, there are wonderful moments in which I realize that in painting I am doing exactly what it is I wanted to do when I decided on an academic and research career in psychology. This declaration deserves some unpacking. My decision for psychology rested on my expectation that the work would be primarily about looking with as much awareness as I could muster at people in the world. Personality psychology, in particular, would be about looking as hard and as sensitively as I could for the distinctiveness in individual lives, and then communicating that in a form that would be clear and engaging to others. Having also selected a phenomenological and existential orientation, my texts would tell others as accurately and convincingly as I could how I saw individuals responding to and creating a changing world (Gendlin, 1997). My intention would be to provoke in my readers and listeners the feelings that I felt as I saw what I saw. Part of my job would be to enable others to care about the depth and complexity of human experience, care enough to craft their own responses to it. There were times in which my work as a psychologist researcher met all these expectations. Nonetheless and sadly, there were also times when it did not.

There were professional demands (traveling to conferences, attending meetings, writing administrative reports, worrying about budgets, etc.) that took time that would have been better spent in close and regular contact with the lives I wanted to understand. There were questionnaires that seemed to obscure rather than represent what others thought and felt. For the sake of getting the work funded, there were compromises and short cuts in research design that enabled me to ask questions I thought important but kept me from learning what it was that my research participants thought important to study about their lives. There were reviewers and editors who decided simple summary statistics would be sufficient, and that quotations from the narratives of individual participants and self-reflexive comments on my place in and possible biasing of my research—material closer to the empirical way of knowing I had come to value—wasted precious journal pages. An accumulation of times such as these left me feeling constrained and stifled in my practice of psychology.

So, it was similar to learning again how and why to breathe and see deeply when I took up the paintbrush. There I was, standing in front of a wonderful French landscape with only my palette and easel separating me from what it was I wanted to depict. And I squinted and squinted and used all the strategies my teacher had shared about how to see the big general shapes and the value contrasts. I loved what I was looking at and I felt driven to let others in on the beauty that I was observing. I was nearly overwhelmed by a commitment to get it right. There seemed nothing more important than creating an image that represented the serenity of the hillside, the power of the old trees, the promise of human celebration in the grape-vines, and the caring between the child and older man who worked with the vines. And then there were all of those decisions: Can the shrub be that size if I have decided the tree across the field from it is that big? What color is that sky, really? How can that rock be so dark if it is so far away? Each decision pointed to many others that had to be made and heightened my sense of commitment and responsibility to those whom I was depicting and those who might view my work. For example, having chosen a particular mix of paints for the sky, I then had to make sure that it would work with what else was on my canvas. I was accountable for all of those choices and then turning them into a representation that would enable others to see the world in a new way. No value-free enterprise this! On that very first painting expedition *en plein air*, I found myself feeling and thinking and acting just as I had hoped I would when, as a young freshman in college eager to make the world a better place, I changed my major from political science to psychology. From that moment on, it was clear that painting would remain part of the rest of my life, and that how I felt, thought, and acted as a painter needed to be replicated in the other parts of my life, as psychology researcher, writer, and teacher.

## WHY THE SPECIAL CONCERN WITH STUDENTS IN QUALITATIVE WORK?

In my painting classes, I celebrate that I am learning something and that there is always something more to be learned. With every painting, there is the experience of having gained both a new skill and the awareness of skills yet to be exercised. One painting sets the stage for the next step of learning. This experience strikes me as different from what I sometimes witness in students who work with narrative and other qualitative methods. They worry about both not having the necessary skills to do the research and not being engaged in the process of gaining those skills. They report an experience that includes feeling a personal lack of the needed knowledge; confusion about how to fill the gap; and probably the most troublesome of all to teachers, the worry that the knowledge, the systematic and coherent body of understanding of how to do qualitative research, is not there to be gotten. This kind of not knowing can hinder students at several of the stages of a narrative project. I do not have all students in mind here, nor is it the case that a student who gets stuck at one point will get stuck at others. Nonetheless, there are a sufficient number of less-than-ideal student experiences in qualitative research for those of us who call ourselves teachers to pay attention. Something happens that we would like to see go more smoothly.

What troubles me might stem from what Josselson, in an introduction to the sixth volume of the Sage Publications series on narrative, describes: " . . . the natural wish of students and beginning scholars is for a cookbook of some kind, a manual that will outline stages or steps in conducting a good narrative study—something that will guarantee success if you follow all the rules" (1999, p. ix). The students may be voicing a general problem. Indeed, in an early and very helpful part of his methods book, Alford (1998)[2] depicts a panic and anxiety that characterize every researcher's projects, including the writing of his methods book. Nonetheless, there seems to be something distinctive about the challenges facing the students in training for narrative and other qualitative research, and reason for teachers to craft additional approaches to training.

In a sociology text that is wise about psychological matters, Alford goes on to claim there are actually two kinds of research anxiety. Along with the one that is inevitable and simply to be accepted, there is another that is unquestionably unproductive and must and can be reduced to enable students to do their work. He targets for change the anxiety that comes from not having what he calls "a working vocabulary" for social inquiry, a vocabulary that is practiced and recognized by a community of scholars (cf. Booth, Colomb, & Williams, 1995). It is this vocabulary, and not the cookbook that Josselson understandably wants to avoid, that I think my students trying to do narrative and other qualitative work are looking for. Painting has provided me a new language. Through painting, I am learning new words and phrases and ways of putting them into action that I think will work for psychology. It is those that I want to share.

## LESSON 1: PUT DOWN WHAT YOU SEE

Actually, there are two lessons here for the price of one. First, there is the point about "what you see," and then, there is an emphasis on getting that down on your canvas or piece of paper.

### What You See

In the approach to painting that I am being taught,[3] there is very much a reality "out there" to which students devote their attention. In

---

[2]This book and the one by Booth, Colomb, and Williams have been wonderfully helpful in my teaching over the last few years. Serving as bridges from painting back to the university, these wise texts by a sociologist (Alford) and a team of professors of English and rhetoric offer important advice for all stages of psychological research and writing.

[3]This is an important qualifier. I am being taught to paint by teachers whose own paintings may reflect some postmodern influences but who encourage in students the development of representational, figurative, and even classical technique. There is a lot of modernity and

figure and portrait work, the model is another person and the student records the reality of that other person. You paint what you see of the other person, from that particular place at which you are standing, at the particular time that you are painting. Yes, if you move ever so slightly to the right or left, or wait just a bit of time while the light changes in the room, the reality of that model will change. And yes, what you see in the model is different from what another student or teacher sees, given the differences in experiences with art and life, not to mention the differences in height from which you view the model. Nonetheless, there is what you see in that place and time, and that is what you draw and paint.

And there are ways of checking on how well you are doing that. You constantly step back from the work to check if the general shapes and values in the drawing[4] on the canvas correspond with what you see in the scene you are painting, checking both positive and negative spaces. Although it can be difficult and demand what can feel like a lot of discipline, the strategy of holding a brush at arm's length to see if indeed what should line up is lining up, to see if proportions are correct, to measure and remeasure the angles, does reveal something—it is a kind of reliability and validity check— and shows you where you need to make corrections.

Having kept up reasonably well with recent psychological work on the self and identity, I certainly appreciate the extent to which the person I am painting is a multifaceted and socially constructed self. Paintings of all genres have been compellingly depicted as both the results and means of such construction. For example, the setting up of a pose is a very deliberate piece of work by painting teachers, influenced by the many other poses they have viewed, their pedagogical aims, and their attributions to the particular model. Also, there is an amazing amount of co-construction, between the person working as model and the teacher, and the model and each of the student painters.[5] Nonetheless, as I paint, I work with an understanding of

---

premodernity in the classroom with references to the work of painters such as Titian, Rubens, Velasquez, Sargent, the Impressionists, and Bonnard and Vuillard. The contract between students and faculty is that, yes, someday we may go out and do our very own unclassical and most postmodern work, but first we learn some fundamentals.

[4] Although I have led with the term, painting, when painting, one is constantly going back and forth between painting and drawing. The first step in a painting is the construction of a drawing on the canvas. Teachers all issue the warning that unless that foundational drawing is correct (has the right proportions, supports a strong composition, etc.), the painting will fail, no matter how skilled one is at mixing colors or applying paint.

[5] These points about social, personal, and co-construction of another were felt in an extraordinary way during a painting session in which the teacher had placed an African American woman dressed from the waist down in beautiful African clothes in a cross-legged seated pose on the floor, and not on the platform that raises the model above the painter's eye-level. I saw before me a beautiful and regal person that I wanted to paint but I was made amazingly uncomfortable by standing above her and looking down as I painted. There was plenty here to deconstruct, the pages in Foucault flew before my eyes. But that wasn't the job at hand. With the help of the model who was also a painter, we put away the easel at which I usually stood, and found a way that I could paint while sitting on the floor.

a distinction between all of these forms of the construction of reality and reality before me. As I paint, I seek to recognize and look through prior social constructions to capture in paint the reality I see in my distinctive way; a way that represents both the individuality of the person I am painting, and a few small truths about what it means to be a person that strike me as transcending the particular individual in a particular pose.

Postmodernism does not seem to get in the way of my painting. Unfortunately, I cannot say the same for some of my students who conduct narrative research. Their reading of the extreme form of postmodernism, one that seems to dismiss the idea of a reality "out there," has engendered a research ennui or even nihilism. For example, a student doing an intensive study of other lives sometimes reaches a point where all he can ask is: "Why bother, if all that I have recorded is just my construction of that other person, who would be interested in that, how can it be presented as the result of serious inquiry?"

I have not yet done all of the work in philosophy, ideology, and moral thought that would be required fully to respond to students' concerns, but I have been able to engage them in strategies learned through painting that they can use to get through the despair and back into work. Here is one of them. Painting teachers repeatedly encourage students to do paintings of their own faces. It is an important source of practice in a field where practice is key: You learn how to draw faces by drawing faces. It also meets the important aim of learning your own face so well that you can hold it in check while you draw another's: Painters try to record and communicate what they see in others and not simply provide viewers with an endless series of their own self-portraits.[6] There is a lesson here about systematic work with and development of the self as a research tool in a postmodern world, or what Brown (1996) calls the "I in Science."

At each stage of the qualitative research process, there are conceptual and methodological tasks that we researchers can first try out on ourselves. I encourage students to apply the conceptual framework that they are constructing and its specific concepts to their own lives. Before bringing them to others' lives, students can evaluate the extent to which their frameworks provoke important questions and reveal something about life. We can write or speak out the questions we plan to ask another. We can transcribe our responses and try out an analysis of the text; bringing to it whatever coding scheme we have developed, and letting our autobiographical text correct and elaborate the scheme, or suggest an entirely new scheme. All of this is part of the attempt to bracket our preconceived notions and bias, and then go on to observe and record what we have seen. All of this can amount

---

[6] There are, of course, exceptions to this. Picasso is probably the most familiar (Rubin, 1996).

to deliberate and systematic exercises in self-reflexivity and thereby, a support for the validity of what we are reporting about the other. If such a methodological system can exist within the arts, why not within the social sciences?

## Putting It Down

Although painting teachers will encourage their students to think long and hard about their subject matter, not to rush into the drawing before they have decided what they are going to paint and what their overall plan for the painting is,[7] the point of the class or painting session is to pick up the brush and put something down on the canvas. This is the case even for the first class of a semester. Students arrive at the studio with the supplies from the list the teacher has distributed before classes start. The instructor begins the first class as she or he does all classes. A model is set up and the students paint. The instructor, new to the student or not, needs to know where each student is in his or her work in order best to teach each student. The only way to establish that is to have the student produce work to show. More than once, I have thought that our psychology classes at the university could do more to involve students and faculty in the actual doing of work in this way.

The lesson holds for the importance of writing in narrative analysis. For most qualitative researchers in psychology, the brush is our computer keyboard; and the painted canvas is the written document that we produce. And similar to the artist, the researcher needs quickly to get something down. Too often, I have seen students get stuck in wanting simply to talk about their work. The talk can become a way of not writing; and that is serious because in most narrative analysis, writing is the way the analysis happens. As you write, you think (Booth et al., 1995). What is essential is the ability to trust that it is in the writing that the analysis happens. Unlike many forms of quantitative analysis, narrative analysis

> . . . requires you to synthesize sources, engage in conceptual analysis, interpretation, judgment, and evaluation, you may not have a clear sense of your results before you start drafting. You may not have a clear sense of your problem. In that case, the act of drafting is what will help you analyze, interpret, judge, and evaluate. (p. 156)

There are many good reasons for a narrative researcher to begin writing as soon as possible, indeed, even on the first day of the semester. For some students who can only now write with a computer, this means scheduling some time each day in front of the screen; others find it helpful to carry

---

[7] As Sam Adoquei, my current teacher, says repeatedly as he circles behind our easels: "Plan your work, and work your plan."

carefully selected journals wherever they go, and write in them whenever inspiration strikes.

## LESSON 2: WORK THE WHOLE CANVAS

When working with a model, as you start a drawing or painting of a human figure, you must decide on how much of the figure you want to put on the working surface. That decision is recorded by the first marks you put on the canvas. One mark represents the topmost part of the figure, typically the highest point of the skull. A second mark represents the lowest part that will be drawn or painted. This could be the bottom of the foot, the middle of the thigh, a place between the shoulders and the elbow— almost anywhere, but never at a joint (painting teachers warn that cropping at a joint creates the impression that the artist has amputated the model and is sure to send a shudder through the viewer of the portrait). Once the top and bottom marks are down on the canvas, you then go on to indicate the critical points and angles that fall between these two marks, and to place on the canvas the edges and points of other objects in the environment of the figure that you want to include in the picture.

As you go on with the work, along with making sure that proportions are correct and shapes are accurate, you need take special care that the different elements in the picture are working as they should in relation to each other. Important to all of this is working on all parts of the canvas, all the time. For example, if you put down a line that indicates a model's shoulder in the upper left quadrant of the canvas, your eyes instantly move to the upper right quadrant and your hand marks something there that in the scene is at the same level as the shoulder. Almost simultaneously, your eyes and hands go to the lower part of the canvas and fill in what needs to be there, in line with what is above it.

Moving and working this way, right and left and up and down, keeps the whole canvas at the same level of completion. Ideally, you want to end every major work session on a painting in such a way that the piece stands on its on. It tells a story that engages a viewer even in the early stages. What you want to avoid at all costs is working one part of the canvas at the expense of others. When you feel especially good about the handling of one part of the subject matter—for example, the drapery on the figure— it is tempting to stay there in that security and try to make it more and more beautiful. The danger of working too long on this piece is that the rest of the canvas goes unattended. The drapery itself will inevitably fail because it is not depicted as part of the overall scene and in relationship with the other pictorial elements. You learn as you work the whole canvas that no part of what you have decided to depict is more important than anything else. Every part exists only in relationship to everything else.[8]

## Setting the Limits

There is an easy parallel to make between the painter's struggle to decide and stick with the plan to take on only so much of a figure and a student's setting limits on a narrative study. There is a tendency in both cases either simply to start and see where that takes you, or to take on too much. But in the studio and in the research field, neither of these strategies is as effective as making a plan for your work, setting a beginning and end in the plan, and working that plan so that everything between the two end points receives attention. Of course, it may become the case in the course of doing the work that your plan needs to be changed. For example, in figure drawing, you may sometimes step back and discover that your plan has produced a not very appealing composition. The plan can be changed at that point; you can replace your bottom mark and crop the figure in a new way. In the same way, with a plan for the research in hand, the student researcher can gain a better view of how his or her work is going and feel more informed around decisions like cutting the number of people who need to be interviewed or adding a focus group to what was originally set as an individual interview study.

## The Whole Canvas

This is a metaphor I frequently use as I work with students on their papers, at all stages, from their drafts of their research proposals through their final version of their research reports. To use it here, I ask the reader to imagine a canvas split into four quadrants: the upper left represents that part of a research paper in which students review the literature, build a conceptual framework, and state research questions or hypotheses; the upper right canvas corresponds to students' handling of methods; and the bottom two quadrants represent evidence and interpretation of that evidence. Working with narratives, the reader may not want to take a linear approach to these sections, but the reader will agree that every research paper somehow contends with all of these sections.

---

[8]I have read psychologists' claims that persons need to be understood in situations, in their contexts, but their claims never struck me as convincingly as did the action of a painting teacher. He took a brush to my painting of a model in a studio and reworked the harsh line that I had left between her skin and the air in the room. By very careful manipulation and repeated overlaying of the paint used to represent skin with that used to represent air, he clearly portrayed another's being as that which is essentially in a particular context.

Too often, I have seen students get stuck in the upper left quadrant of the canvas. As my painting teachers have taught me, I encourage students to work with all of the quadrants, all parts of a research paper. It is important to begin drafting at the earliest of stages what might be called sketches of the whole paper. As they craft the introduction for their research paper, it is essential for students to think about how what they write there has implications for what will need to go in the methods section. I once worked with a student who seemed unable to move on from work with the introduction (there was always another publication to review, there was yet another concept that needed to be rethought, there was a hypothesis that was not quite right, etc.). It was only when I asked very directly if he was afraid to take on methods that we were able to move on in the work. Only then was he able to say that he feared that his casting of his research questions would require interviews with more participants than he would ever be able to find. Facing this conflict directly, we were then able to attend to what kind of interviews would be feasible and quickly move back from there to a suitable recasting of the research question.

It is equally important to move from the upper half to the lower half of the canvas, from the introduction of a conceptual framework and methods to expectations about data and interpretation. If you are interested in a particular stance and a particular way of collecting data, you need simultaneously to think about the implications of those for the various ways that the evidence might emerge, and moreover, what you would make of each of the alternative kinds of results. This may seem a bit too mind-bending, but more than once, in engaging students in this exercise, we discover something very important. We find that, from the very beginning of the project, the student had intended only to come up with one sort of result; typically, the sort that would support the statement that the student felt the world needed to hear. The confrontation with the possibility that the data might look different is critical. At that point, the student can go on motivated by the possibility of discovering something new; or the student can recast their questions so that they address both the research and practical dimensions of the problem that concerns them (cf. Booth et al., 1995).

I close this lesson with a student's reflections on how she worked it:

> it is important to not paint in any one area of the canvas with too much detail before other sections. To keep the level of detail equal across the canvas. It was like an "ooohhhh!" moment that made perfect sense but I had never thought of it in that way before. I think the second section of my paper is what it is because I zoned in on it too early. The result is that the details I thought were clear are not and it doesn't fit as well with the overall paper as I needed it to. I use that metaphor for my life, my work in general, and while working on specific papers. Given the intensity, and peaks and valleys associated with life

as a graduate student, it is impossible to apply this metaphor literally all the time and still remain efficient, but it is a wonderful reminder of the need for balance in all things.

## LESSON 3: SHOW YOUR WORK TO OTHERS, OR THE VALUE OF THE "CRIT"

Painting can be simultaneously the most isolating and most communal of activities. Standing at the easel, your looking and concentration can be so intense that you forget there is anyone else in the room but you and the model, and you lose all sense that time is passing. When you paint, you can go to that "other place" that I have heard jazz musicians say they go to when they play their music. But it is also the case that in painting classes, whether they meet for five times, three times, or once a week, students paint with other students. You watch other people paint. Every 20 minutes or so, there is a 5-minute break. You leave your easel and check out what is going on at others' easels. You talk and you compare what you see. The teacher moves from one easel to another and gives detailed individual criticism to each student. Also, at the end of some classes, teachers will have students line up all of their paintings in one part of the room, creating a gallery of sorts. After some careful looking at the lot, teachers talk about each work on its own and in relationship to the others, and ask students to do the same about their own and others' paintings. You learn a great deal from all of this. At individual sessions with the teacher, you come to see things in your work and in the model you are painting through the vision of someone who sees more nuances that you now do, someone who is working hard to ensure that you will come to see as well as she does when she is not in the studio. In the easel visits and group "crits," you learn about your painting through what someone says about someone else's work. Oftentimes, there are things you cannot see or hear about your own, but when it is put in terms of another's, you finally get it.

Of course, there are times when what you learn is not so pleasant. That person who sees more nuances may ask questions that strike at the core; questions such as: "Suzanne, isn't there more ochre in her skin? Is the background really that green? Is his hand really that large in relationship to his head?" There is seldom just one question. They come in a series, as the teacher sees one problem in your work that enables her to see another, and another, and so on. And there are times when to make the point that I did not get it right (that I got involved in details too early on and did not capture the big shapes at the start, that I did not step back enough, check the proportions and angles enough, etc.), the teacher will wipe off all of the charcoal marks from my page that I come to attach to as my drawing, or take my paintbrush in hand and add that blob of bright white paint to acknowledge the spot of bright light whose value I had underestimated. The lesson here is to be willing to let go of your work, to be willing to start over to ensure that the story you are telling in your painting is the most accurate and compelling story you can tell.

I have frequently wished that the psychology classroom could be more like the painting studio, a place where students are involved in the doing of the work and the sharing of that work. Those moments in which a group of students stare in silence at the transcript of one student's interview are dreadful for all. The student has shared the record of a marvelous interview, a transcript with which he or she is working a discursive analysis. And no one says anything: no conversation about conversation. The reasons for silence appear to be many. Students fear they have not thought enough about the material, worry that they will say something that feels like criticism to the student who did the interview, want to avoid looking not so smart before the teacher and their peers, and are silenced by an odd sense that whatever they say here may have negative repercussions for what might be said about their own work in the future.

Of course it does not always happen this way. There are times when the group is able to get involved in the analysis and everyone leaves the room knowing more about the particular narrative that was reviewed, other narratives they have been collecting, strategies for interviews, and the theoretical frameworks they have been crafting. But the silences are frequent enough for us as teachers to take seriously what it is that stifles the work and the sharing. Too many of us have been socialized as scholars to think that real thinking happens only when we are alone, that we cannot speak until we have thought it all out, and that what we have written (after all that time spent thinking about it) is precious. We need to provide our students with other models for working and other spaces in which they can freely engage in those models.

While we are working on building those new models and spaces, I have found it helpful to tell stories about my experiences from the studio in the research classroom. One day in a course in which we were working with students' proposals for their first major research projects in graduate school, we found ourselves stuck. Michelle Fine and I had read and commented on drafts of the proposals, we had had individual conversations with students about their work, and we had sought to promote student critiques of each other's projects and group discussions. All of this had led to awareness of problems in the work, but students did not seem to want to move on to discuss and make changes.[9] Even those who appeared to be

---

[9] This is a place in our work at which word processors do more harm than good. Too often I have seen students just call up an old file that is already on their computer, or just cut and paste across

on the very verge of making changes were unable to trust that change would better the situation. They simply wanted to hold on to what they had; at least that was something. Having run out of any psychology teacher tricks I had, I decided to tell the story of what had happened to me the night before at a sculpture class.

I was working in clay to make a small statue of the very muscular man who was working as our model. I spent hours pulling and pushing the material until I had what I thought was a pretty good representation of the human form I had observed. My little statue was very handsome. The teacher came by. I saw her looking at one of the arms, and yes, there it was, the distance between one elbow and fingertip was a bit too long. There was no time to say I saw that. The teacher picked up the wire we used to cut up the clay and sliced my little man in two. She said simply: "You came very close to getting it once, you'll be able to do it again, and when you start from the beginning, you will find what you had and more." And so, I kneaded the clay into two simple round balls, and started again into shaping a man.

I received a strong response to this story. One student described her initial reaction as "visceral." Michelle, who is not prone to using psychodynamic references, said she saw castration anxiety sweep across at least half of the room. Whatever kind of anxiety it was, it did not appear to be of Alford's unproductive sort. Students did seem to be able to use the metaphor to take some new steps in their work. One student, reflecting back on this class put it this way:

> Since you were telling this story at a time when we were writing our second-year project proposals, which was for me the first major piece of research-related work I'd done using my own research question, the image of taking a wire to cut through my creation evoked a very strong protective response. I thought I couldn't possibly discard this paper, which clearly needed work, but ... surely there were some thoughts there worth saving? It was very hard to take that advice but you were right, I learned that the thoughts worth saving could be re-created. Starting over made room for fresh ideas and even clearer ways of expressing them.

## LESSON 4: SAM'S RECIPE FOR A GOOD PIECE OF WORK

In a recent painting class, in response to a student who feared that she was not gaining technique quickly enough, Sam Adoquei, our current teacher, responded that she should stop worrying and just keep working.

---

several old files; instead of starting afresh, from the beginning. There continues to be value in old yellow pads and writing things out in pen, in longhand.

Technique would come through the careful doing of the work. He then went on more emphatically to say that technique was *not* the crucial ingredient for a good painting. According to Sam, it takes just three things to make a good painting: inspiration, passion, and conviction.

*Inspiration* in painting comes from having seen wonderful paintings. Being able to create a good painting depends on having on more occasions than you can count stood simply transfixed in front of another painter's work, been unable to stop looking at the piece, known that something has happened to your blood pressure, and felt that the most wonderful thing in life would be to be able to paint *just like that*. Just as the painting teacher sees it essential in the early part of training to expose students to a variety of great paintings, the teacher of narrative inquiry needs to engage students in the study of compelling examples of qualitative work. Students need to marvel at provocative and sound work done by a variety of investigators, over a long time period, in different research settings, on a diversity of topics. It is not just the idea of doing qualitative work that will sustain students; they need actually to have encountered specific pieces of work that inspire them and serve as models.

*Passion*, in painting, whether it is of a landscape, still life, or another person, needs to drive the work. Cezanne loved the apples he painted. As a painter, you feel passionate about both the subject matter and the need to communicate what you see to others. Throughout the process, you must care enough about what you are working on to stick with it, even in the most difficult parts of the work. Also, you need stay engaged enough so that you continue to see new things, to be surprised, to use art like science as a means for discovery.

Unfortunately, many of us in psychology have been exposed to views of science that have led us to think that passion, engagement, and surprise are threats to detached objectivity; and thereby, dangers to the scientific enterprise that depends on distance from what we are studying and skepticism. The job of teaching narrative research includes showing students ways to do another kind of science, one with roots in Dilthey and the American pragmatists and exemplars in psychology and philosophy in the intervening century (cf. Gendlin, 1997). This kind of science provides room for passion and offers our students and ourselves strategies for taking seriously those points in our work where we seem to have lost it. Unless that passion can be restored, the research or teaching project is at risk of not being as effective as it might be.

*Conviction* comes with trusting that you see something very distinctive in what you have chosen to paint and that communicating that something to others is worthwhile and necessary. Also, you know that you can do the painting and do it in a way that will be respectful of those you paint and those who view your work. You and the world have what it takes. This is about confidence and courage. This brings us back to the point about the need for a "working vocabulary" in qualitative research. There is no way I can feel conviction about a painting if I have not gotten the basic structure right, if I have not attended to the values, colors, basic shapes, and plane changes. I need to know those words, what they mean, and how to recognize them in what I or anyone else sees in my painting. Knowing what I need to be courageous about is essential. In narrative research, our students and we need to have a language like this with which we can do and communicate about our research.

## CONCLUSION

Experiences as a painting student have not resolved all, not even most, of my struggles with how best to teach qualitative methods. Nonetheless, for Elijah and me, ways of seeing gained through the practice of one trade enable better seeing of what matters in another. That vision includes the sighting of good fields for planting. Elijah found a field to farm, saw possibilities that others had ignored, and cleared away all the many loose stones. Then, he turned to the rocks that were too big to move. He marked these with buoys that he had made for his work at sea. He carefully placed his brightly painted buoys so that the plow that he would later take to the field would not run aground on the big rocks. For me, narrative approaches constitute a field to be worked for the research questions that my students and I want to pose, questions that we think will enable psychology to show its promise as an academic and social institution. Using approaches and strategies I have learned while a painting student such as those discussed in the painting lessons presented here, I try to remove rocks and everything else that gets in the way of students' research work. In those really tough spots in initial conceptualization, data collection, analysis, and interpretation, I offer painting metaphors to encourage alternate routes and new ways of thinking through and back into the work. What seems most critical is that we all stay hard at work in the field.

## REFERENCES

Alford, R. R. (1998). *The craft of inquiry: Theories, methods, evidence*. New York: Oxford University Press.

Booth, W. C., Colomb, G. G., & Williams, J. M. (1995). *The craft of research*. Chicago: University of Chicago Press.

Brown, J. R. (1996). *The I in science: Training to utilize subjectivity in research*. Boston: Scandinavian University Press.

Gendlin, E. (1997). How philosophy cannot appeal to experience, and how it can. In D. M. Levin (Ed.), *Language beyond postmodernism: Saying and thinking in Gendlin's philosophy* (pp. 3–41). Evanston, IL: Northwestern University Press.

Jewitt, S. O. (1989). *The country of the pointed firs and other stories.* New York: Doubleday. (Original work published 1886)

Josselson, R. (1999). Introduction. In R. Josselson & A. Lieblich (Eds.), *Making meaning of narratives: Vol. 6. The narrative study of lives* (pp. ix–xiii). Thousand Oaks, CA: Sage.

Rubin, W. (Ed.). (1996). *Picasso and portraiture.* New York: Museum of Modern Art.

# 2

# AN EPISTEMOLOGICAL APPROACH TO THE TEACHING OF NARRATIVE RESEARCH

BLYTHE McVICKER CLINCHY

I came to appreciate and to practice narrative research rather late in my career as a psychologist. In school I had been taught that truth was to be found in well-reasoned arguments and tightly controlled experiments, and this was the lesson I continued to teach my own students. Outside of school, of course, I had always learned and taught from stories—the ones I read to myself and the ones I read to my children. But stories, I thought, belonged to "real life," as the students say, not "academics." Now, I know better. Although I fell into narrative research almost by accident, I emerged as a convert. I believe now that narrative is a rich source of knowledge, that procedures for constructing and interpreting narratives should be part of every psychology curriculum, and that if this were to come to pass, academic life would become more "real," more meaningful to students than it is today. In this chapter I tell how I arrived at these convictions and how I have acted on them.[1]

## BECOMING A NARRATIVE RESEARCHER

It all began when my colleague Claire Zimmerman (Clinchy & Zimmerman, 1982) decided to launch a longitudinal study of epistemological development among students at Wellesley College. Our project was inspired by William Perry's (1970) groundbreaking longitudinal investigation of

---

[1]I write mainly about women because most of the participants in my narrative research and nearly all of my students have been women. I do not mean to imply that what I have to say applies only to women. Readers can decide that for themselves.

"intellectual and ethical development" among Harvard undergraduates. Perry's description of the evolution of students' conceptions of knowledge and truth seemed to capture our impressions of our students' development, and we wanted to explore the topic more deeply. We knew nothing of "methods" in narrative research. Nor did Perry; for he was an academic counselor, not an academic researcher. But, as his longtime collaborator, Lee Knefelkamp points out, in her preface to the 1999 reissue of the 1970 book, "He was passionately interested in stories . . . the structures or forms through which we tell them" (Knefelkamp in Perry, 1999, p. xxi). Perry's assumption, shared by many cognitive psychologists, including those of us who have followed in his wake, is that people do not simply "have" experiences; they construct them, although usually unaware that they are doing so, on the basis of their own implicit epistemological premises. Students at different epistemological "positions," in Perry's terms, will construct the same "objective" event—a freewheeling class discussion, for instance—quite differently. Students who believe that there are right answers to every question and that it is the duty of authorities to provide them (a position Perry came to call "dualism") will be frustrated and confused when the professor fails to indicate which opinion is right, while those who believe that all opinions are equally valid (Perry's "multiplicity") will simply opt for the one that feels right, and those who believe it is their responsibility to construct the most reasonable position possible will listen with a critical ear, comparing and contrasting the various views from a variety of perspectives (Perry's "contextual relativism").

Perry's interview technique was scandalously simple: After explaining that they were interested in students' experiences at Harvard, his interviewers asked just one standard question: "Why don't you start with whatever stands out for you about the year?" Although Claire and I used a more structured approach, designed to elicit data codable in terms of Perry's scheme, the purpose of our interview, as with Perry's, was "to obtain from students their own reports of their college experience, in their own terms" (Perry, 1970, p. 19). We, too, looked for stories, not abstractions. Stories, we believed, were apt to be composed in the women's own epistemological terms, whereas the terms in which abstractions were expressed might have been borrowed from someone else—someone in authority, perhaps. The participant's task was to tell the story; the researcher's task was to induce the perspective from which it was told.

While the Wellesley study was still going on, I joined with three other developmental psychologists—Mary Belenky, Nancy Goldberger, and Jill Tarule—in a three-year project (reported in *Women's ways of knowing* [WWK]; Belenky, Clinchy, Goldberger, & Tarule, 1986/1997) involving interviews with a much more diverse sample of women, varying widely in age, social class, and educational background. The four of us shared an interest in epistemological development, but the main impetus behind the enterprise, as we say in WWK, was our sense that many of the women we had encountered, in research and teaching and in our own lives as students, had been ill-served by the colleges they attended. Stories of "alienation, repression and division" (Jacobus, 1979, p. 10) pervaded the data we had collected. Why, we wondered, did education hurt so much and mean so little to so many women? At the start of the project, we saw little connection between the two sets of issues—epistemological development and feelings of alienation; later, we changed our minds about that.

## DISCOMFORT IN THE CLASSROOM

I was now spending half my time doing narrative research. But I was not teaching it. In my classroom, it was business as usual. The department offered a number of "methods" courses in a variety of content areas, and students majoring in psychology were required to take one of them. I enjoyed teaching Psychology 207R, "Research Methods in Developmental Psychology," mainly because it required the students to engage actively in the construction of knowledge. Research on epistemological development at a variety of institutions (e.g., Baxter Magolda, 1992; Clinchy & Zimmerman, 1982, 1985; King & Kitchener, 1994) had shown that many undergraduates took an essentially passive approach to the acquisition of knowledge, relying either on the truths dispensed by authorities or their unexamined intuitions, positions similar to Perry's dualism and multiplicity, respectively, which in WWK we adapted and retitled "received knowing" and "subjectivism." A substantial number of students remained at these positions even after graduating from highly selective, academically demanding institutions. In 207R, I was trying to cultivate the more active approach that in WWK we call "procedural knowing," a position based on the assumption that knowledge is not simply ingested or intuited but constructed, through the deliberate and systematic use of procedures. The procedures central to 207R, neatly codified in "methods texts" for the convenience of teachers such as myself, stressed the need for objectivity, detachment, and critical thinking. We spent an awful lot of time worrying about "error." Students learned how to detect flaws in the design of the research they read about and how to avoid these pitfalls in designing and executing their experiments. They learned, for instance, how to "control" and "isolate" variables so as to eliminate irrelevant "noise" and how to reduce the intrusion of personal bias through procedures like "double-blind observation."

As time went on, I became increasingly aware of the disparity between the procedures I was teaching and the procedures my colleagues and I were using in our research. The approach we used in interviewing women and interpreting the interview data was primarily personal and empathic rather than impersonal and detached. Instead of adopting a neutral perspective "from no position in particular," we allied ourselves with our research participants, struggling to get behind each individual's eyes, to see the world from her particular perspective.

Some of the students I encountered, both in research and in the classroom, seemed to be using a similar approach in their daily lives, although it took me a long time to recognize it. In the Wellesley study, for instance, we asked students to respond to a quotation representing a form of critical thinking that I was emphasizing in 207R.

> Even if something sounds right to me, I'll take a critical look at it and evaluate it carefully, looking for flaws in the argument, and trying to challenge it. Sometimes it helps to play devil's advocate, arguing the opposite of what somebody's saying, thinking of contrary evidence or alternative interpretations.

As I have reported elsewhere (Clinchy, 1996), although some of our interviewees heartily embraced this statement, many did not. For instance, an undergraduate we call Grace said that even when she disagreed with someone, she didn't start arguing in her head; instead, she tried to imagine herself into the person's situation: "I sort of fit myself into it in my mind and then I say, 'I see what you mean.' . . . There's this initial point where I kind of go into the story, you know? And become like Alice in Wonderland falling down the rabbit hole." At the time, we did not connect Grace's comment to the approach we were using in our narrative research. We dismissed it as uncodable in terms of Perry's scheme, thus rendering it epistemologically invisible. Perhaps, I thought, Grace was exhibiting a maladaptive tendency that the psychologist Robert Hogan calls "over-empathizing" (1973, p. 224).

Students in several of my courses often showed signs of this same disturbing tendency. On one such occasion, I was presenting Piaget's research on the child's concept of the lie to a class in child development. Piaget's procedure, I told them, was to present a child with two stories. For example,

> (a) "A little boy goes for a walk in the street and meets a big dog who frightens him very much. So then he goes home and tells his mother that he has seen a dog that was as big as a cow."

And

> (b) "A boy comes home from school and tells his mother that his teacher had given him good grades, but it was not true. The teacher had given him no grades at all, good or bad. Then his mother was very pleased and rewarded him."

Piaget then asks, "Which boy was naughtiest?"

I said to the class, "Which boy was naughtiest? . . . What would *you* say? . . . What would the little kids say?" I was met with 31 blank stares.

The right answer, in terms of Piagetian theory, is that although adults would judge the second boy naughtier, because of his selfish motive, young children would consider the first one naughtier, because his was a physically "bigger" departure from truth. The students knew enough to figure this out, but they just didn't seem to get it. What was wrong with them?

Finally, one of the students said, "Well, if you *had* to say one of them was *naughtier*, I *suppose* you could say the second one, but I wouldn't say that." "What would you say?" I asked. She said, "Well, I'd want to know why he was so worried about grades." At this point a dozen students leapt enthusiastically into the discussion: "Yeah, and that dog must have really scared the other kid. Did the mother know he was afraid of dogs? She needs to get him to tell her more about it." "Maybe he really *thought* the dog was as big as a cow, because he was so terrified." On and on it went. At the time, this discussion seemed to me irritatingly irrelevant—a waste of precious class time.

Later that day I was proofreading a chapter I had written about the relation between women's ways of knowing and their conceptions of morality (Clinchy, 1993). One of the central points of the chapter is that, at least at certain periods in development, and perhaps throughout the life course, many women are reluctant to make judgments of other people's behavior; they are oriented more toward *understanding* the behavior than evaluating it. I report in that chapter that when we asked undergraduates whether they believed Hitler was wrong, a substantial number found it hard to say a simple "yes." It was not that they did not think he was wrong. It was more, as one student put it, that "that's not the question." The women did not perceive it as a productive question. A more productive question to their minds would be, "Why did he do what he did? What were the circumstances that made Hitler happen?" What was Hitler's story? Finally, I "got" what had happened in class that day. "Which boy was naughtiest?" was not the right question. My students were answering a different question, one that was more meaningful to them, one that could be not be answered through experiment, but only by "going into the story."

Gradually, it became clear that some of the women we were interviewing were exhibiting something more than just a proclivity for going into stories; they were describing at least the rudiments of a genuine procedure for doing it, a "way of knowing" that was uncritical but not unthinking. One woman said, for instance, that when someone said something that sounded odd or wrong-headed, she did not usually start arguing with it; she said, "I'll usually try to look at it from that person's point of view, see how they could say that, why they think that they're right, why it makes sense." And another: "I try to look for pieces of the truth in what the person's saying instead of going contrary to them. Sort of collaborate with them." These women cannot be accused of compulsive overempathizing; they know that entering another person's perspective does not just happen, like falling down a rabbit hole, that you have to "try"—try hard—to make it happen. In time, we came to call this approach, the one at the heart of my own narrative research, "connected knowing," in contrast to "separate knowing," the approach that was featured in the research methods course.

## CONNECTED AND SEPARATE KNOWING

Separate knowing is an impersonal way of knowing. Objectivity is required for obtaining valid results, and valid results are achieved, in the writer/teacher Peter Elbow's (1973) phrase, by "weeding out the self." In the methods course great stress was put on the importance of reducing personal bias. When administering tasks to children, for instance, the textbook warned that the experimenter's behavior should remain "constant" throughout the experiment. If two or more students served as experimenter in a single project, they should behave in exactly the same way, and they should treat each child in as identical a fashion as possible. According to this paradigm, both experimenters and research participants are seen as "interchangeable someones," to borrow a phrase from Alfie Kohn (1990, p. 112). To illustrate the danger of differential treatment of research participants, I recounted how I had discovered in listening to tape-recorded sessions of my dissertation research on children's reasoning that, quite unconsciously, I used a different "voice" depending on the gender of the participant— tender and maternal with the girls, brisk and businesslike with the boys. The class and I agreed that this might well have skewed my results. Had I found gender differences in the children's reasoning, I could not assume that these differences had existed prior to the study; I might have created them on the spot. Ideally, we agreed, experimenters would be "blind" to the characteristics of their research participants, but unfortunately in some cases—gender, age, and skin color, for instance—this was not possible.

The students appreciated these points in the abstract but in practice, as they began their projects, they forgot them immediately, for the 4- and 5-year-olds behaved not as impersonal someones but as idiosyncratic, often inscrutable individuals. The students realized that if they were to entice the children into playing their experimental "games," they would have to use a more individualized approach, rather than rigidly adhering to a standard script. The issue was not how to maintain detachment but how to establish an attachment, a personal relationship, with each child. Once this was achieved, nearly all the children responded eagerly to the students' questions. But now the students encountered a further problem: how to make sense of these responses. Far from aspiring to "blindness," they yearned for something like Superman's X-ray vision that would allow them to see straight into the child's mind. Something like connected knowing.

Connected knowing has much in common with Elbow's "Believing Game" or "methodological belief" (1973, 1986). In connected knowing, as in playing the Believing Game, one tries to "believe" if only temporarily, ideas that appear to be unbelievable, looking for what is "right," even in those that seem quite preposterous. Young children's minds are full of preposterous notions, and most of them, such as their views about lies, are, by adult standards, quite wrong. Connected knowers[2] treat the other not as an object, but as a subject—as Alfie Kohn puts it, "an actor, a knower, a center of experience" (Kohn, 1990, p. 100), and in order to understand, they attempt to enter that subjectivity, share that experience. "Was the little boy afraid of dogs?" they ask, and they try hard to imagine what it would be like to be afraid of dogs, to believe in fear of dogs, to "say 'Yes' to it" (Elbow, 1986, p. 279). In reading a book, Virginia Woolf advises, "try to become the author," become his or her "fellow worker," his or her "accomplice," (1932/1948, p. 282)—"sort of collaborate" with him or her. My students intuitively understood, I think, that some such procedure was required if they were to interpret the children's behavior, but they did not know how to do it, and they received little help in standard methods courses like mine. There was not enough time in the semester, not enough room in the textbook or the syllabus, for topics such as "becoming the subject." Separate knowing was the name of the game in my course.

I began to dream about a different sort of course, one that featured narratives, rather than experiments or arguments, as the principal source of knowledge, and connected knowing, rather than separate knowing, as the principal method of constructing it. Fortunately, I had a vehicle at hand, Psychology 317, a seminar on "Psychological Development in Adulthood," which I had taught, in various versions, for years. Because I had never been satisfied with the seminar, I was happy to abandon it in its present form, and because it was not "required" as a prerequisite to anything, I was free to play with it as I chose. I felt some trepidation about teaching narrative research, because I had had no formal training in it myself; nearly all that I knew I had learned by doing. But perhaps, if the seminar were designed to provide opportunities for students to engage in the same sorts of activities that I was pursuing in the research, they too could learn by doing.

I approached this task with missionary zeal, for I no longer believed that epistemology and women's disaffection with education were unrelated. I had come to believe that the emphasis on the values and practices of the

---

[2] I use the term "knower" as in "separate and connected knowers" as a convenience, but of course individuals are not limited to a single approach, and most people probably use different approaches in different domains.

separate mode to the virtual exclusion of connection might lie at the root of the "alienation, repression and division" pervading women's educational autobiographies. Neither connected knowing nor narrative research receives much respect, let alone tutelage; both are regarded as stepchildren within the groves of academe, if they manage to inhabit it at all. The seminar on adult development that I describe in the rest of this chapter represents my attempt to compensate for these twin deficiencies, by cultivating connected knowing in the context of narrative research.

## OVERVIEW OF THE SEMINAR

The seminar deals exclusively with epistemological development from late adolescence through adulthood. By way of entry into a topic that can seem intimidating, given its polysyllabic title and philosophical overtones, we spend the first three weeks or so reading and discussing reports of longitudinal studies carried out in the familiar context of the elite college. During the next five or six weeks, we work within the WWK paradigm. Students read the sections of the book describing the epistemological positions (see Exhibit 2.1), discuss excerpts from Ways of Knowing (WOK) interviews, and write and present a brief memoir applying the positions to their own experience. The next four weeks are devoted to one of the two major projects in the course. Using a version of the WOK interview that is widely used in research, students conduct an interview with a person of their own choosing, transcribe it, code it in terms of the WWK positions, and write a paper based on the coding. The grade for the project is based on its three principal parts: the conduct of the interview, the coding, and the paper. The students also design and execute a final project in narrative research, in which they explore relationships between ways of knowing (drawing on one or more of the theories we have studied) and some other aspect of adult development. In this chapter, however, I shall focus on the earlier project.

### The Interview Schedule

The WOK interview is designed to encourage people to think about and talk about their sense of themselves as "knowers" and how it has developed over time. It begins with a series of open-ended questions, asking how the informants would describe themselves as thinkers (knowers, learners), how they have changed, what they like about themselves and what qualities they would like to develop in themselves in these respects, and whether there were specific experiences and specific persons who have helped and hindered their development. The next section focuses more directly on epistemological assumptions, asking the person to respond to statements

*Exhibit 2.1* Ways of Knowing Positions

- *Received Knowing*: The source of knowledge is external, residing especially in Authorities who know the Truth. Truth can be embodied in words. Truth is single, absolute, concrete, and factual, so a thing is either right or wrong, true or false, good or bad.
- *Subjective Knowing*: The source of knowledge is located in the self. Listening to one's inner voice becomes primary as knowledge is seen as being based on one's personal experience and intuition. There are multiple truths and multiple realities, and all are equally valid, but mine is absolutely right for me. Truth is personal and private and probably incommunicable.
- *Procedural Knowing*: Knowledge is acquired, developed, and communicated through the deliberate and systematic use of procedures.
  *Separate Mode*: focus on analyzing and evaluating different points of view or arguments. Abstract and analytic. Objectivity achieved through detachment, by adhering to impersonal standards and "weeding out the self." Feelings seen as clouding thought. Goal: to construct truth—to test, prove, disprove, convince, and be convinced.
  *Connected Mode*: focus on trying to understand and experience another's perspective, another's reality, and to be understood. Narrative and holistic rather than argumentative and analytic. Objectivity achieved through attachment, adopting the other's perspective. Feelings seen as illuminating thought. Goal: to construct meaning—to understand and be understood.
- *Constructed Knowing*: Knowledge is understood to be constructed, and the knower is assumed to play a role in shaping the known. Use of both separate and connected modes of discourse, possibly integrated into a single approach. Openness to transformation. Goal: to understand the contexts out of which ideas arise, and to take responsibility for examining, evaluating, and developing systems of thought, and to attend to their implications for action. To care about thinking and think about caring.

representing various epistemological positions (e.g., "There's a part of me I can count on—instinct, intuition, whatever. It tells me the truth, the truth for me."). This is followed by an interview on separate and connected knowing that Annick Mansfield and I designed to elicit people's conceptions of the two procedures; how they feel about them; what they see as their benefits, drawbacks, and purposes; when and where and with whom they do and do not use each procedure; and how their use of them has changed over time. Finally, we ask, "Have you ever experienced doing work that you really loved?" and "Can you tell me about a really powerful learning experience that you've had, in or out of school?" Interviewers are encouraged to be liberal with follow-up questions, such as "Can you say more?" and "How so?," asking for clarification, specification, elaboration, concrete examples, and, especially, stories.

## Conducting the Interview

After the students have familiarized themselves with the interview questions, they conduct and record abbreviated "practice interviews" in class. The students work in pairs, each member interviewing the other, while I, wearing my separate knowing hat, cruise from one pair to the next, pointing out what they are doing wrong. Two "errors" are at once apparent, and they frequently recur in the "real interview" that the students goes on to conduct. The interviewers are too apt to assume that they understand what the interviewee is saying, and they are too likely to interject their own views. They find it impossible to adopt the "voice" urged upon them in one of the course handouts: "Don't just converse," it says.

> Do not give your own opinion, but do express your understanding. For example, you can say, "I think I know what you mean," but not "I feel that way too." Do not reinforce or praise the person. On the other hand, *do* reassure the person and maintain the flow of talk by little interjections like "mmm-hmmm," "yeah," "I see," and reflecting back the person's words.

To the students, this approach feels highly artificial, which indeed it is; it is not what they thought "connected interviewing" would be like. Before beginning the interview project, they had read about connected knowing; they claim that they understand it and even that they do it. Most of them believe that they are "good listeners," but in fact, without training, few of us are able to listen "objectively" in the connected sense, that is, to hear the other in the other's own terms. Students bring to the interviewing the less arduous modes of listening they use in everyday life; they assimilate connected knowing to the conversational mode. The conversational mode does come naturally. It is the voice that takes part in the "real talk" that students tell us they cherish, the deep sharing of stories that goes on among friends late into the night in the residence hall, the kind of talk that builds relationships. Real talk requires equal participation, while the asymmetrical approach that is urged on them in the handout ("Don't give your own opinion") seems to take the interviewer *out* of relationship with the interviewee. Connected knowing, as practiced in narrative research, does not come naturally to these women; it must be learned, and the learning involves the unlearning of more natural forms of discourse.

Encountering connected knowing in this extremely self-effacing form can be disturbing to students, but by exaggerating the contrast with everyday talk, it helps them to recognize it as a genuinely deliberate procedure. In this austere form of connected knowing—a caricature, perhaps—there is no more room for agreement than for disagreement, no more room for praise than for blame, because all such expressions distract both interviewer and interviewee from what must remain the exclusive focus of attention: the perspective of the interviewee. At the start, when students are not yet in control of connected knowing, they need to practice something approaching this severely disciplined form, to maintain the intense effort to understand.

Although connected interviewers are not supposed to converse with the interviewees, they are expected to "collaborate" with them, by speaking as well as listening. To my novice interviewers, however, the self-effacing ways of speaking I recommend—little interjections such as "mmm-hmmm," "yeah," "I see," reflecting back the person's words, and expressing uncertainty, as in "You mean . . . ? I'm not sure I understand . . ."—seem scarcely more active than silence. They are familiar with this manner of speaking, for women use it often in everyday life, but, in common with society as a whole, they assume that "maintenance talk," (Fishman, 1978) such as other forms of maintenance work (cleaning the house, collecting the trash) takes little thought or training. They do not expect to be asked to use it in school, and, indeed, some of their professors are at pains to exclude it from the classroom. A colleague of mine in economics insists that her students develop "a public voice" for use in class, a confident, decisive, authoritative voice: "I say to them, 'I don't want you talking in class the way you talk to your friends in the residence hall. I don't want to hear all that hesitation and vagueness and uncertainty.' I tell them that if the CEO asks you how many factories the company should build, and you say 'F-i-i--i-ve . . . ?' [rising intonation] while the guy next to you says firmly 'Seven!,' seven will be built and the guy will be promoted above you." Of course, in this context, she is right: The situation she presents is a contest, and the prize goes to the one who knows more (or appears to know more). The interview, in contrast, is not a competition between knowers; it is a collaboration between thinkers, and it calls for a form of discourse similar to the poet Emily Dickinson's "epistolary voice," as described by Erika Scheurer, a voice intended not to assert or announce, but to explore and engage, a voice suggesting a "*mind thinking*," rather than a mind "*having thought*" (1995, p. 99; emphasis in the original).

In school, however, students believe they are to present themselves as minds having thought. In their essays they are expected to "speak with authority" (Bartholomae, 1985, p. 156), or, as an undergraduate interviewee put it, "to sound like we know what we're talking about." Asked, "What's the purpose of class discussion?", an undergraduate replied, "It's to show the teacher how much we know." In this climate, it is not easy for my students, as interviewers, to assume a mantle of ignorance, to adopt "a deliberate conscious naiveté" (Kvale, 1996). I assure them, however, that in grading their performance as interviewers I will regard expressions of doubt and uncertainty and "little interjections" as evidence of competence rather than lack of expertise.

## Coding the Interview

After typing their transcripts into the computer, the students proceed to classify passages in terms of epistemological position, copying blocks of text from the transcript into the appropriate categories of a "Reader's

Notation Sheet" also typed into the computer. Beneath each entry they write a brief explanation of the grounds for their judgment. The notation sheet allows coders to distinguish between ambiguous passages (which could be seen as illustrating either one category or another or perhaps both) and those which seem clearly to illustrate a given position. The notation sheet encourages the coder to view her person as an evolving rather than a static entity: Space is provided for noting evidence of transitions in the past and hints of possible future transitions—the person's "growing edge." Where does the person seem to be heading? What sorts of experiences might empower the person to "gain a voice" and to claim the powers of his or her mind? Coders are encouraged to reread and reinterpret, adding new passages and reshuffling old ones, using the notation sheet as a place for thinking rather than having thought, saving their conclusions for the papers they will write on the basis of the coding.

To guide them in their coding, the students have a handout containing brief definitions of the epistemological positions (see Figure 2.1). Nearly everyone complains that the definitions are not elaborate enough to permit easy coding, and they are right. I do not intend the handout to serve as a cookbook, any more than I want the interview schedule to serve as a questionnaire. The skeletal nature of the definitions forces the students to reread their texts (especially WWK) for more detail. More important, I hope to convey that this task is not, as so many "school" tasks are, an exercise in "received knowing," in which one looks to authority (teachers and texts) to provide clear-cut rules for obtaining absolute truths. I want the students to regard WOK theory as a work in progress, rather than a finished product. By noting passages that seem relevant but do not "fit" the scheme, students may contribute to its amplification and revision. I want them to see that, given the "schematic" nature of the WOK categories, and given the inherent ambiguity in their data, they will have to weigh alternative interpretations, and sometimes they will be unable to arrive at a single satisfactory "answer."

Although students operating initially from a received knowing perspective would like more structure, those who take a subjectivist approach would prefer less. These are the students who irritate their English teachers by treating poems as mirrors or ink blots, asserting that "whatever you see in the poem, it's got to be there." On the assumption that "whatever you see in the [interview], it's got to be there," subjectivists would prefer to base their "interpretations" on their immediate gut reactions. By insisting that they view their data through the lens of the scheme, as well as their own eyes, I mean to suggest that, at least for this assignment, all opinions are not equally valid; interpretations must make sense in terms of the coding categories. The categories, it is hoped, serve as a somewhat objective (in the sense of external) rein on subjectivism, at least by narrowing the range of possible meanings.

Connected knowers, as do subjectivists, resist the notion of imposing external criteria on the data, not because they want to "go with their guts," but because true understanding, in their view, depends on seeing the other in the other's own terms. Pigeonholing an interviewee in terms of the WOK scheme, "slapping a label on my person," as one woman said, is seen as reductionistic; it treats the person as an instance of a category, rather than as a unique, multifaceted, particular other. There is clearly something right about this concern, and we do not dismiss it or even resolve it; we use it as a basis for exploring a number of paradoxical issues. For instance, we say, paraphrasing a remark attributed to Lawrence Kohlberg, "We code the interview, not the person" (but in connected knowing, are not the knower and the known inextricably intertwined?). We say that any particular narrative research project will illuminate certain aspects of the participants as persons while leaving others in shadow. There is more to individuals than their epistemological assumptions (but it is claimed in WWK that these assumptions "shape the way we see the world and ourselves as participants in it" (Belenky et al., 1986/1997, p. 3). We say that the WOK scheme is to be regarded not as a method of evaluation, but as an instrument of understanding. (And yet it seems at times to be implied—WWK is incoherent and inconsistent on this point—that the scheme represents a developmental progression. Is it not "better" to be a procedural knower, who really thinks, than a subjectivist, who just reacts?) Our data are *co-constructed* by a particular interviewer and her interviewee. Because the interviewer herself is an instrument in the research, we cannot assume that a different interviewer, even if using the same interview schedule, would elicit the same data (but we do assume some similarity, even though we cannot prove it).

## The Self as Instrument

This last point leads to the question of bias, or what Elbow calls "projection in the bad sense," the tendency to see the other in the self's own terms. While separate knowers try to avoid bad projection through "self-extrication," connected knowers do it through "self-insertion" or "projection in the good sense" (Elbow, 1973, p. 149). They use the self to understand the other. Procedures for extricating the self, being clearly defined as impersonal general rules, are relatively easy to teach. One can ask, on an exam, "What is a double-blind experiment?" and the answer is easy to grade. Specific techniques for using the self cannot be so precisely codified, because they are neither impersonal nor objective: The precise form they take depends on the subjectivity of the "self" that is being used. Qualitative researchers, however, have made useful general suggestions.

In qualitative research, Grant McCracken says, "the investigator serves as a kind of 'instrument' in the collection and analysis of data." "Detection proceeds by a kind of 'rummaging' process. Investigators must use their experience and imagination to find (or fashion) a match for the patterns evidenced by the data. . . . The diverse aspects of the self become a bundle of templates to be held up against the data until parallels emerge" (McCracken, 1988, pp. 18–19). The investigator constructs the parallels, by conjuring up "metaphorical extensions, analogies, associations" (Elbow, 1973, p. 149), and instead of waiting passively for a person or a text to strike a chord, we can, by "fine tuning" (Margulies, 1989, p. 16) the instrument of our subjectivity, increase the likelihood of its "empathic resonance" (Howard, 1991, p. 189). Instead of simply "letting" the other in, we can prepare our minds to receive it by engaging in arduous systematic self-reflection.

McCracken advises that, before embarking on qualitative research, the investigator should construct a "detailed and systematic appreciation of his or her personal experience with the topic of interest. . . . The investigator must inventory and examine the associations, incidents and assumptions that surround the topic in his or her mind" thus "preparing the templates with which he or she will seek out 'matches' in the interview data. The investigator listens to the self in order to listen to the respondent" (McCracken, 1988, pp. 32–33). Although McCracken and other qualitative researchers suggest that investigators interview themselves, my students find it difficult to attain "intrapsychic empathy" (Schafer, 1964, p. 251) on their own. In the seminar, they engage in a number of exercises designed to encourage self-reflection: They write memoirs about their own epistemological development, and they literally "listen to themselves" in reviewing their tape-recorded responses to the practice interview. But it is class discussion that helps the most.

## Collaborative Connected Knowing

Both separate and connected knowers benefit from collaboration with others. Separate knowers need external critics, "friends willing to act as enemies" (Torbert, 1976, quoted by Reason & Heron, 1995, p. 139). Connected knowers need friends willing to act as friends, people who will take the time to draw them out, help them to explore and to articulate their own thoughts and feelings. Elbow remarks that it is easier to play solitaire in the doubting game than in the believing game (1973, p. 175), and I agree. It is easier to internalize a partner in the doubting game, because the rules of that game are codified within discourse communities, and anyone who knows the rules will do: The partner is an "interchangeable someone"

(Kohn, 1990, p. 112). Berkowitz and Oser found that once adolescents achieved the ability to integrate a partner's argument with their own and to anticipate weaknesses in both, the partner became "superfluous . . . because one can now fully anticipate the other and take a more objective perspective on one's own reasoning, critically examining it as if from an outside perspective" (1987, p. 9). Because the partners in connected knowing are not interchangeable someones, but particular persons whose unique perspectives cannot be anticipated and so cannot be internalized, connected collaboration would seem to be essential in narrative research; when the self is the instrument of understanding, two or more selves are more likely than one to come up with a match providing a clue to the meaning of a narrative passage.

In nearly every meeting of the seminar, students work together in groups of various sizes, usually devoted to the interpretation of common texts extracted from transcripts. Most of these sessions are conducted in the connected mode. Members are encouraged to come up with a multiplicity of meanings. Ideally, one interpretation builds on another, rather than competing with it, and the "resolution" that is achieved is not a choice or a compromise but a creative "co-construction." When, as often happens, there is disagreement among members of the group or within an individual, it is not seen as evidence of error (interrater or intrarater unreliability), for, as Ruthellen Josselson says, "narrative research is a meaning-making endeavor with multiple truths" (Josselson & Lieblich, 1999, p. xi). At least one of my students seemed to take this message to heart; in her evaluation of the seminar, she wrote, "I learned that ambiguity is good."

But ambiguity has its dangers. For students who retain a belief in absolute, objectivist Truth ("dualism" in Perry's terms, "received knowing" in WWK's), "multiple truths" is an oxymoron, and research that cannot produce "facts" is an exercise in futility. The students who enter my seminar, as with advanced students at similar colleges, almost never adhere to this position (although they sometimes feel that their professors do). Subjectivists, however, do sign up for the seminar. I welcome them, for my experience suggests that, although narrative research presents special challenges to their present position, it also offers special opportunities for advancement to a more reflective position. I think, for instance, of a third-year undergraduate we call Sue, who was interviewed by one of the seminar students. Subjectivists such as Sue are no more capable of connected than separate knowing, but they tend to be less resistant and more receptive to it. Although Sue never says that she would like to attain skill in analysis or argumentation, she repeatedly expresses despair over her inability to understand other people's thinking and to make others understand hers. Over and over, she reports that she can make no sense at all of her teachers' and classmates' thoughts ("I can't see where they're coming from"), and she cannot express her own thoughts in a form that makes sense to them: "There's no way that I can make them see my thought," she says, "although I would love to. They're just never going to see where I'm coming from." Asked, "What are you like in class?" she said, "I'm quiet. . . . And I - I absorb rather than give. . . . I just—I am a mute." Sue experiences the classroom climate as "extremely critical": "There's so many things that I just want to say, you know? But I feel I'm better off if I just shut up, because I don't want to have my thoughts attacked." Sue realizes that she "can't think," and she would like to know how, but she needs to be in a situation in which she is encouraged to think *with* other people rather than *against* them.

At first, students such as Sue enter into seminar discussions with gusto. In the cozy climate of this class they feel free to express their interpretations, confident that no one will try to shoot them down. But of course, they are not really listening to anybody else; they do not know how.

Given enough students of this ilk to form a critical mass, potentially collaborative discussion threatens to disintegrate into parallel play. At this point I am apt to distribute a handout listing "Rules for Playing the Believing Game" (derived from Elbow's [1973] account), which tells students how to behave in class when listening to a classmate or examining a text: "Draw on your own intuitions, experiences and beliefs to try to project yourself into the experience of the person," and "Act as an advocate of the person, trying to help other players enter into the interpretation by pointing out believable features of them, offering analogies and metaphors, etc." For a designated period of time, in an atmosphere combining playfulness and rigor, all of us try hard to abide by these rules and enforce them on other members of the group.

No one finds it easy to play this game. Subjectivists find it especially difficult at first, but in fact, they have the potential to become adept at it. Although they do not yet have the procedures they will need for engaging in connected narrative research, they do have a basis for learning those procedures, for subjectivism has much in common with connected knowing. Both are personal ways of knowing. Both subjectivists and connected knowers use the self, its feelings and intuitions, as an instrument of understanding. Both would agree that understanding occurs only when there is some "parallel" between the person and the object of understanding; it has to click. It has to feel right. This is not connected knowing, but it is not a bad beginning. As Jerome Bruner wrote, "With science, we ask for some verification (or proof against falsification). In the domain of narrative . . . we ask instead that, upon reflection, the account correspond to some perspective we can imagine or 'feel' as right" (1986, p. 51–52). For subjectivists, the click of connection happens or it does not. Through playing the Believing Game they can learn procedures for making it happen, procedures for constructing the parallels. It is hoped that in "trying on" the meanings experienced by others, "going into" other people's stories, students will learn that experiences are constructed, and that, given the proper tools, they can be deconstructed and reconstructed.

## RECONSTRUCTING THE THEORY

As well as using WOK theory to help them understand their interviews, I want the students to use their interviews to deepen their understanding of the theory. I remember how, despite numerous readings, I never really "connected" to Erikson's theory of human development until, as a graduate student in his seminar on life history, I used it as scaffolding for a semester-long project on the intersecting lives of Helen Keller and Annie Sullivan. I did not "learn" Erikson's scheme and then proceed to "apply" it in interpreting the data; the data deepened my understanding of the theory, as well as the reverse. Terms used by the literary scholar Louise Rosenblatt help me to say what I mean: "Literature," she has written, "provides a *living through*, not simply *knowledge about*" (1938/1995, p. 38). My reading of Erikson had provided me with "knowledge about" his theory. For instance, I knew about the developmental stage in which young children and their caretakers engage in a "battle for autonomy" which, if all goes reasonably well, results in the child's gaining "a sense of self control without loss of self esteem" (1968, pp. 108, 109). But, as I became engrossed in Annie's terrible struggle to tame this wild child and help her reclaim the powers of her own mind, against the child's ferocious resistance, I felt I was "living through" Eriksonian theory and understanding it for the first time.

Data can also lead to reconstructions of theory, of course. Carol Gilligan's conception of the moral orientation of care grew out of her inability to "hear" what women were saying in terms of Kohlberg's "justice" orientation. The questions on epistemology that we used in interviewing women in the WWK project were derived from Perry's scheme, but gradually it became clear, as we said in our preface to the second edition of the book, that "many of the answers the women gave to the 'Perry questions' [as we called them at the time] could not be wedged into the 'Perry scheme.'" "In this instance, as in others," we wrote, "when the data the women provided diverged from the theories we had brought to the project, we forced ourselves to believe the women and let go of the theories" (Belenky et al., 1986/1997, pp. xiii–xiv).

In providing a space on the notation sheet for "responses that don't fit," I mean to leave room for students to regard the WOK scheme with a good parental eye, both critical and empathic. I want them to assist in its development, to help it to grow up. Josselson and Lieblich have written that "the most challenging aspect of narrative research is the process of movement between interview data and conceptual framework." Too often, they say, researchers "do not manage to go beyond the presentation of a good story to some kind of wider, theoretical meanings or implications" (1999, p. x). Too often, too, students find it difficult to really love their academic work if it serves no purpose beyond themselves. "I do it, and I get my grade," as one undergraduate said, "but it doesn't mean anything." Narrative research becomes a more powerful learning experience for students when they perceive it as contributing to the construction of theory. If students can experience themselves as members of a community engaged in the creation of knowledge, they may get a glimpse of what it means to be, in the language of WWK, a "constructed knower," the most sophisticated epistemological perspective we identified among the women we interviewed. I do not claim that many—even any—of my students reached such an exalted position, and I realize (but don't seem to regret) that they are perhaps more confused at the end than they were at the beginning. I like to think, though, that at least some of them emerged from the seminar with more complex conceptions of the nature of truth than they held at the start and with more faith in the power of their own good minds.

## REFERENCES

Bartholomae, D. (1985). Inventing the university. In M. Rose (Ed.), *When a writer can't write: Studies in writer's block and other composing-process problems* (pp. 134–165). New York: Guilford Press.

Baxter Magolda, M. (1992). *Knowing and reasoning in college: Gender-related patterns in students' intellectual development*. San Francisco: Jossey-Bass.

Belenky, M., Clinchy, B., Goldberger, N., & Tarule, J. (1997). *Women's ways of knowing: The development of self, voice, and mind*. New York: Basic Books. (Original work published 1986)

Berkowitz, M., & Oser, F. (1987, April). *Stages of adolescent interactive logic*. Paper presented at the Biennial Meeting of the Society for Research in Child Development, Baltimore.

Bruner, J. (1986). *Actual minds, possible worlds*. Cambridge, MA: Harvard University Press.

Clinchy, B. McV. (1993). Ways of knowing and ways of being: Epistemological and moral development in college women. In A. Garrod (Ed.), *Approaches to moral development: New research and emerging themes* (pp. 180–200). New York: Teachers College Press.

Clinchy, B. McV. (1996). Connected and separate knowing: Toward a marriage of two minds. In N. R. Goldberger, J. M. Tarule, B. McV. Clinchy, & M. F. Belenky (Eds.), *Knowledge, difference, and power: Essays inspired by women's ways of knowing* (pp. 205–247). New York: Basic Books.

Clinchy, B., & Zimmerman, C. (1982). Epistemology and agency in the development of undergraduate women. In P. Perun (Ed.), *The undergraduate woman: Issues in educational equity* (pp. 161–181). Lexington, MA: D.C. Heath.

Clinchy, B., & Zimmerman, C. (1985). Growing up intellectually: Issues for college women. In *Work in Progress*, No. 19. Wellesley, MA: Stone Center Working Papers Series.

Elbow, P. (1973). *Writing without teachers*. London: Oxford University Press.

Elbow, P. (1986). *Embracing contraries*. New York: Oxford University Press.

Erikson, E. (1968). *Identity: Youth and crisis*. New York: Norton.

Fishman, P. M. (1978). Interaction: The work women do. *Social Problems, 25,* 397–406. Reprinted in B. Thorne, C. Kramarae, & N. Henley (Eds.). (1983). *Language, gender and society* (pp. 89–101). Rowley, MA: Newbury House.

Hogan, R. (1973). Moral conduct and moral character: A psychological perspective. *Psychological Bulletin, 70,* 217–232.

Howard, G. (1991). Culture tales: A narrative approach to thinking, cross-cultural psychology, and psychotherapy. *American Psychologist, 46,* 187–197.

Jacobus, M. (Ed.). (1979). *Women writing and writing about women*. New York: Harper & Row.

Josselson, R., & Lieblich, A. (1999). *Making meaning of narratives. Vol. 6 in The narrative study of lives*. Thousand Oaks, CA: Sage.

King, P., & Kitchener, K. (1994). *Developing reflecting judgment*. San Francisco: Jossey-Bass.

Knefelkamp, L. (1999). Introduction. In W. Perry (Ed.), *Forms of intellectual and ethical development in the college years*. New York: Holt, Rinehart, & Winston.

Kohn, A. (1990). *The brighter side of human nature: Altruism and empathy in everyday life*. New York: Basic Books.

Kvale, S. (1996). *InterViews: An introduction to qualitative research interviewing*. Thousand Oaks, CA: Sage.

Margulies, A. (1989). *The empathic imagination*. New York: Norton.

McCracken, G. (1988). *The long interview. Qualitative research methods series* (Vol. 13). Newbury Park, CA: Sage.

Perry, W. (1970). *Forms of intellectual and ethical development in the college years*. New York: Holt, Rinehart, & Winston.

Reason, P., & Heron, J. (1995). Co-operative inquiry. In J. Smith, R. Harré, & L. Van Langenhove (Eds.), *Rethinking methods in psychology* (pp. 122–142). Thousand Oaks, CA: Sage.

Rosenblatt, Louise M. (1995). *Literature as exploration* (5th ed.). New York: Modern Language Association. (Original work published 1938)

Schafer, R. (1964). The clinical analysis of affects. *Journal of the American Psychoanalytic Association, 12,* 275–299.

Scheurer, E. (1995). "Near, but remote": Emily Dickinson's epistolary voice. *Emily Dickinson Journal, 4,* 86–107.

Woolf, V. (1948). How should one read a book? In *The common reader, Series 1 and 2* (pp. 281–295). New York: Harcourt Brace. (Original work published 1932)

# 3

# QUALITATIVE RESEARCH IN PSYCHOLOGY: TEACHING AN INTERPRETIVE PROCESS

ANNIE G. ROGERS

A psychologist trained as a clinician in the 1980s, deeply versed in developmental traditions and the study of personality in psychology, as well as psychometrics and statistics, I did not learn qualitative research as a graduate student. After I had finished my degree I began to learn qualitative methods—drawing from books, courses, more knowledgeable colleagues, and a group of researchers whose methods were entirely qualitative. For the past decade I have explored and written about qualitative methods with colleagues (Rogers, Brown, & Tappan, 1993) and with students. This work included creating a new method, interpretive poetics, used to explicate layers of conscious and unconscious associations in language data (Rogers et al., 1999). I have also mentored students working with me on qualitative research projects and taught courses on research interviewing, feminist methodology, and developmental qualitative research. Increasingly psychologists are waking up to the potential of qualitative methodology as a viable paradigm of research in itself, yet I think many departments greatly underestimate what it takes to train students to become strong qualitative researchers. Lacking an understanding of what qualitative research is and what good qualitative research looks like, we mistakenly superimpose the standards of quantitative studies on qualitative projects.

In this chapter, I discuss what I think it takes to train psychology students in qualitative research through an interpretive process that is grounded in the logic of qualitative research. I begin with the particularity of my individual experience of becoming a qualitative researcher, move on to my experience of teaching qualitative methods to doctoral students and creating a qualitative method, and finally suggest some ideas for qualitative research training and guidelines to evaluate qualitative research in psychology departments.

# MY LIFE AS A QUALITATIVE RESEARCHER

I read this phrase and instantly it resounds with a title of a film, "My Life as a Dog." The little boy in this film narrates his position in a first-person voice. We enter his world from a child's eye point of view, hearing directly his thoughts and fantasies about his mother's dying and his identification with a dog sent up to circle the earth in space forever. I, in turn, identify with this child through my own childhood, and also as a qualitative researcher. My father died when I was five years old, and, starting at age 10, I wrote letters to him I buried in the ground, the only way it seemed possible to send mail to the dead. As a teenager, I mailed my letters in the local mailbox with only my father's name, knowing they would end up in the "dead letter" mail in the post office—a wonderful metaphor for how to communicate with someone dead. These acts, I knew, were more imaginative rather than realistic, but they allowed me, nevertheless, to enter the world I was creating. What I kept creating was the interpretive possibility that my father did actually read my one-way epistolary narrative—jarring continuously against the knowledge that he did not.

In adulthood, my experience of becoming a qualitative researcher has followed a somewhat similar psychological track. What I was learning as a student about how to conduct (read quantitative) research kept continuously jarring against the knowledge of its limitations, and more critically, the fear that by becoming a psychologist I would lose my distinctive voice as a writer. Yet considering even the possibility of qualitative research seemed akin to launching myself indefinitely in space in relation to my field and most closely allied colleagues. As a novice psychologist I wanted to enter and learn about the imaginative worlds of childhood and adolescence, focusing on gender as a central interpretive theme. I selected Jane Loevinger as my advisor and mentor. I was not drawn to her as an internationally known psychometrician, but as a brilliant interpreter of human development though an ingenious little device—a sentence completion test (Loevinger & Wessler, 1970). I was fascinated to learn from her how to read signs of ego development in a range of responses to colloquial sentence beginnings: "What gets me into trouble is—"; "A good mother—"; "Sometimes she wished that she—". In my dissertation work, I added to the interpretive possibilities of her test by proposing and demonstrating how to read the sentence completions for themes of moral voice (Gilligan, 1982) in order to test gender hypotheses (Rogers, 1987, 1999). However, I was also deeply frustrated with the limitations of quantitative research and its conventions of writing. I wrote my dissertation each day under American Psychological Association (APA) strictures, but each evening I wrote in a very different way about my clinical internship, in the voice of a fiction writer depicting a detailed, layered, metaphoric understanding of psychic life (Rogers, 1995).

Following my doctorate, I came to the Harvard Graduate School of Education to join Carol Gilligan and her students as a postdoctoral research associate and a member of the newly formed Harvard Project on Women's Psychology and Girls' Development. I was intrigued by a method of reading interviews Carol and her students had created (Brown et al., 1988). What was so intriguing to me was the possibility of portraying layers of psychic life through a polyphony of voices (see Brown & Gilligan, 1992; Gilligan, Brown, & Rogers, 1990; Rogers et al., 1993). Overlapping this time, I directed a study in collaboration with Carol Gilligan called "Strengthening Healthy Resistance and Courage in Girls." This three-year study involved annual interviews with girls of various classes and ethnic backgrounds, as well as an intervention project, a Theater, Writing and Outing Club designed for two groups of girls in different schools. Suddenly I was engaged in a participant observation and indeed ethnography—observing in classrooms, taping and transcribing conversations about our group meetings with the girls each week. I needed to interpret these materials, as well as interview narratives with the girls, and the girls' artwork and journal entries. Working on data analysis with a group of graduate students,[1] we were pressed to invent new ways of interpreting rich data sets in relation to an evolving theory of girls' psychological development (Brown & Gilligan, 1992; Rogers, 1993).

During these years as a doctoral student and postdoctoral research associate, I continuously grappled with questions of epistemology, methodology, and evidence. My two mentors could not have been more different in the ways they thought about these issues in psychology. It was not possible for me to choose between quantitative and qualitative methods because I saw the complexity and integrity of Loevinger's way of working quantitatively with sentence completion data, and the tremendously creative theoretical possibilities of Gilligan's qualitative, voice-centered approach to interview narratives.

When I finished my postdoctoral research, I began to teach a course in feminist qualitative research methods at Harvard, a title that puzzled my colleagues. What in the world was feminist qualitative research?! I remember vividly my identification with the little boy in "My Life as a Dog." As a newly appointed faculty member I was flying, it seemed forever, in some outer orbit of darkest space in relation to my training and the early promise of my research career. For all of that, the discussions I had with my students each week in class were riveting. We talked about our lives and what drew us to particular questions, the construction of science and scholarly

---

[1] The students working on this project were Kathleen Curtis, Kathryn Geismar, Amy Grillo, Kate O'Neill, and Heather Thompson. Carol Gilligan was the principal investigator of this research, which was funded by the Lilly Endowment.

interpretations, what could and could not be counted as science, as psychology, as social science. These conversations were also necessarily inquiries about gender, race, class, and sexuality as point of view, whether privileged, erased, or never articulated. We played these themes into the nitty-gritty everyday questions of designing and doing and writing qualitative research.

During these early years of my teaching, I learned that mentoring students through a process of becoming qualitative researchers is a complex and risky business. Almost all students questioned the legitimacy of their research in a broader climate of skepticism and wondered where they would publish their work. Some students wanted to follow passionate personal interests but did not know how to connect their questions to a theoretical puzzle, creating research that had personal meaning *and* meaning in psychology. Other students were facile in thinking theoretically but placed their most interesting questions and personal experiences of doing research in the footnotes of their proposals. I tried to steer my little boat of mentoring along a channel between these two extremes.

During these first years teaching, my role often shifted from teacher to learner and from authority to collaborator with my doctoral students. This was especially true when I invited a small group of students to work on a qualitative research project extending over several years.[2] In the course of this research on children's narratives of relationships, we became aware of a poignant elusiveness when children began to speak about difficult and disturbing relationships in their lives. In data analysis discussions, the students and I wanted to understand a range of a child's relationships, including her or his relationship with the interviewer. Someone in our group offered an initial interpretation and others created variations on it. We asked for clarification and challenged ideas, but not until they had been articulated first and explored at some length. We saw that we were treating interview texts as though they were poems to be read in layers through a multiplicity of associated interpretations. As we began to name the process of our listening, we initially drew on the idea of "a poetics of research" defined as "a sensitivity and responsiveness to emergent images and the associative logic of poetry" (Rogers, 1993, p. 268). This way of working with children's narratives captured the complexity of figurative thought in language, as well as the elusiveness and silences we noticed in these narratives. Over time we recognized the value and potential of this approach as a method. Naming it an interpretive poetics, we decided to write about the theoretical and methodological basis of this method (Rogers et al., 1999). The students were involved fully as collaborators in a long creative and

---

[2] The research project, *Telling All One's Heart: A Developmental Study of Children's Relationships*, was funded through grants from the Mailman Family Foundation and the Milton Fund from the Harvard Medical School.

intellectual project. Critical to the process of our research and the time to develop and write about a new method were grants and funded apprenticeship opportunities that enabled us to work as a team over a period of several years. If qualitative research had been denigrated and dismissed in our department, or had not been funded, our sustained collaboration could never have happened.[3] As it was, we had a priceless opportunity to learn together the rigors and riches of thinking through and conducting a qualitative research project and creating a new method. This experience, more than any other, showed me how to collaborate with doctoral students while teaching them how to conduct qualitative research.

## SUGGESTIONS FOR TEACHING AND EVALUATING QUALITATIVE RESEARCH

Qualitative research is sometimes called narrative research because it seeks to understand the particular details of a story or stories in historical and social contexts (Bruner, 1986). I began with a series of stories about my life as a qualitative researcher to portray in some detail the particularity of my point of view as someone learning and teaching in this field. Narrative research commonly connects such personal stories with a research process. I could go on now to interpret what I have said further—as a form of discourse, as illuminating a time in intellectual and social history, as an allegory for other experiences outside the academy, as a symptomatic narrative based on anxieties and solutions discovered in childhood. I could go on, but will not. By now that you know enough about my learning and teaching qualitative methods, and my purpose is to jump off into another kind of discourse. I shift now to making suggestions and lightly offering some guidelines for teaching qualitative research to colleagues.

The challenge of teaching qualitative research is particularly fractious and fraught in psychology. Although psychology is a field in which methods matter a great deal, we have had an ambivalent and resistant relationship with qualitative research methods, lagging behind the other social sciences in acceptance and knowledge of qualitative research (Zeller & Farmer, 1999). This resistance on the part of psychologists is rooted in historical positivist traditions as well as contemporary misconceptions (see Rogers, 2000, for further discussion). I have heard qualitative research described as anecdotal, unscientific, and relatively easy to learn—the sort of expertise students might pick up in a single course offering. In my experience, however,

---

[3] The students involved in this work were Mary Casey, Jennifer Ekert, Jim Holland, Nurit Sheinberg, and Vicky Barrios, and each were funded through research apprenticeship grants from the Spencer Foundation.

teaching qualitative research to graduate students is a daunting undertaking that requires the provision of multiple courses and careful mentoring with an experienced researcher. What is particularly difficult is that the huge majority of academics in psychology were never trained in a qualitative paradigm of research and therefore can only transpose what they know about quantitative research to qualitative projects. Understandable as it is, it results in poorly designed qualitative research.

What are some unique challenges in the design of qualitative research? Whole books address this question, and I will not pretend to be able to do justice to it in a few pages (cf. Maxwell, 1996). However, there are some aspects of qualitative research design that may be pointed out quite succinctly, and I hope may be of some use when considering student research projects and proposals.

Rather than working in a hypothetical-deductive model of research where predefined questions are based on specified hypotheses to be tested, students writing qualitative proposals often work on exploratory questions that emerge over time. Researchable questions commonly become clear only after one has been involved in a research project for a considerable period. This involves initial research designed to define a problem to be explored, including the formulation of questions. Questions in turn depend on more open-ended research relationships, which often include an element of surprise, and often require fine-tuning suppositions and areas of inquiry after initial data analyses. This kind of poking about in one's data can seem like what we used to call "fishing" in quantitative studies, but it is not only legitimate to do in qualitative work, it is often *necessary* in order to formulate good, researchable questions. Initial phases of a qualitative study can yield very rich and usable data, and because students invest a considerable amount of time and labor in data collection, it is not unusual to use these data in a larger project.

Qualitative research questions may sound odd to the ear of someone trained exclusively to do quantitative work. We are used to hearing questions that inquire into group differences and seek to explicate interesting sources of variation. Questions that focus on description or process, and pertain to specific situations and limited groups may sound strange. Qualitative researchers often begin descriptively: "What do adolescents in Hospital X experience as inpatients?" Not only is this question basically descriptive, it also specifies a place and a limited group. The purpose of such a qualitative project is not to research adolescents in general or even a specific subgroup, but to investigate adolescent experiences in a particular setting. This initial question may lead to another question after talking at length with the teenagers: "How do adolescents in Hospital X make sense of their own mortality when faced with a life-threatening illness or accident?" This question focuses on a process, and I would surmise, rests on considerable familiarity with the adolescents in the research setting, as well as with developmental research. Qualitative research questions tend to focus on process rather than variance, are specific with respect to place, and draw on a relatively small group that is not meant to serve as a sample of a larger population.

In a qualitative study, researchers are commonly involved in long-term and relatively intimate relationships with participants that are both research relationships and social relationships in a particular context. Scholars trained to give standardized treatments, administer tests, or create particular experimental conditions in relation to research participants may see qualitative relationships as messy compromises to the neutrality and rigor of a research project. Common methods of qualitative data collection, such as participant observation in which one actively joins the group one is studying (a method anthropologists use regularly), may seem to psychologists like further muddying already murky waters. Most psychological researchers will spot possibilities of bias and social reactivity in almost any qualitative research project. I would argue, however, that such wariness misses the uniqueness of the researcher in relationships with participants in a qualitative paradigm. Working in long-term relationships with participants (who are seen as whole persons with their own agendas, wishes, intentions, subversions, and perspectives on the researcher), a qualitative researcher wants to learn his or her own part in the process of relating in order to identify biases, assumptions, and social reactions in such encounters. One aspires to be influenced and changed by the process, and to grapple actively with the intersubjective nature of understandings gleaned from complicated social relationships. Worries that become most pressing concern responsibility to participants, appropriation of their voices, documents, and lives for purposes that may serve only the researcher, and the ever-present necessity to be clear, honest, and open about all aspects of the research with participants.

Students trained in psychology departments are likely to feel that the gap in conceptions of good research between qualitative and quantitative approaches becomes a widening chasm when it come to data analysis and writing. Turning to professors for guidance and legitimacy, students do not know how to communicate across a metaphoric divide. "I feel as though I am just waving across a chasm, you know, trying to say 'hello, this [analysis] is valid too, isn't it?' . . . Whatever they are hearing it's not what I've been saying. . . . I feel I'm just, like I'm just signing in a foreign language or something," one student told me. I can readily understand this student's frustration, and can remember clearly the mistranslated version of her experience from the other side too. Data analysis in qualitative work is hardly ever entirely predictable and seldom goes exactly as planned, even when one has spent considerable time planning and predicting what will be required. This messiness and unpredictability would be a nightmare in quantitative research but is often a boon to qualitative work. To the extent that students can tolerate ambiguity and question their interpretations continuously, the process of data analysis will lead to a crumbling of conceptions, theories, and plans. Far from a disaster, I have seen this kind of analysis repeatedly yield fresh insights and more accurate descriptions and ideas of interest and benefit to psychology, and sometimes to research participants too.

Although I was trained as a graduate student to write in a third-person voice and to eliminate all evaluative language from my text, the kind of writing required in nearly all APA journals, this way of writing is terribly suited to qualitative research studies. I encourage my students to write in a first-person voice, to claim their choices and interpretations throughout a research document, and to write through telling details rather than authoritative broad conceptions. The attempts by students to write from a neutral, distanced, third-person point of view results in the worst qualitative research studies I encounter. Strong and trustworthy research allows me as a reader to agree or to doubt what is presented by hearing the details of a particular, specific, limited, and subjective voice on the page.

A common question about qualitative research is what should we be teaching? What do students in psychology need to become knowledgeable qualitative researchers in today's academy? Ideally, students have the opportunity to take a series of courses and begin their research while engaged in these courses. In my experience, students benefit from learning the logic of an interpretive process at every stage of their development as qualitative researchers, rather than learning a potpourri of qualitative methods.

First of all, students need a course that grounds them in the logic of qualitative research, which is inductive and highlights the meanings of events and experiences in particular social, historical, and cultural contexts. Students need to understand theories of qualitative research, including various epistemological positions such as phenomenology, hermeneutics, constructivism, feminism, and critical theory. Students are often bewildered to discover serious debates and conflicts among qualitative researchers and scarcely know how to locate their own projects. In order to situate their fledgling research questions and plans in these debates, students must first grasp differences in approaches that often also dictate particular choices around data collection, analysis, and writing.

Second, it is important to learn an array of qualitative researcher skills. Almost always this involves some trial-and-error practice so that students can appreciate the skills required, for instance, to conduct good exploratory open-ended interviews, or to take useful and detailed observational notes, or to select historical or contemporary documents for analysis. These skills can be taught, practiced, and learned in coursework and through apprenticeship research experiences. No matter how these methods are learned, it is crucial to provide students with constructive feedback on the quality of data collected in relation to a specified purpose or set of questions posed.

Third, students must grapple with an array of data analysis tools and select ways of working that do not obscure the richness and complexity of qualitative data. Data analysis techniques might include open coding, thematic coding, plotting themes in conceptually clustered matrices, and various forms of discourse analysis, as well as broad analytic practices such as reflective memo writing, checking interpretations with participants, and proofing the accuracy of transcribed interviews and texts. My experience is that sometimes students embrace these methods as though having methods makes research strong or "rigorous." It is far more important for students to learn how to ask questions about their own research process, including what they need to learn more about or explore in greater depth to strengthen an emerging interpretation. These questions in turn guide students to make good choices in data analysis from what is now a staggering array of possible choices drawn from various fields and available as software programs. In short, students need to learn over time how to think through the logic of qualitative data analysis, rather than rely on methods as a magical solution to making sense of research data. Small data analysis seminars are a wonderful forum for such learning.

Fourth, and crucial in the process of learning qualitative methods, students ideally learn to think about qualitative research as a series of theoretically informed choices and modifications involved in data collection, analysis, and writing. Qualitative research is an iterative, exciting way to contribute to knowledge by telling a detailed, empirical, and theoretically interesting story about a particular project. Theoretically informed writing choices are critical, whether a study takes the form of interview-based interpretations, an ethnography of a culture or subculture, or a portrait of a place and time in history. The process of thinking theoretically begins with the formulation of research questions in response to an articulated theoretical puzzle. If students begin with descriptive questions about a particular interest in the absence of any theoretical base, their work later resembles perhaps interesting journalism and has little to offer psychology as a field because the research itself was never conceptualized in relation to conversations in the field. Ideally, through data collection and analysis, students are in a position to write a theoretical story with a strong evidentiary base. In the process of analyzing data and writing, they also learn how to search for disconfirming data, and to consider rival theoretical interpretations.

As academics granting degrees in psychology, the question of what is good qualitative research becomes pressing (see Brizuela, Steward, Carrillo, & Berger, 2000, for a discussion of qualitative research across various disciplines). Certainly there are examples of shoddy and misinformed student research using both quantitative and qualitative methods. But we are still better prepared to spot problems in quantitative research proposals and dissertations, and we stand on rather thin ice when making judgments about qualitative projects. Unfortunately applying the known standards of good quantitative research to quantitative projects can lead to terrible qualitative research studies. We are not entirely without standards for evaluating good qualitative research proposals and studies, and I am startled to still hear stories from students about not being able to do a qualitative project in their department because faculty cannot agree on standards for such work. Qualitative researchers, even a group representing a diversity of positions and disciplines (Henwood & Pidgeon, 1994), do agree on some qualities of good research. At the risk of discovering just how many qualitative researchers might disagree with me, I am going to take a stand here on what good qualitative research looks like. I do not mean to be definitive, only to offer a few guidelines that in my experience hold up in project after project.

1. As with any research, good qualitative research is open to question and is therefore transparent with regard to the formulation of research questions, data collection, and analysis, revisions in process over time, and limitations of the research.
2. Qualitative research tends to focus on cultural and social contexts in which individuals or groups construct their lives and should therefore be designed for particular contexts and provide enough detailed information to ground interpretations in a specific time and place.
3. Qualitative research also highlights processes, for example, individual, social, developmental, and historic ways people construct meanings and act in the world—and therefore should clarify not only what happens in a particular time and place, but *how* it happens, and *how* meanings get created.
4. Qualitative researchers typically raise questions that cannot be answered definitively or with a single strong interpretation—and good qualitative research commonly proposes multiple interpretations and raises new questions.
5. Qualitative research addresses a theoretical puzzle through narrative data and methods of analysis—good qualitative research then goes on to elaborate on or to challenge theory in a particular field or across disciplines.
6. At a time when the ethics of good research are being reviewed and questioned, the ethics of qualitative research are especially thorny. Good qualitative research consciously grapples with the entwined issues of power and responsibility in relationships with individuals or groups that are often more lasting and

intimate than is commonly the case with quantitative research projects.

Psychology has a rich, if forgotten, history of qualitative research studies (see, for example, Dollard, 1937). Embracing this tradition means teaching students how to consider qualitative research as an interpretive process. Making a place for qualitative research in graduate education can only strengthen psychology as a discipline, helping the next generation of psychologists to join an increasingly interdisciplinary effort to address local and global human concerns.[4]

## REFERENCES

Brizuela, B., Steward, J., Carrillo, R., & Berger. J. (2000). *Acts of inquiry in qualitative research*. Cambridge, MA: Harvard Educational Review.

Brown, L., Argyris, D., Attanucci, J., Bardige, B., Gilligan, C., et al. (1988). *A guide to reading narratives of conflict and choice for self and moral voice*. Cambridge, MA: Harvard Graduate School of Education, unpublished monograph.

Brown, L., & Gilligan, C. (1992). *Meeting at the crossroads: Women's psychology and girls' development*. Cambridge, MA: Harvard University Press.

Bruner, J. (1986). *Actual minds, possible worlds*. Cambridge, MA: Harvard University Press.

Dollard, J. (1937). *Caste and class in a southern town*. Garden City, NY: Doubleday.

Gilligan, C. (1993). *In a different voice*. Cambridge, MA: Harvard University Press. (Original work published 1982)

Gilligan, C., Brown, L., & Rogers, A. (1990). Psyche embedded: A place for body, relationships and culture in personality theory. In A. Rabin, R. Zucker, R. Emmons, & S. Frank (Eds.), *Studying persons and lives* (pp. 86–147). New York: Springer.

Henwood, K., & Pidgeon, N. (1994). Beyond the qualitative paradigm: A framework for introducing diversity within qualitative psychology. *Journal of Community and Applied Social Psychology, 4*, 225–238.

Loevinger, J., & Wessler, R. (1970). *Measuring ego development: Construction and use of a sentence completion test*. San Francisco: Jossey-Bass.

Maxwell, J. (1996). *Qualitative research design: An interactive approach*. Thousand Oaks, CA: Sage.

Rogers, A. (1987). *Gender differences in moral thinking: A validity study of two moral orientations*. Unpublished doctoral dissertation, Washington University, St. Louis, MO.

---

[4]I would like to thank my four reviewers for critical questions and ideas that pushed my thinking and writing.

Rogers, A. (1993). Voice, play and a practice of ordinary courage in girls' and women's lives. *Harvard Educational Review, 63*(3), 265–295.

Rogers, A. (1995). *A shining affliction: A story of harm and healing in psychotherapy.* New York: Viking/Penguin Books.

Rogers, A. (1999). Understanding changes in girls' relationships and in ego development: Three studies of adolescent girls. In A. Blasi, L. Cohn, & M. Westenberg (Eds.), *Character development: On the contributions of Jane Loevinger's ego development theory* (pp. 145–160). New York: Erlbaum.

Rogers, A. (2000). When methods matter: Qualitative research issues in psychology. *Harvard Educational Review, 71*(1), 75–85.

Rogers, A., Brown, L., & Tappan, M. (1993). Interpreting ego development in girls: Regression or resistance? *The Narrative Study of Lives, 2*, 1–36.

Rogers, A., Casey, M., Ekert, J., Nakkula, V., & Sheinberg, N. (1999). An interpretive poetics of languages of the unsayable. *The Narrative Study of Lives, 6*, 77–106.

Zeller, N., & Farmer, F. (1999). "Catchy, clever titles are not acceptable": Style, APA, and qualitative reporting. *Qualitative Studies in Education, 12*(1): 3–19.

# 4

# RESEARCHERS AS PROTAGONISTS IN TEACHING AND LEARNING QUALITATIVE RESEARCH

COLETTE DAIUTE AND MICHELLE FINE

Teaching a course on qualitative research in a graduate psychology program, as we have done since the mid-1990s, is a narrative enterprise and challenge. We think of our primary task in this introductory course as one of researcher development—helping students develop theories of research and their own roles in the research process, thus becoming the protagonists of their own research narratives. Narrative discourse is powerful because it integrates knowledge and subjectivity—an integration that is typically avoided in psychological research training. Building on these integrative qualities of narrative, our course guides students through issues in developing a researcher stance—a stance that is necessarily interpretive and requires self- and social-consciousness.

The context for the course is the social/personality psychology doctoral program in which we both teach. The program prides itself on offering an array of courses well furnished with critical theory, feminist theory, critical race theory, and methodological diversity. Many of our graduate students, by now, have a growing fluency in both qualitative and quantitative methods. Teaching and learning research methods occurs within a specific culture— represented by the discourse of that research paradigm. Across our classes in theory, methods, and ethics, we ask students to interrogate: What constitutes truth? What influence does/should a researchers' point of view have on research questions? Who are the research participants and what is my relation to them? Why pursue these questions at this point in history? What constitutes significant work, work worth pursuing? What are "data" and "results"? All of these questions form the grand narrative of our courses. As a faculty we accept an obligation to teach students to be literate across a variety of methods. But that does not mean it is always easy.

Caught between questions of "Is this science?" much less "Is this psychology?" and "What's my role in all of this?" students sometimes become confused, anxious, and doubtful as they develop socially and personally meaningful research they can sustain through qualifying projects, dissertations, and eventually a research career. To teach research methods for methodological multilingualism that meets ethical standards crucial to psychological studies in the 21st century, we encourage students to develop a researcher self within a clearly stated interpretive stance, a stance about social research as well as about the specific topic and questions of inquiry. We explain to students that making this research narrative explicit is useful in all phases of their projects, including designing a study, maintaining ethical standards, reporting results, drawing implications for future research and practice.

In this chapter, we tell a story about how we try to do this. First, we explain how narrative theory helps us organize the teaching of qualitative inquiry as a developmental process. We then isolate issues that evolve in the course, extract key theoretical notions that students grapple with, and specify the kinds of questions or "speedbumps" (Weis & Fine, 2000) students confront as they wander into the praxis of qualitative research.

## TEACHING QUALITATIVE RESEARCH AS NARRATIVE

Narrative has been defined in numerous ways by psychologists, literary theorists, and linguists, with definitions differing in interesting ways based on scholars' prevailing theories and research missions. Although narrative discourse and ways of knowing are complex, some characteristics have emerged that provide a useful frame for teaching qualitative research methods.

Narratives depict sequences of events, with the presumed order moving from some beginning—often the past—to an end point, later in time. Chronologies might alter artistically with flashbacks and leap into the future, but the presumed narrative logic is the forward movement of time. Many courses on research methods are narrative as they enact steps in the research process: moving swiftly through phases of finding a topic and rationale; doing a literature review; creating research questions to test specific aspects of a theoretical model; crafting research design, methods, and instruments; and gathering data through a sequence of analyzing data and reporting and interpreting results. Such a narrative research sequence has practical value and salience. It is most consistent with experimental research epistemology, yet some presume it is also the basis for qualitative research. In teaching qualitative methods, we emphasize the recursive nature of the research process, in which ongoing theoretical reflection may change the course of data analysis, and revised research questions may be the result of the process. Writing, as we discuss later, is also often a phase of data analysis, and thus creating discursive themes to explain data may lead to data analysis. Such recursiveness can be unnerving to researchers trying to hold themselves to a chronological sequence, and, of course, the process can go awry if there are no standards to assess its success.

Narrative has also been described as a developmental discourse. The stories we tell create lives in the interpretive search for meaning. Numerous theorists and researchers reaching back into human history have explained how telling the story of one's life or community creates that life consistent with cultural, social, and historical contexts (Gates, 1992; McAdams, 1993, 1996; Polkinghorne, 1988; Spence, 1982). This life-making function is dynamic because narratives do not merely report on the life that is lived nor the community that has developed. The narrative process is a search for meaning, so the telling and the told, the hearing and the written, are inextricably linked, as is the individual narrator in the social milieu of discourse (Bruner, 1986). The search for meaning in narrative is, moreover, interpretive in that the narrator selects every detail, whether consciously or not, to tell the story in a way that also reveals why it is being told (Labov & Waletzky, 1967/1997). This interpretive function of narrative takes it out of the realm of mere reporting and embeds it in researcher subjectivities and social relations.

Teaching qualitative research as narrative usefully builds on these developmental and interpretive qualities of narrative, which we argue, are as central to research as following a sequence of steps. With the assistance of writings by other qualitative researchers, sharing our research experiences, and building students' research projects into the course, we guide students to develop their interpretive stances as researchers.

Not surprisingly, this process of developing a stance engages students intellectually and emotionally because it complicates the time-honored wall between science and self. Intense reactions often erupt in the form of provocative questions students have asked recurrently over the six years we have taught the course. We present these questions in this essay as they circle around issues of truth and objectivity, researcher-stance, researcher/ participant communication, search for meaning, and authority. We take the position that posing these questions must be taught alongside strategies for observing, interviewing, analyzing data, writing up results, and using other techniques typically involved in methods courses.

We present examples of key questions in *italics* throughout the text, questions voiced by students that constitute crucial discussion points in the course.[1] We read these questions as constitutive of learning and teaching in a qualitative methods course, hoping that researchers pursuing regression analyses or life history interviews will think through these issues, as well. While these questions have been gathered from students entering the space of qualitative research, we expect that all leave the course with a dedication to probe these issues for all kinds of social research, qualitative and quantitative, regardless of material gathered, methods practiced, and settings engaged.

## QUESTIONING TRUTH AND OBJECTIVITY

As with us, many of our students have been socialized as undergraduates to think about research as a discipline of distance, objectivity, and truth that by necessity lacks personal connection and passion. In this course, we challenge—from the first class—these constructions of disengagement and attempt to illustrate how research is affected by researchers' goals, plans, beliefs, and practices. In short, our sensibilities as people living specific lives influence how we read and create research. Becoming aware of one's researcher stance and assessing this stance critically are milestones in the development of a social researcher.

We introduce the notion of a qualitative *stance* early in the semester. By qualitative stance we signal a critical epistemological position taken up by a researcher in relation to the questions asked, materials collected, practices of analysis and interpretation used, and process of writing (Kidder & Fine, 1996). A qualitative stance toward teaching and researching means that we teach, and we invite students to research, through an epistemology in which knowing is produced in critical dialogue and action (Collins, 1991; Freire, 1982; Haraway, 1991; Rosaldo, 1993). By assuming a qualitative stance, educators and researchers are often bold in initial steps, resisting distance from the project. But we are always prepared to be wrong. Social research and teaching are seen as opportunities to learn. The elusive nature of "truths"—indeed their multiplicity—grows to be a pleasure rather than a frustration. Qualitative researchers never assume to know more than informants do, and, at the same time, we never assume informants' words simply speak for themselves.

To articulate these points, we draw from Kenn Gardner Honeychurch (1996) who writes, "all theories and methods of research, however, presuppose a particular worldview and also determine the ways in which individuals experience, and subsequently privilege, particular knowledges and approaches over others. . . . The biases of powerful and regulatory regimes

---

[1] Quotes from students are drawn from more than six years of student–faculty interaction and are paraphrased, rather than direct quotes.

were . . . mistaken for knowledge" (pp. 339, 346). We also read Sandra Harding (1993) who challenges what she calls the "God's eye view" version of objectivity and argues instead for "strong objectivity" in which the investments, commitments, and standpoints of researchers are acknowledged and then critically analyzed. There is a strong recognition of social science as a human enterprise stretching toward ever-partial truths.

Our teaching project is to create a context in which young researchers develop a recognition that social research is always constructed and contingent, that no construct or life or community preexists language or social relations; that research is about evidence, framing, and reframing. What students "know" to be "true" or "natural" is quickly revealed as one theory among many possible theories. So some brave students ask:

> "So, this may be a bad time to ask, but what does this have to do with science?"

> "Maybe I'm a control freak, but if someone is murdered, there is a truth; this table is real; I am actually a graduate student—These are truths. Why are we talking about partial truths?!"

Course activities are designed to help students make visible their theories of research and social theory. This process involves keeping track of questions, concerns, doubts, and contradictions, writing journal entries to reflect on these issues, and then producing brief papers over the course of the semester to integrate these issues with the aspects of students' theoretical stance and methodological approaches about which they are more certain. Instructions for short papers, such as the following, help students integrate their emotions and their epistemologies, which shatter and develop.

### Reflections for Developing Theory

Write a brief (three page) statement stating your theoretical framing and possible frames that you think your research participants might bring to your study. Reflect on conceptual, ethical, methodological, or any other issues that arise in relation to this theoretical framing, including strategies and worries you have about mis-framing.

Assignments like these raise issues and acknowledge the choices that researchers make. These papers offer a productive context in which to create theory and generate variations on a research design. In the process, for example, of deciding what to ask in an interview or how to ask it, students have to consider the understandings and issues that participants might bring to the research.

## THE DEVELOPMENT OF RESEARCHER SELVES

As students "get" the constructed nature of their work, quantitative and qualitative, their anxieties sometimes rise about themselves as scholars.

In teaching toward a researcher stance, we refuse to turn research methods into a set of decontextualized techniques. The learning of research methods is, instead, often an emotional journey because it means challenging and perhaps disrupting some long-held assumptions about knowledge and role of the researcher in knowledge inquiries. Student reactions range from resistant to thrilled, engaged, fearful over losing control, and delighted with the journey of qualitative work. Once students acknowledge their researcher selves, they begin to reflect thoughtfully:

> *Why am I pursuing this research question, and with what consequence to whom?*

> *Why do I, as a White researcher, want to study youth violence in an African American urban neighborhood, rather than a neighborhood more like my own childhood community?*

> *Because of my experience as a new mother, and the difficult issues that no one was willing to talk about, I want to study the hidden discourses of new motherhood, but how do I invite women to talk about the unspeakable without putting words in their mouths?*

In response to these questions, we guide students toward course readings and activities with the goal of making explicit their understandings about research and about the topics that interest them. We ask students to ask themselves: "*Why is your topic interesting to you as well as to the field? What do you really want to know, and why are these participants the ones who can add insight?*"

We encourage students to see themselves as co-constructing the lives and communities with whom they study. Understandably, the explicit insertion of the researcher shaping the story rather than simply reporting it discomforts some student researchers eager to don the symbolic white lab coat. As one student wrote to us in the course, "All my traditional assumptions about my separation from the research, having no preconceived ideas, me being the scientist who discovers . . . are turning upside down. I spend hours crying about what I have lost."

We encouraged this student, for example, to dig under her original question to raise up successive questions about the assumptions and goals of her research. Such emotionally charged reactions thus become material to advance thinking about the research process with questions such as, "*Why are these 'traditional assumptions' so valuable to me? What are these assumptions protecting me from knowing and keeping me from hearing?*"

A large piece of our work in the classroom involves inviting students to be clear about the relation of their research selves to the questions they ask, the voices they hear in their data, the theories they write through. We ask students to be clear about how they will learn, read, see, and confront what they do not want to hear or cannot. Will they explicitly seek counter voices? Will they have a group assist in interpretation and analysis? Will they include a set of codes that work in opposition to where their researcher self is positioned? How will they analyze material that confirms and material that disconfirms their theoretical position? Will they search for the outliers, seek contradictions and commit to an analysis of differences within the study (Bhavnani, 1999)? This may end up feeling like a lot of responsibility for beginning researchers, some of whom came to the class just to learn how to construct codes or run a focus group.

Although philosopher Sandra Harding has not written on the emotional consequence of such teaching, she has noted the radical collision that can occur when feminist social science meets up against traditional epistemologies. This is a collision that is analogous, for some students, to the confrontation between a qualitative stance and traditional psychology. Harding wrote,

> Once we undertake to use [women's] experience as a resource to generate scientific problems, hypotheses, and evidence to design research [for women], and to place the researcher in the same critical plane as the research subject, traditional epistemological assumptions can no longer be made. These agendas have led feminist social scientists to ask questions about who can be a knower (only men?); what beliefs must pass in order to be legitimated as knowledge . . . ; what kinds of things can be known (can 'subjective truths,' ones that only women—or only some women—tend to arrive at, count as knowledge?); the nature of objectivity (does it require a "point of viewlessness"?); the appropriate relationships between the researcher and her/his research participants (must the researcher be disinterested, dispassionate, and socially invisible to the participant?); what should be the purposes of the pursuit of knowledge . . . ? (1993, p. 181)

By asking students, as emergent researchers, to reflect on their stance, their questions, the assumptions they bring to the work, the passions, interests, and "blind spots" they can anticipate, they too confront long-held assumptions about what constitutes knowledge, objectivity, appropriate relations of researchers and participants, and the purpose of social research. At our peril, we share our experiences and resistances to doing the same.


## RESEARCHER/PARTICIPANT COMMUNICATION

The search for meaning is implicitly dependent on collecting multiple perspectives. In qualitative work, these perspectives may converge; but more likely, if the data collection is well done, they also conflict. The readings make clear that participants' reflections gathered in interviews or observations must be considered in terms of relevant social, cultural and political contexts. The sociocultural engagements of these participants play a role in their views of research and the topic under study. These views are complex and dynamic.

As Lisa Delpit (1995) reminds us, "People of color are, in general, skeptical of research as a determiner of our fates. Academic research has, after all, found us genetically inferior, culturally deprived and verbally deficient" (p. 31). Oliva Espin (1999), likewise, reminds researchers that the language in which an interview is conducted may convey relation or distance: "Even among immigrants who are fluent in English, the first language often remains the language of emotions. Thus, speaking in a second language may 'distance' the immigrant woman from important parts of herself" (Espin, 1999, p. 138). And yet allowing us no easy answers, Espin goes on to say, "Conversely, a second language may provide a vehicle to express the inexpressible in the first language ( . . . because the person censors herself from saying certain 'taboo' things in the first language)" (Espin, 1999, p. 138).

Race, ethnicity, language, gender, sexuality, disability, context, place—all forms of power affect relations between researchers and participants. Moreover, even "within groups" people vary, and people vary within themselves across time, place, language, and method. Finally, participants' views of the worlds often differ radically from researchers' views of the world. Qualitative research lifts up this stew of perspectives for social analysis. Once this is apparent, students begin to think through their delicate relations with research participants:

> Do I tell someone—like a middle school kid—in an interview that I find his language to be offensive, or that he is being sexist? If I don't say anything, am I letting them believe it's ok to talk like that? But if I do say something, am I losing important information?

In qualitative inquiry, it is now well recognized that different methods produce different kinds of data; that participants—even from the same "group"—vary enormously and that participants—even within the same person within a single interview—may contradict him/herself; and that participants do not all see the world as researchers do. These contradictions are the stuff of qualitative analysis and tough choices qualitative theorists need to explore.

> If the respondents tell me that "race" or "gender" is irrelevant, that they don't matter in their everyday experiences, but the data suggest that men and women, African Americans, Latinos, and Whites, actually speak through very different discourses, am I betraying my informants by employing a race or gender analysis? Is this theory building? Is it unethical?

> What if the very constructs I am interested in understanding are not meaningful—or are offensive—to my respondents? That is, I interview her as a battered woman but she sees herself as a lawyer, mother of two who was hit by a former husband? She does not want to be defined by the violence, but

*instead by her accomplishments. Is this her denial—or is my theoretical frame just wrong?*

In qualitative research projects, a collision of evidence is far more likely than simple confirmation of a researcher's a priori hypotheses. Triangulation, construct validity, and generalizability as unproblematic concepts may be called into question. Take, for instance, construct validity, the *raison d'être* of qualitative work. With qualitative methods we seek to learn, from participants, how they view the world, what a construct means or does not mean to them, where they situate the borders on a construct and what they believe constitutes that construct. But once people are interviewed, surveyed, observed, or involved in a focus group, the very constructs we thought we were studying are typically unpacked and stretched out of shape. Sometimes they are unrecognizable and just plain fall apart. The analytic task for the young researcher, then, is to resuscitate or retheorize the construct, to make sense amid conflicting bits of evidence. At this point, we try to help students see the dialectical relation of theory, codes, and perspectives through what Strauss and Corbin (1994) call "conceptual density."

> *At this AIDS organization, nobody talks about the virus in the same ways. For some people it's just another problem in a long list of life struggles, and for others it is the only issue they deal with. How can I refer to HIV as a "trauma" when half of my respondents don't?*

> *But the women who live in the shelter think the shelter is a "success" if they stay for only one day and then go back home—because they got out of the violence. But the Board of Directors thinks they need to leave their abusive husbands and be self sufficient. How do I talk about the "success" of the program when they all disagree on the definition of success?*

Another writing assignment builds the issues of researcher/participant communication into more formal questions of research purpose as the foundation for design.

### Research Purpose
Write a two-page statement about the goals of your research and the research "stance" you have in relation to these goal. What is it you want to find out? Why? What are the constructs and outcomes you are studying? What might you learn that would discomfort or disrupt your initial conceptualizations?

Students, at some point, realize that unpacking the construct, from multiple points of view, is not the end of the research but is, in itself, a research project and that constructs only stand still if we refuse to ask or hear how participants "make sense" of their lives.

# SEARCH FOR MEANING THROUGH METHOD

On the basis of theoretical stance and having raised difficult issues of purpose, ethics, and relationship to research questions and participants, the appropriateness of different techniques are then relevant to the search for these socially and personally grounded meanings.

*What if I get different information in the focus groups and the individual interviews? Which is true?*

*Can I use both qualitative and quantitative methods?*

In classes focused on specific methods such as interviewing, focus group, participatory action research, or narrative analysis, and classes focused on analysis plans such as thematic, content, psychoanalytic, discourse, conversational analyses, and the integration of qualitative and quantitative methods (Bogdan & Biklen, 1992; Emerson, Fretz, & Shaw, 1995; Kitzinger, 2001; LeCompte & Preissle, 1993), research is articulated as a developmental process. Across methods, there is a commitment to recursive reflection and review of the data, the codes, the interpretations, and the writings. Such a commitment extends seeing the unseen, hearing the unheard, and speaking the unspeakable. And there is a recognition that different methods indeed produce different kinds of data and that this variation is useful for—not a distraction from—theory building.

Students learn that in Michelle and Lois Weis's research on poor and working-class young adults in urban America (Fine & Weis, 1998) and Colette's study of young people's social development, especially around issues of conflict and violence (Daiute, 2000), in the beginning of our analyses we generated "theoretical" codes based on previous research and conceptual models foundational to the research. The data analysis process then involved reading for those codes but also, and in a separate phase of reading, examining the material for what those a priori codes missed or misrepresented. Such grounded qualitative readings involve, for example, looking for discourses of "outliers," or atypical cases, and patterns that contradict or extend the explanations and arguments in organizing the emerging results.

We noted, in Michelle and Lois's materials, that the stories women told in individual interviews about male violence were very different from the stories told in focus groups. For White women in particular, it was only in the individual interviews that they would reveal evidence of such violence. In Colette's study, reading children's writing about conflict and violence in terms of social developmental patterns offered some expected patterns of difference across 7- through 10-year-olds, while subsequent critical readings illustrated how assumptions from developmental theory were disconfirmed by details in the data missed by codes. Alternative patterns of social explanation emerged across narratives of social conflict written by children from different race/ethnicity groups, in how they represented rights and responsibilities in community and interpersonal relations (Daiute & Jones, in press), and in how addressing issues of injustice defied normative patterns of narrative coherence (Daiute, 2000). In some instances, we wanted to account for the silences (e.g., about domestic violence, racism, or youth conflict) and fill in the missing "spaces" in our theoretical architecture. In minilectures about such findings in our research, we try to model a commitment to move recursively between method, evidence, and theory; to revise, collect more evidence, and to seek contradictions, fractures, and nuances. By so doing, we invite a kind of recursive theorizing that challenges the traditional linear format of literature review, method, data analysis, and discussion so prominent in psychology. Indeed, we admit that the "ending" of a qualitative empirical article may require that the "beginning" be rewritten, because constructs shift. Other literature may need to be scanned, a new code added, a closer analysis entertained. Then, the question that inevitably erupts is,

> Does it take "longer" to complete a qualitative study than an experiment or a survey?

We think not. But qualitative work does benefit from an intellectually open mind stretching toward theoretical sophistication, developed over time, over evidence, with colleagues, over coffee and wine.

## ON ANALYSIS AND WRITING

Once students (and we) appreciate that social relations, "variables" and "themes" are constructed, then meaning making becomes a doubled project: Informants search for meaning when we ask them questions, and researchers search for meaning across all aspects of qualitative research, including when writing. We read Laurel Richardson who describes writing as a search for meaning (1994):

> I write because I want to find something out. I write in order to learn something that I didn't know before I wrote it. I was taught, however, as perhaps you were, too, not to write until I knew what I wanted to say, until my points were organized and outlined. No surprise, this static writing model coheres with mechanistic scientism and quantitative research. . . . The model has serious problems: It ignores the role of writing as a dynamic, creative process; it undermines the confidence of beginning qualitative researchers because their experience of research is inconsistent with the writing model; and it contributes to the flotilla of qualitative writing that is simply not interesting to read because adherence to the model requires writers to silence their own voices and to view themselves as contaminants. (p. 517)

Thinking about the process of meaning making across data collection, analysis, and writing again raises conflicts about science and self, often expressed in relation between data collection and data analysis.

*If my research questions keep changing, how do I ethically inform my respondents about my most recent questions?*

*How often do I remind informants of their rights. . . . is bathroom conversation, talk in the "after interview," elevator small talk—ethically considered "data?"*

*But I already did my literature review on divorce, and the data all lead me to write about domestic violence . . . do I have to do another literature review?*

The search for meaning includes and demands a rigorous plan for analysis. This explicit request for an analysis plan often intimidates students, especially those attracted (erroneously) to the seeming looseness of qualitative work. For guidance, we read Gail Hornstein (1994), feminist biographer, who wrote, "Part of the seductiveness of writing a life is that it fosters the fantasy of perfect understanding. You start by imagining your research participant as misunderstood and unappreciated, someone in need of rescue. Then you convince yourself that you are the first to recognize her, to see fully who she was. In a union that is more lamination than marriage, biographer and subject fuse their interests, allowing each other to speak in one voice" (p. 53). Hornstein, as does Patricia Hill Collins (1991) and Mari Matsuda (1995), asks us to consider how researcher and researched—race, class, gender, sexuality, and quirks of biography—influence what we see, hear, delete, and critique and how we develop social analysis. The social analyses that informants narrate weave delicately with the growing analysis of the researcher. Thus sense is "made," theory born.

At several phases across the creation of their research projects, we ask students to write, review, and rewrite if necessary research questions and to consider several approaches for inquiry into these questions. Writing good research questions captures issues of theory, purpose, and process, so we spend considerable time on the nature of qualitative research questions and what they imply about method as well as theory.

### Research Questions

By today, you should hand in to us and bring copies for other students a statement of the research questions you are pursuing, with a brief statement about some of the theoretical assumptions and goals motivating these questions, as well as issues of concern in relation to them. Also suggest two possible methodological approaches to addressing these questions. That is, we want you to move toward developing the question(s), recognizing that many of you will want to build in enough flexibility for new questions to emerge in the research process. The idea of this assignment is to provide experience creating and critiquing theoretically based and practical research questions as the basis for sound, reflective research. This paper should be no more than three pages (which should also provide experience at succinct theorizing).

Working on research questions at different stages in the project piques different concerns. Research questions early in the process tend to sketch broad outlines of an inquiry, implying some aspect that is particularly salient to the researcher, such as an interest in a specific topic, theoretical perspective, or method. Qualitative research, for example, tends to value interviewing as a research interaction because it involves participants' direct expression, so early versions of qualitative research questions often imply interviewing as a method. Ongoing critique of research questions, however, should require increasingly explicit rationales for interviewing in relation to or instead of other modes of data collection. From such a process, students also become aware, for example, that given the nature of their theory, their interest in gathering a certain kind of data such as interviews, or the current state of the art in the area they are researching, they may have to revise questions to ask "how" something happens and to seek descriptions rather than to ask about comparisons.

## AUTHORITY

At some point, recognizing their own hands in the construction of social research and analysis, students struggle with questions of power and authority. If social relations and social research are constructed, whose analysis prevails in the writing? Whose language should be used—mine or theirs? How much authority do I give away to informants? Thus, they ask,

> In what language do I interview, for respondents who are not native English speakers?

> If I interview participants in their native language, isn't my translation always an act of revision and distortion?

> Sometimes I worry that if I involve my participants as researchers, it would be just because I am scared of writing through my own position.

> How much veto power do I grant informants? Can they change my final research report if they disagree with my conclusions? Do I want to give away so much?

In the search for meaning, what we ask, how we ask it, how we analyze the material, and how we write matters. There is no neutral voice and no escape from theoretical authority. The research setting and the analysis plan are always filled with theory, politics, and difficult choices.

This search for meaning and struggles with authority may be particularly problematic for students who think they are participating in research which "empowers." Some students new to qualitative methods often carry a romance into the classroom, wanting to "hear unheard voices" as though these voices were raw, innocent, authentic, uncontaminated, and unaffected by the co-construction of the research relationship. The desire to hear unheard voices may pervert into a way of not seeing, not hearing, and not engaging participants in all their complexity. The romance with qualitative research may camouflage students' troubles with critical analysis and theoretical authority. We learn to be wary when students say,

> "Qualitative research is much more ethical . . ."
>
> "Qualitative research gets closer to the truth . . ."
>
> "I just think numbers are too distant . . ."
>
> "I want to hear unheard voices . . ."
>
> "I don't want to change anything that the youth said to me. Too many scholars have messed with their words, telling them what they really mean. Theory is a cover; it's an act of colonialism to theorize the voices of oppressed youth . . ."

At this point in the course, students are usually thrilled having collected narratives of "personal experience," but nervous about "imposing" analysis or theory. We remind them that even or especially those historically "unheard voices" must be theorized, connected to broader historic and current social arrangements (cf. Mills, 1959; Smith, 1999). People speak through a language of "experiences," but this language at once reveals and obscures. We then read historian Joan Scott's (1992) outstanding essay, "Experience" in which she writes: "To put it another way, the evidence of experience, whether conceived through a metaphor of similarity or in any other way that takes meaning as transparent, reproduces rather than contests given ideological systems—those that assume that the facts of history speak for themselves. . ." (p. 25). Scott insists that words are neither innocent nor ideologically free, and always in need of critical analysis and theorizing.


## CONCLUSION

As teachers and researchers continuing to learn ourselves about qualitative inquiry, we feel an enormous responsibility to guide and support students as they deconstruct prior notions of truth and objectivity, challenge the presumed value of researcher distance, rethink what constitutes standpoint and "bias," and discover with trepidation the importance of researcher authority and theory. Our measure of success is not whether or not a given student pursues a qualitative dissertation, but whether or not all of the students bring a critical eye to the research enterprise; to any research enterprise, involving numbers or words, constructs or lives—not *so* critical that they cannot work (which also happens), but no longer uncritically accepting the practices of social science. There is, then, a bold pedagogical project: the teaching of critique and humble co-construction, creativity and reflexivity, the courage to design and engage research as action in the world.

We have crystallized, in this chapter, a kind of master narrative, despite ourselves, one with a beginning, middle, and end, a linearity of progress, and not enough reflection about our own engagements and screw ups in the course. Thus, we admit, this master narrative, too, is semifiction. Throughout the course we meet often, change directions, and alter the syllabus to "fit" our dominant narrative. The course is always informed by our problems with research. The course inevitably provokes changes in our understandings of our research and our teaching. So we, too, are delightfully subjects of a developmental process.

## REFERENCES

Bhavnani, K. (1999). Tracing the contours. In H. Afshar & M. Maynard (Eds.), *Dynamics of "race" and gender* (pp. 26–40). London: Taylor & Francis.

Bogdan, R., & Biklen, S. (1992). *Qualitative research for education: An introduction.* Boston: Allyn & Bacon.

Bruner, J. (1986). *Actual minds, possible worlds.* Cambridge, MA: Harvard University Press.

Collins, P. H. (1991). *Black feminist thought: Knowledge, consciousness, and the politics of empowerment.* New York: Routledge.

Daiute, C. (2000). Narrative sites for youth's construction of social consciousness. In L. Weis & M. Fine (Eds.), *Construction sites* (pp. 211–234). New York: Teachers College Press.

Daiute, C., & Jones, J. (in press). Diversity discourses: Reading race and ethnicity in children's writing. In S. Greene & D. Abt-Perkins (Eds.), *Talking, reading, writing, and race: Contributions to racial understanding by literacy research.* New York: Teachers College Press.

Delpit, L. (1995). *Other people's children: Cultural conflict in the classroom.* New York: New Press.

Emerson, R., Fretz, R., and Shaw, L. (1995). *Writing ethnographic fieldnotes.* Chicago: University of Chicago Press.

Espin, O. M. (1999). *Women crossing boundaries: A psychology of immigration and transformations of sexuality.* New York: Routledge.

Fine, M., & Weis, L. (1998). *The unknown city.* Cambridge, MA: Beacon Press.

Freire, P. (1982). Creating alternative research methods. Learning to do it by doing it. In B. Hall, A. Gillette, & R. Tandon, (Eds.), *Creating knowledge: A monopoly?* (pp. 29–37). New Delhi, India: Society for Participatory Research in Asia.

Gates, H. L. (1992). *Loose canons: Notes on the culture wars*. New York: Oxford University Press.

Haraway, D. (1991). *Simians, cyborgs, and women: The reinvention of nature*. New York: Routledge.

Harding, S. (1993). Rethinking standpoint epistemology: "What is strong objectivity?" In L. Alcoff & E. Potter (Eds.), *Feminist epistemologies* (pp. 49–82). New York: Routledge.

Honeychurch, K. G. (1996). Researching dissident subjectivities: Queering the grounds of theory and practice. *Harvard Educational Review, 66*, 339–355.

Hornstein, G. A. (1994). The ethics of ambiguity: Feminists writing women's lives. In C. E. Franz & A. V. Stewart (Eds.), *Women creating lives: Identities, resilience, and resistance* (pp. 51–68). Boulder, CO: Westview Press.

Kidder, L. H., & Fine, M. (1996). Qualitative inquiry in psychology: A radical tradition. In D. R. Fox & I. Prilletensky (Eds.), *Handbook of critical psychology* (pp. 34–50). Newbury Park, CA: Sage.

Kitzinger, C. (2001). Resistance in women's talk: Thinking positively about breast cancer. *International Journal of Critical Psychology, 4*, 35–48.

Labov, W., & Waletzky, J. (1997). Narrative analysis: Oral versions of personal experience. *Journal of Narrative and Life History, 7*, 207–215.

LeCompte, M., & Preissle, J. (1993). *Ethnography and qualitative design* (2nd ed.). San Diego, CA: Academic Press.

Matsuda, M. (1995). Looking to the bottom: Critical legal studies and reparations. In K. Crenshaw, N. Gotanda, G. Peller, & K. Thomas (Eds.), *Critical race theory: The key writings that formed the movement* (pp. 63–79). New York: New Press.

McAdams, D. P. (1993). *The stories we live by: Personal myths and the making of the self*. New York: William Morrow.

McAdams, D. P. (1996). Personality, modernity, and the storied self: A contemporary framework for studying persons. *Psychological Inquiry, 7*, 295–321.

Mills, C. W. (1959). *The sociological imagination*. London: Oxford University Press.

Polkinghorne, D. (1988). *Narrative knowing and the human sciences*. Albany: State University of New York.

Richardson, L. (1994). Writing: A method of inquiry. In N. K. Denzin & Y. S. Lincoln (Eds.), *Handbook of qualitative research* (pp. 516–529). Thousand Oaks, CA: Sage.

Rosaldo, R. (1993). *Culture and truth: The remaking of social analysis*. Boston: Beacon Press.

Scott, J. W. (1992). Experience. In J. Butler & J. W. Scott (Eds.), *Feminists theorize the political* (pp. 22–40). New York: Routledge.

Smith, L. T. (1999). *Decolonizing methodologies: Research and indigenous peoples*. London: Zed Books.

Spence, D. P. (1982). *Narrative truth and historical truth: Meaning and interpretation in psychoanalysis*. New York: Norton.

Strauss, A., & Corbin, J. (1994). Grounded theory methodology: An overview. In N. K. Denzin & Y. S. Lincoln (Eds.), *Handbook of qualitative research* (pp. 273–285). Thousand Oaks, CA: Sage.

Weis, L., & Fine, M. (2000). *Speedbumps: A student-friendly guide to qualitatative research*. New York: Teachers College Press.

# 5

# LEARNING TO LISTEN: NARRATIVE PRINCIPLES IN A QUALITATIVE RESEARCH METHODS COURSE

SUSAN E. CHASE

On the first day of my qualitative research methods course, I tell students that even if they never do qualitative research again in their lives, this course will help them to develop strong listening skills. Many of them are nonplussed by this promise. They already think of themselves as good listeners—do we not all think the same? Besides, "good listener" is not one of the skills they hope to list on their resumes. Yet, by the end of the semester, even the most skeptical are convinced that listening well is a difficult, important, and useful skill.

In my course—which enrolls undergraduates in sociology, anthropology, psychology, communication, and education—I introduce students to a range of qualitative research methods: participant observation, life history/oral history, and autoethnography. I concentrate, however, on in-depth interviewing as a method. Over the years, I have found that the best way to teach students how to conduct research based on in-depth interviews is to use the principles of narrative analysis. In this essay I show how those principles inform my teaching practices and how they encourage students to listen well.

## THE PRINCIPLES OF NARRATIVE ANALYSIS

In the social sciences, and particularly in the tradition of qualitative research, the term "narrative analysis" typically indicates two major principles. The first is that narration is a major way in which people make sense of experience, construct the self, and create and communicate meaning. The second is that personal narratives, no matter how unique and individual, are inevitably social in character. Thus, in one way or another, narrative

79

analysis combines a focus on people's actual stories with some form of analysis of the social character of those stories.[1]

The second principle merits some explanation because narratives are social in a number of ways. To the extent that a narrator tells her story to an audience, whether that be an interviewer, a friend, the public, or herself (as in a diary), her narration has an interactional component. During an interview, for example, the narrator tells her story to a particular person, who may shape the telling of the story by encouraging, empathizing with, interrupting, or resisting it. In addition, the form and content of a person's story must be socially recognizable if it is to be meaningful to self and others. In terms of form, stories typically have at least a beginning, middle, end, and a point—an answer to the question "so what?" (Labov, 1972; Riessman, 1993). In terms of content, a story usually resonates with some genre familiar to the narrator's community. For example, in American culture at large, familiar narrative genres include the success story (overcoming obstacles to reach one's goal) and the quest story (finding one's true self by facing particular challenges; Aisenberg & Harrington, 1988; Heilbrun, 1989; Rosenwald & Ochberg, 1992). Narratives are also social in the sense of reflecting broad social, cultural, ideological, and historical conditions in which they get told and get heard. For instance, gay and lesbian coming out stories and sexual assault survivor stories are a product of late 20th-century Western societies. These stories were not told 100 years ago (at least not as they are told today), and they may not be prominent or recognizable in the same way 100 years from now (Plummer, 1995). Finally, narratives are social in the sense of playing a role in specific communities as well as in a society at large. Gay and lesbian coming out stories have produced new understandings of sexual orientation, and those altered understandings have transformed not only individuals' lives, but also wider cultural meanings, politics, and legal issues concerning sexuality (Plummer, 1995).

The value of narrative analysis in the social sciences lies in the integration of these two major principles in research practice. When we listen carefully to the stories people tell, we learn how people as individuals and as groups make sense of their experiences and construct meanings and selves.

---

[1] For various social science discussions of the meaning and importance of narrative, see Brown (1987), Chase (1995a), DeVault (1999, chap. 5), Gubrium and Holstein (1997), Hunter (1990), Josselson (1996), Josselson and Lieblich (1995), Maines and Ulmer (1993), Mishler (1986), Richardson (1990), Riessman (1993), and Rosenwald and Ochberg (1992). It is also important to note that even within qualitative research the term "narrative" has different meanings, each of which is useful in its own way. William Labov (1972) defined the term narrowly to refer to a specific linguistic form that is distinguishable from other kinds of talk. Catherine Riessman (1987, 1990, 1993) expanded this definition by suggesting that there are several different kinds of linguistically identifiable narratives, such as habitual or episodic narratives. "Narrative" can also refer more broadly to a life story about some aspect of the narrator's experience that is of deep and abiding concern for him or her (Chase, 1995b).

We also learn about the complexities and subtleties of the social worlds they inhabit. We gain deeper understandings of the social resources (cultural, ideological, historical, and so forth) that they draw on, resist, and transform as they tell their stories (Chase, 1996).

What is the relationship between these principles of narrative analysis and qualitative research generally? On the one hand, I think most qualitative researchers would agree that these principles are integral to the in-depth interview method; most researchers who conduct in-depth interviews are interested in the meanings people construct as they talk about their lives, as well as in the social contexts and resources that enable and constrain those meanings. On the other hand, I find that many researchers who conduct in-depth interviews do not put these principles into practice in the course of actual interviews. In describing how I teach qualitative research methods, I will argue that qualitative researchers *should* take seriously the principles of narrative analysis and that these principles have consequences for research practice, in particular, how we write interview questions and how we conduct interviews. By contrast, when it comes to the analysis of in-depth interviews, I will argue that narrative analysis is one form among other equally valuable methods of data analysis.

## CHOOSING A RESEARCH PROJECT

My students and I begin the course by reading studies based on different qualitative research methods and discussing issues and ideas central to all qualitative research: the role of subjectivity, the meaning of objectivity, situated knowing (Harding, 1991), ethical problems, relationships between the researcher and researched, and the rights and responsibilities of both. On the theory that doing is the best way of learning, however, I organize the bulk of the course around students' individual research projects.

To guide them in choosing a project, I ask students to think of a group of people whose lives or experiences are especially interesting to them. Whose stories would they most like to listen to? In other words, I instruct students to begin with people's lives rather than with a research question per se. This beginning point may seem to bypass the important issue of how to conceptualize research problems or questions that are appropriate to qualitative research methods. But I find that asking students to focus on a group of people they are interested in is a no-fail method of ensuring that their projects will be grounded in qualitative principles generally and in narrative principles specifically.

Many students have been trained to think of research as beginning with a hypothesis that they will then test, an assumption drawn from quantitative methods. Even though we discuss the questions researchers seek to answer in the qualitative studies we read early in the semester, most students find it difficult to resist quantitative assumptions when it comes to their projects. Asking them to come up with a group of people they find interesting rather than a research question is a good way of disrupting those assumptions. To the extent that all qualitative research is grounded in an interest in the meanings people construct in their social worlds, asking students to focus on a group of people encourages their immersion in people's lives. Furthermore, this way of beginning makes it easy for students to ask for people's stories when it comes to writing interview questions.

At the same time, by conceptualizing their research projects as about a specific group of people, I implicitly direct students to certain kinds of research questions: What are the experiences of such and such group of people? How do they give meaning to their experiences, their lives, their selves? What meanings do they develop? What cultural, ideological, and other social resources do they draw on or resist? How do they draw on or resist those social resources in making sense of their experiences?

Recently, my students' projects have included studies of strippers, homeless people, women with eating disorders, local gay activists, women survivors of sexual assault, women of color who date White men, law students, and foreign-born mothers who are raising their children in the United States. Although each student had a particular interest in the group he or she chose—often times, but not always, students choose groups they belong to—each of these groups is also interesting in a broad sociological sense. Even at the beginning of the semester students can articulate some version of the sociological import of their projects. Strippers' stories will tell us something about gender relations and women's occupational opportunities; homeless people's stories will reflect limited life chances and our society's treatment of poverty; anorexic and bulimic women's stories will draw on cultural ideals about women's bodies; gay activists' stories will resist heterosexism in our society; sexual assault survivors' stories will speak to gender oppression and overcoming victimization; the stories of women of color who date interracially will address racial ideologies and race relations; law students' stories will tell us about their socialization into a competitive and prestigious profession; foreign-born mothers' stories will include strategies for negotiating the differences between two cultures.

To put a different spin on this, each of these groups of people has a story to tell that is not only sociologically significant but also culturally interesting. By culturally interesting I mean that the stories these groups of people have to tell tap into issues that most members of our society would find familiar and (in some sense) important. Strippers, for example, have a story to tell about how they deal with American society's simultaneous aversion to and demand for their work and how they manage (or do not manage) to develop a strong sense of self in the midst of that contradiction.

Asking students to choose a group they are interested in, then, becomes a way of asking them to choose a group that has a culturally interesting story to tell. This is a no-fail method because students' particular interests (similar to narrators' particular stories) are inevitably shaped by social, cultural, and ideological dimensions of the world around them. This, then, is another more subtle sense in which narrative principles underlie my instructions to students to choose a group of people whose stories they would like to hear.

## WRITING INTERVIEW QUESTIONS

When it comes to writing interview questions, there is nothing subtle about how narrative principles inform how I teach research practice. I instruct students to organize their interview questions around the life story the narrator has to tell. In the broadest sense, this is some version of, "Tell me what it's like to be an exotic dancer." Or, "Tell me the story of how you became politically active in the gay movement." Or "Tell me what you have done to survive the trauma of sexual assault." Although the broad question organizes the interview as a whole, I require students to write an extensive interview guide that anticipates all of the possible areas that narrators might cover. My instructions for writing the first draft of their interview guides include this:

> A good way to begin is to jot down all of the issues or areas you want to cover in the interview. Then write a series of questions for each of those issues or areas. After that, think about a good way to order or organize the questions. Some of your interview topics lend themselves well to a chronological ordering of questions. How you order the questions is very important—you want your questions to flow from topic to topic, rather than jump around.

Students often find it difficult to understand what appears at first as a contradiction: I require them to write lengthy, detailed interview guides, and to rewrite them until there is a flow—oftentimes, but not always, a chronological flow.[2] And yet I tell them that apart from their first major opening question—a question that invites a life story—they should ask questions that follow from close listening to the narrator's story rather than ask questions from their interview guide. Why, some students complain, do they have to spend so much time on their interview guides if they are supposed to put them aside during the interviews? I tell them that a well-constructed interview guide prepares them to be open to a wide range of

---

[2] We read Catherine Riessman (1987) and discuss how some narrators may organize their narratives in ways that are not chronological.

stories their interviewees may tell, and it helps them to know what in general they want to hear about. But once they are prepared in this way, inviting and listening well to this person's particular story should be their main goal. Many of their interview questions will be answered without even being asked.

I find that preparing to listen well by writing a thorough interview guide is a critical but underemphasized part of the research process. Most qualitative researchers who conduct in-depth interviews are interested in how people make sense of their experiences and so their questions aim to elicit people's experiences and perspectives. However, when a researcher uses narrative principles to guide her interviewing practices, she develops interview questions that focus on specific, concrete life stories. In my view, the principles of narrative analysis ground the best interviewing practice rather than being one viable option among others. In this sense, close attention to narrative principles could improve immensely the data qualitative researchers gather.

An example will help here. Sometimes my class reads parts of Sharon Hays's *The Cultural Contradictions of Motherhood* (1996). This is a fascinating study of the clash between two contemporary ideologies: the ideology of self-interest that governs behavior in the public world of work and the ideology of intensive mothering that implores mothers (and mothers in particular, as opposed to fathers or any other caretakers) to invest selflessly a tremendous amount of time, energy, and money raising their children. Hays conducted in-depth interviews with working-class and middle-class mothers to find out how mothers who do and do not work outside the home come to terms with the contradiction between these ideologies.

In a chapter titled "Intensive Mothering: Mothers' Work on Behalf of the Sacred Child," Hays speaks to us as readers before she introduces the voices of her interviewees:

> As you listen to these mothers, it may seem at times that they are simply speaking in clichés, trite truisms, and all too well-worn phrases. But clichés and truisms should not be underestimated or discounted— they often highlight recurring cultural themes. Ultimately, our familiarity with many of the phrases used by these mothers is a measure of the deep and pervasive power of the ideology of intensive mothering and the extent to which all of us recognize at least portions of its logic. (p. 98)

I agree wholeheartedly that the ideology of intensive mothering is familiar; it is the dominant cultural discourse about mothering in contemporary American society. But to the extent that Hays's interviewees spoke in clichés and trite truisms, that is at least partially because many of her interview questions were not aimed at inviting life stories.

In the appendix we find Hays's interview guide and in a section of the interview called "Ideas about Child Rearing," we find some of the questions that formed the basis of the chapter on intensive mothering:

> How would you describe a good child as opposed to a bad child?
> How do you think they become good or bad children? (p. 180)

These questions are abstract—they instruct an interviewee to speak in generalities rather than about her experiences. Indeed, they invite ideological talk, clichés, and trite truisms; they do not invite stories about personal experience.

> When your child grows up, what kind of qualities would you like to see in him or her? (p. 180)

This is a much better question because it is grounded in mothers' everyday experiences, which are likely to include thinking, hoping, worrying about, and perhaps planning for the child's future.

> Do you think of yourself as a good and competent mother? (p. 180)

Even though this question allows the respondent to focus on herself, it asks for self-evaluation without asking for a story that would contextualize that evaluation. It may also invite defensiveness—there is obviously a good answer.

> Do you think people hold mothers responsible for how their children turn out? Do you think this is fair? (p. 180)

These questions also pull a mother away from her experience and ask her to theorize about people and mothers in general.

The interview excerpts Hays offers show that the mothers sometimes did tell personal stories in the course of answering her questions. Nonetheless, it is clear that many of her questions were not aimed at *inviting* stories (Chase, 1995b; Mishler, 1986). If Hays were to address my critique, I suspect that she would say she is interested in the logic of cultural ideologies and how people express those ideologies. The methodological and theoretical difference between Hays's perspective and mine turns on the question of how researchers should go about accessing those ideologies and their logic. The principles of narrative analysis recommend that we ask people about their life experiences rather than ask them sociological questions—questions about cultural ideologies or questions that ask them to generalize about others' experiences. I believe that we learn more about those ideologies by listening to how people express, use, and transform them through their stories. Hays is a good example of a qualitative researcher who does not embrace, at least in practice, the principles of narrative analysis. My argument is that embracing those principles leads to stronger interviewing practice and thus better qualitative data.

This is how I would rewrite this section of the interview guide to invite narrators to tell their specific motherhood stories:

> When your child grows up, what kind of qualities would you like to see in him or her?
>
> What do you do now, at this point in your child's life, to encourage those qualities?
>
> Can you tell me about a recent occasion when you felt you did an especially good job at that?
>
> How about a recent time when you had trouble with this or felt you didn't do so well?

The stories a woman tells about her specific experiences and her feelings about her experiences will provide much deeper and more nuanced examples of how she has internalized or rejected or transformed ideologies about good mothering than her responses to questions aimed at producing descriptions of those ideologies. From the point of view of narrative analysis, cultural ideologies are not interesting in themselves because we all know what they are just by virtue of being competent members of our society. What is interesting is what people do with those ideologies. And that is only available to us through people's full, detailed stories.

Emily Martin's *The Woman in the Body* (1987) offers a counter-example. Although she does not use the terminology of narrative analysis, her interview guide shows that narrative principles inform her approach. Martin is interested in the metaphors women use to understand their bodies and in how the instrumental, technological language of science and medicine shape women's understandings of their biological processes. Thus, she interviewed middle- and working-class women about their experiences of menstruation, pregnancy, childbirth, and menopause. Here are her questions from the section of her interview guide on menstruation:

> How did your family regard menstruation? What did you know about it before your first period, from your parents, siblings, friends, books, or school?
>
> What was it like the first time you menstruated?
>
> How did you feel about menstruating during your early years?
>
> Were there any special practices or restrictions at school, work, or home about diet, exercise, bathing, or anything else during your period?
>
> What significance in your life did beginning to menstruate have?
>
> How would you explain menstruation to a young girl who knew nothing about it? How did you explain it to your daughters? (p. 205)

All of these questions invite an interviewee to speak about her own experiences. Even if a woman has nothing to say in response to some of these questions, she will clearly hear that it is her experience that the interviewer wants to listen to. The one exception is the hypothetical question: "How would you explain menstruation to a young girl who knew nothing about it?" As a general rule, I instruct students to stay away from hypothetical questions because they move the narrator away from her actual experience. Yet, when an interviewer focuses closely on a narrator's stories, an occasional hypothetical question may work very well. If, for instance, a woman is deeply immersed in her memory of early menstruation experiences, she might move easily to how she would explain menstruation to a young girl who knew nothing about it. Through this hypothetical exercise she might communicate what she would have liked others to say to her when she was a girl.

As students write and rewrite their interview guides, we work collectively on orienting their questions toward narrators' life stories, anticipating a wide range of possible experiences, and making sure that their interview guides prepare them to listen closely to whatever stories the narrator has to tell about this aspect of his or her life. Students learn that most abstract or opinion-oriented or sociological questions (such as many of Hays's) can easily be translated into questions focused on life stories (Chase, 1995b).

## INVITING LIFE STORIES DURING INTERVIEWS

The best discussion I have read of actual interviewing practices is found in chapter 4 of Robert Weiss's book, *Learning From Strangers* (1994). He wrote (with one modification in the first sentence):

> In the great majority of research interviews you will want the respondent to provide specific concrete descriptions of something he or she has [experienced or] witnessed. This includes both scenes and events in which the respondent participated and the respondent's own thoughts and feelings. A task in almost every interview is to communicate to respondents that this is what is needed. (p. 66)

Although other qualitative researchers may say similar things, Weiss includes long examples that demonstrate what he means. Similar to Martin, he does not use the terminology of narrative analysis, but his examples show that he instructs students to invite full, detailed, concrete life stories. We read Weiss's chapter before students start interviewing and we read it again later in the semester. The first time around some students have difficulty understanding what is wrong with his examples of bad interviewing. After they have conducted some interviewing of their own, they can easily see the difference.

I find that the hard work for students lies in learning to communicate the level of concreteness and specificity needed—that is, inviting a full story. Weiss gives examples of probes to facilitate this: " 'Could you tell me about a time that displays that at its clearest?'; 'Is there a specific incident you can think of that would make clear what you have in mind?'; and 'Could you tell me what happened, starting from the beginning?' " (p. 71). Respondents, he suggests, and I agree from my experience and from that of my students, do not usually go into such detailed concrete descriptions of specific events because we are asking for more than they would give in the course of ordinary conversation. Weiss recommends the test of visualizability to determine whether or not we have heard enough. "Can you call up the scene and imagine who is there in the setting being described and how the participants relate to each other? If you were to stage the scene in a theater, would you know what people to put there? Would you know who is saying what? Would you be able to move the plot forward?" (p. 80). He confesses that this is a difficult standard to reach. Indeed I find that people sometimes anticipate my asking for specifics by saying "I can't think of a specific example, but . . . ." And yet there are other times when a simple probe such as "do you have a specific incident in mind?" leads to a wonderfully detailed story.

Most students are quite anxious before they conduct their first interview. By this point they know that a lot goes into getting a good interview and they are afraid of failure. So I ask them to write about their worst fear. Usually they are most afraid that the interview will be over in 15 minutes, that they will ask all of their questions and the narrator will answer each question with one sentence and that will be it. We talk at length about what students can do to avoid this possibility: If possible, choose for your first interviewee someone you expect will be comfortable talking about his or her experiences; acknowledge your nervousness to the other person and ask for his or her patience with your inexperience; do not start the interview itself until you and the interviewee are relaxed. But most importantly we talk about how to interrupt an interviewing process that is heading in the unproductive question–answer, question–answer direction. I share with students an example of my own from a study of how university students on different campuses come to terms with issues of race, gender, and sexual orientation (Chase, 2000). One participant, a gay man active in the gay, lesbian, bisexual organization on his campus, was very willing to talk to me but was racing through his coming out stories. I interrupted him to explain what I needed:

**Susan:** Do you mind if I interrupt?

**Joe:** No not at all I'm kind of rambling.

**Susan:** No no it's fine it's fine. It would just be helpful to me if we could go into some of the details of this story that you're telling and let me just explain why I'm asking detailed questions. It's because in this project one of the goals is to get students to really listen to and understand people who are different from themselves and the best way to do that is to really have full and detailed stories. The person is more human the richer the story is, the fuller the story is. You know what I'm saying.

In class, I play this part and the next 30 minutes of the interview tape because it demonstrates not only my direct attempt to get Joe to slow down and immerse himself in memories of his coming out process, but also how long it takes to get to the stories that really display his experience (in the case of this interview, another 15 minutes). This is helpful to students because they are accustomed to reading in social science studies the best stories, data, or examples that qualitative researchers come up with. It helps them to find out that even experienced researchers have to work hard to get a full story and that it is fine if some interview talk consists of the interviewer and interviewee working toward the full stories.

As students gain experience as interviewers, they gain confidence in their skills at inviting and listening to narrators' stories. One problem students sometimes encounter at this point is their fear that they are being intrusive. One time I used in class an excerpt from a student's interview that I felt displayed beautifully her good interviewing skills. As we discussed what the student, Marshan Oliver, had done well, she confessed that she had felt nosy asking such detailed questions.[3] Her project was about women of color dating White men and the interview was with a friend. Both she and the interviewee are African American and both had White boyfriends at the time of the interview. They had discussed their situations with each other before, but during the interview Marshan asked questions she would not normally have asked her friend. Here are some of the questions she asked (to conserve space I will skip the narrator's responses [indicated by ellipses] until the end):

**Marshan:** A good starting place is how you all met. Can you tell me about that? . . .

So what was that like? What were you feeling knowing that he had gone out of his way to get back in touch with you? . . .

So you didn't remember his name and were embarrassed right? . . .

So you were surprised not only by his friendliness but how he didn't care about race right? So what happened after that initial meeting? . . .

What kinds of things started getting complicated? . . .

---

[3] I use excerpts from Marshan Oliver's interview transcript with her permission.

So what were peers or your friends' reactions like as the two of you got more serious? . . .

Who was saying those things? . . .

When they said this what was your response or what were you thinking? . . .What was your response to Black men calling you a sell out? . . .

So what were the reasons people were saying that you were with him? Can you remember a particular moment?

**Takiesha:** One day in the cafeteria this boy sat down with me and just asked me, "Why are you with him?" And he continued to say, "Was it because no one else wanted you that you are with him? Because I would be with you, you know."

**Marshan:** Hmm when he said that to you what were you thinking? What was going through your mind?

**Takiesha:** I was *livid*. I could not believe he had the balls to say something like that to me. What he was basically saying was that "I'm Black and you are Black so if no one else wants you then I'll be with you." I just got up and left the table. I mean the balls of someone and for that person to be Black. Well I started thinking about that and he must not be friends with any of the Black guys that used to try to talk to me if he thought that I couldn't get a date or whatever because my phone was always ringing.

Even though I have left out most of Takiesha's responses, we can hear the outline of her story in Marshan's questions. In class, we talked about how Marshan's close attention to the details of Takiesha's story encouraged her to express herself fully. We can visualize the scene in the cafeteria and we can feel Takiesha's anger and sense of personal injury. Interestingly, no one listening to the tape or reading the transcript felt that Marshan's questions were intrusive or nosy. No one got the sense that Takiesha felt her privacy was invaded.[4] Rather, Marshan's questions clearly arose from Takiesha's story and were directed at inviting her to tell her story fully. With practice, students become more comfortable asking about and listening to a fuller story than they would normally hear in everyday conversation.

Another problem that students sometimes encounter is interviewees who seem to talk too much about apparently irrelevant aspects of their lives. It is true that occasionally interviewees really are unwilling to tell their stories, but more often than not, as we listen closely we find that apparently irrelevant stories turn out to be deeply relevant. For example, the student whose project was about people living in homeless shelters was

---

[4] There may be times, however, when interviewees find researchers' questions intrusive (see, for example, Phoenix, 1994, and Edwards, 1990). Although we need to be aware of this potential problem, I find that students tend to err in the opposite direction: They are overly reticent to ask difficult but relevant questions.

particularly interested in finding out how they deal with the indignities of homelessness. One respondent who had recently moved into an apartment seemed uninterested in the student's questions and kept telling stories about her new neighbors and about her new home. As we listened to this narrator's stories, it slowly became clear that she was resisting the thrust of the interview questions—that homeless people are victims and that indignities define their lives and selves. Here the interview experience itself prompted the student to rewrite her questions. Indeed, while they are writing their interview guides, I strongly encourage all students whose research projects have to do with inequalities of any kind to make room within the interview for positive experiences and for strategies of dealing with oppression. In American culture, the narrative genre that gives us resources for speaking about oppression and discrimination also encourages us to speak about surviving, resisting, or at least preserving dignity in the midst of indignities. In other words, American culture discourages narrators from defining themselves primarily as victims.

Examples such as this give students a particular listening lesson: Our interview guides need to cast the life story net far and wide enough if we are to hear all kinds of life stories relevant to our projects. I share with students how I learned this lesson. During a long interview with one of the women superintendents my coresearcher, Colleen Bell, and I studied, the superintendent pulled out pictures of her family and began talking about each person. I remember waiting politely for her to finish with this digression so we could get back to her work stories, the ones that interested me most. Only later did I realize what seemed so obvious as I delved into the narrative themes in her interview: Her interest in sharing her family photos was perfectly coherent with what she was telling us about work—she was exhausted from the stresses of her very public job and was moving to a less stressful job in order to spend more time with her family. If I had listened more carefully to what she said about family members as she showed us the photos, I might have gained more insight into her decision to make a major career move (Chase, 1995a, chap. 4).

## INTERPRETING NARRATORS' STORIES

Inviting a narrator's story and following it closely during an interview is one kind of listening skill; interpreting what he or she is saying is another. We spend a good deal of class time listening to portions of the students' interview tapes. To protect narrators as much as possible, I set specific ground rules for this activity: We do not listen to the tapes of interviewees who work or study on our campus; we only listen to the tapes of off-campus interviewees who give us permission to do so; and we promise not to talk about the interviews with anyone outside of class.

We begin listening to tapes after students have conducted their first interview and we continue for as long as the exercise is useful. During these weeks, students are also working on other exercises. After each interview, they write an interview summary, in which they address methodological issues, and an interview index, in which they summarize the content of the entire interview. Then they type at least eight pages of transcript. For the first interview, I require them to type at least three pages of what I call "process transcribing," which focuses not only on content but also on nonlexicals such as pauses, sighs, stammering, and laughter, and to the extent that they can remember, facial expressions and body language (see Chase, 1995a, pp. 38–39).

Before we listen to an interview tape in class, the student sets the stage by explaining the context surrounding the excerpt we will hear. As we listen we follow along on the transcript. The lessons students get out of listening to and discussing each others' interviews are many, beginning with how hard transcribing is (inevitably a few words are missed or misheard or are ambiguous), and how hard it is to capture speech on paper. I encourage each student to evaluate his or her interviewing skills in this part of the interview: Does the tape/transcript show that she or he was listening well? What we spend the most time on, however, is interpreting what we are hearing. We listen to the tape (usually no more than 10 minutes) three times and then we each write "codes" in the margins of the transcript. Next, we work collectively on what I call "interpretive comments." In class we do this verbally, but students eventually write up their interpretive comments. Here are my instructions for the interpretive comments:

> When you come to a natural stopping point in the transcript (for example, a change of subject, the end of a story, or simply a point where you know interpretation is needed), stop coding and write about what is going on. Focus specifically on this passage (not the entire interview) and try to answer such questions as these:
>
>> What is this person doing or communicating (especially if that is different from what he or she is saying)?
>>
>> How does the interaction between you and the interviewee facilitate or hinder his or her story or ideas?
>>
>> What do you think is important or particularly interesting about this passage?
>>
>> What social factors (for example, social structures, ideologies, or social processes) help you to understand what is going on here?
>
> Include whatever else you want to write about that is relevant to this portion of the transcript. For example, if the themes that arise here are repeated throughout the interview, mention that. The two extremes that you want to avoid are being too descriptive on the one hand and overinterpreting on the other hand. Do interpret what is being said and

try to articulate your reasons—give evidence—for your interpretations. This is a good place to entertain possibilities and alternative interpretations. You want to speculate rather than jump to conclusions.

Here is a transcript from Katrina Grantham's project, the student who interviewed women with eating disorders ([p] indicates a short pause).[5]

> **Kay:** I mean the days when I'd go [p]
> the times when I'd go a few days without eating um [p]
> it's hard to describe like the way that feels like after two or
>     three days [p] you are on such a high it just feels like
>     you're on such a high and that you could keep on going
>     forever you've got so much energy cause you just feel like
>     you're so in control it's a huge adrenaline rush it's [p]
> I'd almost compare it to [p] like runner's euphoria you know you
>     just keep on going and you think that you can supersede this
>     world you know you're like superhuman you go and [p]
> and you just laugh at everyone who thinks that they have to eat
>     [p] (laugh) who thinks that they have to eat to stay alive
>     and to keep going it's like "look at me oh I haven't eaten
>     you know I don't eat I can do this and I'm living" [p] and
>     [p] after two or three days without eating you just feel so
>     such a high and you're so [p] on cloud nine

Katrina wrote the following for her interpretive comments:

> This portion of the transcript shows that Kay thinks her story is important and she wants to get it right, to find the right words to communicate her experience. Her pauses in this section as well as throughout the interview, especially during topics like the rape that are difficult to talk about, show again that she wants to make people understand. In this section, she also says several sentences in one breath, which I have tried to denote by indenting everything that is basically in one breath. She talked at a very rapid rate in this section, and that could be because she was talking about positive feelings. Kay is describing how good it felt to starve herself because she felt in control and also because her body reacted like it was on a high. She talks about having pride in herself and feeling superior to others. Because Kay compared herself to others, especially other girls, regarding weight, beauty, and eating habits, it makes sense that she chooses to differentiate herself strongly from others. She held herself to higher standards, such as not having to eat at all, and she was proud that she was different and better than others. The overall feeling in this passage is of happiness, pride, and wonderful feelings.

---

[5] I use excerpts from Katrina Grantham's interview transcript, interpretive comments, and later from her final analysis, with her permission.

Katrina's interpretive comments capture nicely the complexities of this passage. She listens to how Kay speaks as well as to what she says. Using the evidence of those "hows" and "whats," Katrina articulates what Kay is communicating: her feeling of superiority over others, her pride in her self-control, and her euphoria. Katrina does not mention, at least here, Kay's use of the impersonal "you." Deciding whether that linguistic choice indicates that Kay is distancing herself from her experience or connecting herself to others in a similar situation would depend on finding patterns or evidence in the rest of her interview (Chase, 1995a, pp. 148–149; Laberge & Sankoff, 1979; Riessman, 1990, p. 100). Katrina also could have focused on the discourse of self-control and achievement, which Kay draws on to tell her story. Note, as well, that Kay does not tell a story about a particular incident (in many other places she does). Nonetheless, Kay's description is very detailed about the high she got from not eating. (As she continued she spoke about the crash after the high.)

One crucial lesson that comes out of the exercise of listening collectively to interview tapes is that students learn that even interviews they thought were terrible almost always end up being richer than they thought. The student who interviewed local gay activists about how they became politically active was very disappointed with his first interviewee's refusal to talk about his emotions. We discovered through our collective listening to the tape that even though he did not *describe* his emotions and indeed ignored the student's prompts about feelings, he communicated quite clearly how he felt through the stories he told. The student who interviewed foreign-born women who are raising their children in the United States was frustrated by her first interview, which lived up to her worst fear: It lasted only 15 minutes. Yet our collaborative listening allowed us to hear how much the interviewee was communicating even in her abbreviated responses to the student's questions.

This exercise—listening collectively to interview tapes—gives students confidence. We reinterpret disaster interviews as rich sources of data. We also temper the impulse to jump to conclusions about what a narrator is saying by asking, "How do you know? What evidence do you have from the interview?" And perhaps most importantly, we learn together that hearing what someone is communicating is a matter of slowing down, of listening again and again to a narrator's stories.

## FINDING THEMES AND WRITING AN ANALYTICAL REPORT

When students have completed all of the follow-up work for each of the four interviews they have conducted (summary, index, eight pages of transcript, coding, interpretive comments), they are ready for the next step in the listening process. Here are my instructions:

1. Take a separate sheet of paper, label it with the interviewee's pseudonym, and make a list of all of the codes you had written on the transcripts. The point of this is to have in one place all of the codes for that interview. Then make a copy of all of your interpretive comments for that one interview (separate them from the transcript) and keep them with the sheet of paper with the list of codes for that interview. In other words, this step is a matter of separating your codes and interpretive comments from the transcripts so that you can study your initial analyses in themselves.

2. Categorizing. Look at your lists of codes and your interpretive comments for all of the interviews. Try to name several broader categories that pull together sets of specific codes and/or ideas expressed in your interpretive comments. Don't worry if some of your initial codes/comments fit nowhere. You may end up with three or four or five or even more broad categories. It doesn't matter how many—that will vary from project to project. When you have settled on your broad categories, write them on a separate sheet of paper. Explain in a paragraph or so the meaning of each category and what kinds of material it collects from your interviews.

3. Show which material from the transcripts fits into each category. At this point you need to return to the transcripts themselves, not to the pages where you have listed your codes and copied your interpretive comments. Do this by using the cutting and pasting mechanism of a word processing program. Alternatively, you can xerox your coded transcripts and cut them into pieces in order to rearrange them by category. (If you do the latter, you will probably need to tape them to other sheets of paper.) This process is often called "cutting and pasting"; Weiss (1994) calls it "sorting." Make sure each interviewee's name or initials appears on each excerpt.

Typically, students find this part of the analytical process tedious. And it certainly can be. I require it, however, to encourage their immersion in the data and their immersion in their preliminary interpretations of the data. I want them to resist jumping to conclusions about what they think they have heard. It is another step in the listening process. Sure enough, some students find that this exercise leads them to themes they had not anticipated.

After coming up with their categories, I ask students to write a final analysis or report based on one category that pervades all of the interviews.

This, of course, is what most qualitative researchers do with in-depth interview data. My instructions for the final analysis are similar to what Weiss (1994) called an "issue-focused" analysis:

> Choose one of your broad categories and examine it across as many interviews as possible. Weiss (1994) calls this "local integration." Look at the excerpts you have for that one category or issue and think about the meaning of that category for each of your interviewees. Try to articulate (analyze, pull apart, etc.) what that category or issue is about for your interviewees. Write this analysis up by examining a series of examples from your interviews. Here is where you want to focus on patterns, themes, similarities, and differences between your interviewees with respect to that one category or issue. Do use direct excerpts from your transcripts, even long excerpts, but don't "let the quotes speak for themselves." Make sure every transcript excerpt is followed by your analysis of it. Interpret what is being said, how it fits into the category, and how it compares to the other respondents' quotes you are looking at. Your original interpretive comments should be useful at this point. You can even use them word-for-word if that seems appropriate. If you know that your interpretations are speculative, which I suspect will be the case many times, acknowledge that and discuss the evidence you have that supports your interpretation.

Katrina Grantham decided to write her final analysis on the theme or category she called "daily reality—thoughts and feelings." She described it in this way: "This category . . . provides a look inside the minds of the interviewees and gives us an idea of the mental and emotional scope eating disorders have. Topics include food as a daily focus, being scared, emotional pain, denial, and good feelings about the disorder." Here is an excerpt from Katrina's final analysis:

> One surprise that came out in my interviews was that the women did associate some positive feelings with their eating disorders. First, they gained a sense of self-worth and self-esteem from the fact that they could control their eating. For example, Kay says, "the day that happened, I mean like, after my parents left [p] um like I was proud of it (laugh) proud of the fact that I lost so much weight and that they noticed." She also loved "the feeling of absolute control and absolute power over [p] what I consumed and what I was [p] like how much weight I lost." The other women echoed this sense of pride in their ability to starve themselves or control their eating. Because many of them felt like they were never good enough in most areas, when they could discipline their bodies they took great pride in it. . . . It's much easier to understand why so many women hold onto their eating disorders for so long when we realize some of the good feelings that come along with it.

Katrina's last statement is very powerful. We can see that she developed this idea by finding "good feelings" across the women's interviews. At the same time, Katrina's idea is grounded in the earlier process of listening closely to individual narrators' stories. In this sense, conventional qualitative data analyses are enhanced by the principles of narrative analysis.

At the end of the semester students typically feel as if they have just begun their projects rather than that they have just finished them. This, I tell them, is how I hope they will feel. In a sense they have completed pilot projects and now they are ready to begin research in earnest. When they give their oral presentations, I encourage them to talk about what they would do next, how they would continue, if they could.

My own sense of what would come next is twofold. In a course I might call Qualitative Research Methods II, I would have students begin by making explicit the research questions underlying my original instructions to them to choose a group of people that interested them. This would require them to develop a stronger sense, from the start, of where they are going and why their projects are both sociologically important and culturally interesting. In addition, I would include the principles of narrative analysis explicitly in the analytical part of their projects. This means two things. I would have them analyze at least one narrator's interview by following the themes and patterns *within* that interview. And I would have them look more closely at the relationship between interviewees' narratives and the social resources and constraints (cultural, ideological, and so forth) that they draw on in telling their stories. In other words, I would guide students in honing yet another listening skill, this one based in the second principle of narrative analysis: hearing how the social world is embodied in individuals' stories. In Katrina's interviews, for example, women with eating disorders draw on the powerful American discourse of self-control and achievement. The important questions are: How do they use this discourse? Do we learn anything new about that discourse by listening to how women appropriate, resist, or transform it? And do we learn anything new about eating disorders as social phenomena?

Why do I feel the need to wait for a hypothetical second semester to fully use the principles of narrative analysis in the analytical part of the course? Several years ago I tried to integrate these ideas about what I would do next into my one-semester course. I learned that I was asking too much by listening to my students' frustrations with these additional assignments. I decided that it was enough for one semester to expect students to develop the skills of writing interview questions, conducting interviews, and inter-preting them through the first principle of narrative analysis. It was enough to learn to listen well in these ways to the life stories people have to tell. In addition, although I think the first principle of narrative analysis should inform in-depth *interviewing practices*, I do think that *analyses* based on themes or patterns across interviews are valuable in themselves even though such analyses are not specifically grounded in narrative principles. Taking the next step of using narrative principles to ground analytical procedures, however, would require more developed analytical skills. Learning to hear how the social world is embedded in individuals' stories would require a strong understanding of the concept of cultural ideologies and discourses, as well as the ability to hear how individuals constantly use, make sense of, resist, or transform those cultural resources and constraints.

## REFERENCES

Aisenberg, N., & Harrington, M. (1988). *Women of academe: Outsiders in the sacred grove*. Amherst: University of Massachusetts Press.

Brown, R. H. (1987). *Society as text: Essays on rhetoric, reason, and reality*. Chicago: University of Chicago Press.

Chase, S. E. (1995a). *Ambiguous empowerment: The work narratives of women school superintendents*. Amherst: University of Massachusetts Press.

Chase, S. E. (1995b). Taking narrative seriously: Consequences for method and theory in interview studies. In R. Josselson & A. Lieblich (Eds.), *Interpreting experience: The narrative study of lives* (Vol. 3, pp. 27–44). Thousand Oaks, CA: Sage.

Chase, S. E. (1996). Personal vulnerability and interpretive authority in narrative research. In R. Josselson (Ed.), *Ethics and process in the narrative study of lives* (Vol. 4, pp. 45–59). Thousand Oaks, CA: Sage.

Chase, S. E. (2000). Universities as discursive environments for sexual identity construction. In J. F. Gubrium & J. A. Holstein (Eds.), *Institutional selves: Troubled identities in a postmodern world* (pp. 142–157). New York: Oxford University Press.

DeVault, M. (1999). *Liberating method: Feminism and social research*. Philadelphia: Temple University Press.

Edwards, R. (1990). Connecting method and epistemology: A White woman interviewing Black women. *Women's Studies International Forum, 13*(5), 477–490.

Gubrium, J. F., & Holstein, J. A. (1997). *The new language of qualitative method*. New York: Oxford University Press.

Harding, S. (1991). *Whose science? Whose knowledge?: Thinking from women's lives*. Ithaca, NY: Cornell University Press.

Hays, S. (1996). *The cultural contradictions of motherhood*. New Haven, CT: Yale University Press.

Heilbrun, C. (1989). *Writing a woman's life*. New York: Ballantine.

Hunter, A. (Ed.). (1990). *The rhetoric of social science research: Understood and believed*. New Brunswick, NJ: Rutgers University Press.

Josselson, R. (Ed.). (1996). *Ethics and process in the narrative study of lives* (Vol. 4). Thousand Oaks, CA: Sage.

Josselson, R., & Lieblich, A. (Eds.). (1995). *Interpreting experience: The narrative study of lives* (Vol. 3). Thousand Oaks, CA: Sage.

Laberge, S., & Sankoff, G. (1979). Anything you can do. In T. Givón (Ed.), *Discourse and syntax. Syntax and semantics* (Vol. 12, pp. 419–440). New York: Academic Press.

Labov, W. (1972). *Language in the inner city: Studies in the Black English vernacular.* Philadelphia: University of Pennsylvania Press.

Maines, D., & Ulmer, J. T. (1993). The relevance of narrative for interactionist thought. *Symbolic Interaction, 14,* 109–124.

Martin, E. (1987). *The woman in the body: A cultural analysis of reproduction.* Boston: Beacon Press.

Mishler, E. (1986). *Research interviewing: Context and narrative.* Cambridge, MA: Harvard University Press.

Phoenix, A. (1994). Practicing feminist research: The intersection of gender and "race" in the research process. In M. Maynard & J. Purvis (Eds.), *Researching women's lives from a feminist perspective* (pp. 49–71). London: Taylor & Francis.

Plummer, K. (1995). *Telling sexual stories: Power, change and social worlds.* New York: Routledge.

Richardson, L. (1990). Narrative and sociology. *Journal of Contemporary Ethnography, 19,* 116–135.

Riessman, C. (1987). When gender is not enough: Women interviewing women. *Gender & Society, 1*(2), 172–207.

Riessman, C. (1990). *Divorce talk: Women and men make sense of personal relationships.* New Brunswick, NJ: Rutgers University Press.

Riessman, C. (1993). *Narrative analysis.* Newbury Park, CA: Sage.

Rosenwald, G. C., & Ochberg, R. L. (1992). *Storied lives: The cultural politics of self-understanding.* New Haven, CT: Yale University Press.

Weiss, R. (1994). *Learning from strangers: The art and method of qualitative interview studies.* New York: Free Press.

# 6

# LISTENING TO HOLOCAUST SURVIVORS: INTERPRETING A REPEATED STORY

HENRY GREENSPAN

In this chapter, I focus on a course—really, one moment of a course—that I have been teaching since 1988 at the Residential College of the University of Michigan. Titled "On Listening to Holocaust Survivors," the class is one of our first-year seminars offered during students' first semester in the college. It thus serves as an initiation in several respects—for most students, to the study of the Holocaust and of survivor testimony in particular; to university courses and the seminar format; and, quite essentially, to the challenges of critical listening itself.

The interpretation of Holocaust survivor testimony has preoccupied me for almost 30 years, and the approach I take in my course reflects my work on testimony more generally.[1] As a clinical psychologist and playwright, I have been centrally concerned with *how* survivors retell: not only their use of narrative form but also survivors' specific, situated uses of repetition, silence, and voice. The relationship between survivors and their listeners has also been focal, particularly the impact of listeners' expectations, and survivors' perceptions of listeners' expectations, on what is actually retold. Finally, I have been interested in the ways a survivor's testimony evolves over time, over the course of several retellings, in the context of an evolving relationship between survivor and listener. Therefore, rather than relying on single "oral history" or "testimony" interviews, my work has involved interviewing the same survivors many times, in some instances over many years. Based on that experience, I have come to believe—and will illustrate in what follows—that some communications *essentially* require telling more than once.

---

[1] This work is most fully summarized in Greenspan (1998) and is adapted here by permission of Greenwood Publishing/Praeger. The work was also used in part in Greenspan (1999).

All these dimensions are central in my first-year seminar. Here, I describe one specific class exercise that we do toward the middle of the semester. The relevant background is this:

Leon (a pseudonym) retold the story of a prisoner's execution in each of three different interviews I conducted with him over two months in 1979. The prisoner, a man named Paul Lieberman, had been caught trying to pass a loaf of bread to his sister, who was starving in a nearby camp. Lieberman was shot by SS-corporal Schwetke a few days later. It was apparent in each of Leon's retellings that he did not remember having told me the story before, and this was the only episode that he repeated in this way. This story, therefore, seemed to be quintessentially Leon's testimony—a recounting that appeared to have a mind and a memory all its own. Even further, at each of his retellings, Leon noted that this memory, because of its horror, was precisely the kind of thing he rarely does remember, let alone retell. So here we have a man repetitively remembering what he says he hardly ever does remember yet without remembering that he keeps remembering it. And, therefore, I ask my students, as I have asked myself, what it may be about this memory that makes it, simultaneously, so compelling *and* so horrifying for Leon to recount?

What follows are the texts of Leon's first two recountings of the episode. I should say, however, that there are two important differences between their presentation here and the way my students receive them. First, the students have read much of the transcript of each interview, and so they have access to a context that the excerpts alone do not provide. Second, the students have read Leon's *own* reflections about the significance of this episode. As I will describe, I directly asked Leon about the story's importance, and why he thought he might have repeated it, at the start of his third retelling and again in a fourth interview a few weeks later. Thus the students' interpretations are meant to engage with Leon's own.

### Leon's First Retelling of the Story of Lieberman's Execution

The memory is selective, no question. And the selection is probably toward suppressing traumatic events and concentrating on others that have some human or redeeming quality. It's funny—about 15 years ago someone visited who was in one of the camps with me. In this camp we were unloading supplies for the SS. And we were talking like it was the good old days! For example, we were once in a freight car and there were broken cases of wine. The wine was still in the bottles. We drank some when the SS couldn't see us. And when a case wasn't broken, we made *sure* it was broken! And the few instances like that—we made them into the good old days!

And after a while we caught ourselves. What tricks the memory plays! It slides over all the unredeemed trauma, and suffering, and pain. And we didn't mention the time when we buried our friend who was shot. He went with us to the Jewish cemetery to turn over the grave-stones and carry them back. Because whenever there was no other work, they took us in trucks to the cemetery. And we broke up the stones with sledgehammers, because we were paving a muddy road, a muddy field in the camp, with those stones. And we were always going to the cemetery to perform this work. And once they caught one of our fellows in a minor infraction. He had stolen a loaf of bread to give to his sister who was starving in another camp. Sometimes she was marched by our camp. First they beat him up. Lieberman was his name, Lieberman. Then they told this fellow to come with us to the cemetery. They shot him right there. A young fellow. And we buried him right at the cemetery where we were taking the stones. And somehow or other while discussing this time with the other fellow who was visiting, we never mentioned it. We just mentioned those other, better times.

## Leon's Second Retelling of the Story of Lieberman's Execution

You only go into it when you feel somebody really wants to know. Somebody cares. That will prompt you to open up. Although still to a limited degree. You won't open up the floodgates. And dare to let it completely take you over. You only do it to a limited extent.

But it can just come up—I was talking with someone who was interviewing me, some years ago. And I was really trying to remember. And I remembered a scene—I was in a little camp, and one of the Jewish fellows was caught stealing a loaf of bread. Because his sister was in a starvation camp nearby. So he tried to smuggle it to her. And they caught him and beat him up severely. And we thought that this was the end. But then they took us out to the Jewish cemetery. When-ever there wasn't enough work in the camp, they took us out to the cemetery. To overturn the Jewish monuments, the grave-markers, and bring them back to the camp. To break them up and pave the muddy roads. And they asked this fellow to come along. And the SS corporal, who drove the truck, he asked this fellow to walk ahead of him. And he pulled out his Luger and he shot him. And we buried him in the Jewish cemetery.

And the funny thing was, I vaguely recollected this incident. Oh, I think I mentioned it once before to somebody. But now I remembered the name of the corporal, the SS corporal, Schwetke. And I remembered the name of the Jewish boy, Lieberman. See, before the war, I had an excellent memory. Perfect recall. But after the war, something happened. I have no memory at all. I carry notes in every pocket. Names—it all has to be written down. Even visiting relatives. But here I came up with this memory. And I could see the scene—all of a sudden this lithe, young, 19-year-old boy, full of life—what was his first name? Paul. Paul Lieberman. He just lay there with his head shattered. And we digging the hole, wondering who is going to be next.

## SAVORING A NAME

What, then, can be said about this episode and its retelling? For my students—perhaps reflecting the way their thinking has already been influenced by psychology—they tend to think first in terms of personal significance. They know from the transcript that Leon also had a sister in this camp; that she had also been menaced by SS-corporal Schwetke; and, although she survived, Leon had been able to do little to help her. So perhaps, my students speculate, Lieberman's action represented to Leon what he was not able to do himself—an interpretation which does, in fact, have power in the context of Leon's reflections as a whole.

Typically, my students also focus on Leon's comments at the end of his second retelling about being able to remember names. Describing his loss of memory after the war, particularly his memory for names, Leon exclaims, "But here I came up with this memory," and he repeats, virtually savors, Paul Lieberman's name in particular. Is this story, then, also Leon's victory over the loss of memory, the loss of names? Is it even, suggest my most perceptive students, itself a kind of monument, constructed by this man with notes and names in every pocket, whose work had once been to break up Jewish gravestones?

When Leon reflected further on this memory in our third interview, he said more about names as well as about the terror of the episode as a whole. He noted,

> This had a traumatic impact on me. Because here I was working with a fellow. . . . One moment he's living and breathing, and the next moment we're burying him with a hole in the back of his skull. . . .
>
> This Schwetke was a truck driver and not known for any special brutality. We got to know the SS. This was a very small camp, and we were there for over a year. We knew them by name. We knew their traits.
>
> So to see both the victim and the executioner, to have acquaintance-ship with both—acquaintanceship in the sense you knew what made them tick—it must have made an impression on me sufficient that I retained it.

At least up to the point of the shooting, then (Leon will say more about what happened after), both executioner and victim are known and named. And we might wonder: Does this, in fact, provide the memory something "human," some "redeeming quality" in Leon's terms, and therefore, despite what Leon says, ultimately make it *less* traumatic than his other memories of the destruction? And is that also partly why the Lieberman story is repetitively retold?


## ATROCITY AS TRAGEDY

At this point in the term, my students are not inclined to second-guess a survivor—if he says it was traumatic, it was traumatic. At the same time, at least some are ready to follow the idea that what may be most striking about the Lieberman story is how *untypical* it is of the Holocaust more generally. Rather than the degradation and extermination of a people, here we have a single victim executed, in Leon's phrase, because of an "infraction." Indeed, as noted, Lieberman's infraction—sequestering bread for his starving sister—was an act of valor and resistance. Even when such acts were possible during the destruction, they were generally irrelevant to the fate of victims—all were doomed in any case. Equally untypical, as Leon notes, is to know the name, not only of the victim, but even of the executioner—even to feel he is a kind of "acquaintance," as he was of Lieberman's as well. And, almost bizarre, Lieberman is buried in a Jewish cemetery—the very cemetery that is itself being unearthed, pulverized, and scattered on the muddy roads.[2]

Here, then, we have a "crime," a punishment, a named victim, and a named executioner, all held together by a coherent unfolding of context, action, and response. The Lieberman story, in other words, clearly *is* a story: within its terms, a story and a plot of a familiar kind. Lawrence Langer's preface to *The Age of Atrocity* (1978, pp. xi–xiv) has been part of an earlier class discussion, and his distinctions between tragedy and atrocity are (ideally) now recalled. Tragedy requires some controlled image of the number of dead—not the pits and heaps and ravines of bodies, dead and dying, that characterize atrocity. In tragedy, even terrible events are still within some version of acceptable human fate—which is exactly what atrocity's arbitrary "wasting" of people aims to attack. In tragedy, victims are still identifiably living and human; not atrocity's doomed, defeated, or "walking dead." This is what allows us to feel sympathy for tragedy's victims, in contrast with the dread, disgust, or numbed malaise that atrocity evokes. By these criteria, then, while immersed in an ocean of atrocity, the Lieberman story more closely resembles tragedy: the failed but heroic resistance of an attractive young man—"lithe" and "full of life" as Leon remembers—cut

---

[2] This analysis of the Lieberman story is also given in Greenspan (1998, pp. 159–161).

down by his oppressor. Such stories not only allow retelling; they virtually compel it.

All this, then, on the side of what makes the Lieberman story tellable and, of course, hearable as well. As my students know, Leon *also* came to distinguish between this memory and his later memories of Auschwitz. Responding to my own question about the difference, he noted,

> People hadn't become ciphers yet. They were still, up to that moment, human beings. With a name, with a personality, And when they were gone, their image was retained. But the mass disappearing into the gas chambers—, they're just a mass of people going—, like in a slaughter-house.

Leon also agreed that having names and bounded circumstances made recounting more likely. In response to my questions about the Lieberman story, he began to talk more generally about recounting in our third and fourth interviews and offered a phrase—the idea of "making a story" out of what is "not a story"—that has become central throughout my work on retelling and in this course. He reflected,

> How do you describe a nightmare? ... It is not a story. It has to be made a story. In order to convey it. And with all the frustration that implies.

In fact, as my students know, Leon was feeling a certain amount of frustration even as he spoke. This was because he absolutely did *not* agree with my suggestion that the episode, however tellable, might be any less traumatic. And so he tried to explain better the nightmare from which it was retrieved,

> Yeah. Yeah. Yeah. You see a cause and effect relationship—a crime and a punishment. But, see, this is a good example of how hard it is to convey. You pose the question. I owe you an explanation. There are a few elements you couldn't have known.
>
> You see, in a perverted sort of way, the SS were proud of this camp. We had become their expert workers. They used to show us off! They used to say, in German, they never saw *Juden* work in such a fashion. Despite the killing all around us, we imagined this was a little island of security. And the Lieberman incident destroyed the whole thing.
>
> You see, this was the moment of truth. Lieberman was a favorite. Even to them, to the Germans, he was a favorite. He had smiling black eyes, with so much life in them. All of a sudden we see no one's life is worth a damn. The very Germans you thought took this almost paternal interest—they would kill you with as much thought as it takes to step on a cockroach. And so our pipe-dream was shattered right there. It was suddenly and dramatically shattered, along with Lieberman's skull.

Leon then described the "shattering" from the inside—one of the most vivid descriptions of engulfing terror that I have heard in 20 years of conversations with survivors. And it becomes clear that this, and not Lieberman's burial, is the real end of this story: an end but not an end*ing*; the cessation of the story but not its conclusion. Because, as Leon says, this end really had nothing to do with the universe—narrative and otherwise—retold to that point.

> It was a feverish feeling. A feverish feeling. A terrible intensity. . . .
> When Lieberman was shot—the moment before there was sun—, even in a cemetery you were conscious of the world around you—, but with this execution, the whole thing came to a standstill. It is like—, the only reality left over here is death. Death—and we performing—like a mystic ritual. I wasn't aware of *anything* around me.
>
> There would have been six of us. Six left. Six automatons digging the hole. . . . And even the SS man Schwetke, he ceased to be real. All of a sudden, he has left this known-to-you universe. And become something else. . .
>
> This is probably what makes it so unbelievable. This pure landscape of death. . . . Even sound, even sound would be out of place. There is no sound actually. There is no sound.

## THE LESSONS OF LISTENING

I am more than a little resistant to reduce such recounting to classroom lessons—even lessons in terror. But listening hard to Leon—and to my own listening to Leon—does, I think, help remind my students that nothing is easier than to think we follow survivors when we do not: Nothing is easier than to mistake the tragedy recounted for the atrocity endured, the "made story" for the "whole story," the one name savored for the slaughterhouse recalled.

On one level, then, what my students learn from an exercise such as this applies to their listening to Holocaust survivors in general. And, indeed, it emerges that Leon's story of Lieberman has important formal similarities with other survivors' narratives, both written and spoken, that we consider in the course. These accounts may also be retold more than once, or their special status may be indicated by their appearing fully formed in a narrative that seemed to be about something else. As with the Lieberman story, these stories also tend to focus on a single person—often a favorite of the prisoners or even of the guards—who undertakes some act of resistance. The attempt fails, the resister is caught and executed, and the despair that follows, recalled as consuming and collective, is always much more than the story might initially suggest. Rather, it is as though the death that these memories retell recapitulates all the other losses that the recounter has known—the loss of other people, of course; but also the loss of hopeful illusion, of the "known-to-you universe," of tragedy and responsiveness and tellable stories themselves.[3]

Although leading to so much loss, these accounts are themselves a provisional restoration. They *are* tellable stories. And through their retelling it becomes possible, for both recounter and listener, to respond emotionally to the wider destruction—most particularly, to begin to grieve. Thus the initial hunch of some of my students that the Lieberman story may be itself a kind of monument—a memory that is also a memorial—bears fruit. Later we consider several accounts of the resistance and execution of Mala Zimetbaum, a story that appears many times within women's memoirs of Auschwitz. Mala's story would have been memorable in any context—she was probably as close to a heroine, even a romantic heroine, as Auschwitz could allow. Already well-known in the camp, she succeeded in a dramatic escape with a Polish prisoner who was her lover. The two were caught, but even at her execution Mala continued to resist, cursing her killers and slashing her own wrists. In her memoir, Lena Berg reflected on the significance of Mala's story and particularly of her capture and execution:

> Every community has its legend, its myth; that of Auschwitz was a romance involving Mala, a girl who worked as a messenger, and her lover, a Warsaw Pole who also had a camp job. She was proficient in several languages, and universally admired in the camp for her intelligence and beauty. One day all Auschwitz was electrified by the news that Mala and her lover had escaped, he in an SS uniform and she in that of a wardress. . . . Mala's fate became our own main concern. . . .
>
> Mala's death shocked the camp to the core. She had been our golden dream, a single ray of light in our dark lives. Prisoners who might momentarily be taken to the gas chamber, who lived in the shadow of the crematoria through which millions of human beings had gone up in smoke, wept bitterly when Mala was killed. One death moves the imagination more powerfully than millions; one death is a drama throbbing with emotion; a million, only dry-as-ashes statistics.[4]

---

[3] Along with the story of Mala Zimetbaum noted in the body of the chapter, such repeated or special stories that we consider in class include Elie Wiesel's much discussed account of the "pipel," the "sad angel" who was "loved by all" (1960) and Leon Wells's account of Marek in his memoir of the Janowska camp (1978). Wells's memory of Marek is particularly close to the Lieberman story. Marek was a young inmate, favored by both guards and other prisoners, whose execution proved that no one had protection. "Marek is our symbol . . . ," Wells wrote, "Even if the lieutenant likes us, promises us a 'long life,' takes care that we get enough food, our end will be the same as Marek's— sudden death. . . . We must not try to comfort ourselves with hope again" (p. 161).

Although it is, of course, a memoir "one-generation-removed," Art Speigelman's *Maus* (1986) also contains a story of resistance and execution that has a unique capacity to evoke emotional response—in this case, many years later. The only episode from his father's recounting that Art retells twice, and for which he twice depicts and confirms Vladek's tearful reaction ("It still makes me cry!"), is the story of the hanging of the "black market Jews" (pp. 84, 132–133).

[4] Lena Berg's memoir is included in Donat (1978, p. 311).

My students thus learn that even *within* the terror the imagination craved what could be told and, in that telling, what could be grieved. Even there, stories were cherished and retrieved, although not without dissolving again within the common, unstoried death.

Through all of this, there is also a more general lesson about what Holocaust survivor testimony is and what it has to teach us. Most of my students arrive in the course sharing the popular assumption that testimony is equivalent to "oral history" and that what it provides are "eyewitness accounts" of events that historians would otherwise describe more generally. It is almost never the case, however, that the students' most pressing questions about survivors' experiences center on events and their documentation. Beyond what survivors witnessed and endured, my students want to know how it affected them: How do they go on? Do they have faith? Can they trust or forgive? What do they now think about the world? When pursued through survivors' own reflections, these questions speak more properly to "oral psychology"—or even "oral theology"—than "oral history" in the usual, documentary sense.

In any case, it is clear that the significance of the Lieberman story, as we discuss it in class, does not reside in the event that it recalls—the bread, the capture, the killing. Its significance is rather in the fact that it is this event that is remembered at all, and remembered repeatedly, even while its repetition itself is not remembered. To say it differently, the event to which the Lieberman story finally draws us is not so much Lieberman's act of resistance as Leon's act of remembrance—what he recalls, what he retells, and how the two are and are not the same. Although one might suppose that students would find such questions about the forms of recounting abstract—particularly in comparison with historical content—the opposite is the case. That is because the phenomenon that is most immediately before them is not "the Holocaust" but rather the survivors attempting, somehow, to retell it. Even more so, when the survivors are literally before them— when, later in the course, Leon and other survivors join us in class—and the students are able to attend directly to their efforts to retell. Listening to those efforts *as* efforts (and not simply as results) creates a kind of engagement that, in my own teaching experience, is rarely equaled—a point to which I will return at the end of these reflections.

On the broadest level, the time spent dwelling in Leon's and other survivors' recounting teaches students about the role of narrative in general; and, above all, about its role in their own lives. Thus discussion eventually turns to the ways all of us "make stories" that, simultaneously, convey and conceal actual memory and experience. We discuss the variety of considerations that may apply: the ways that actual experiences may be too complex, too confusing, too provocative, too shameful, too private, or too common to convey without the help of a "made story" of some kind or other. In this context, we also discuss where we find such stories—or, more accurately, from where we borrow them. And, perhaps most essentially, we talk about the difference between the perspectives of the recounter—who knows, on some level, how much has been shaped and sculpted—and the listener, who may imagine (forgetting for the moment their own recounting) that the received fragment is, indeed, the "whole story," or at least its essential core.

There is a poignancy in our consideration of the last point that is not easy to describe but may itself be the essential core of the "story" that the class itself recounts. It concerns the fragility of all human communication—its inevitable limits and uncertainty because of its reliance on forms (and, I suppose, beings) that are themselves inherently limited and uncertain. When, in their course evaluations, my students write about the most important thing they learned, this is usually what they say. Beyond all that they have absorbed about the Holocaust and its survivors, they write that understanding someone else's experience is a much more tenuous process than they had thought. They also write about now knowing that that process is always full of choices—whether to pursue a conversation further or to accept that, for whatever purposes, one has understood enough. Needless to say, the issues here are not simply epistemological but profoundly moral: How much understanding does anyone "deserve"? And, assuming a willing recounter, how much understanding is any would-be listener obliged to attempt?[5]

In the case of Holocaust survivors, at least, my almost always generous students usually answer the last question: "as much as possible." And so there is a special intensity when survivors visit the class, which comes mainly during the last third of the course. That intensity certainly borrows, in part, from the survivors status simply "as survivors"—the ones who were actually there. Likewise, there is an inevitable drama (not necessarily productive), after so much time has been devoted to survivors' words and texts, to meet at last the people themselves. But I believe the intensity also derives from all the time we have spent analyzing recounting as a process. Knowing what can be entailed in survivors' choices of specific words, the students hang on every one, and consider (in classes that follow) why the survivor chose those and not others. They anticipate stories made for "not stories" and think about what is not said as much as about what is. They are aware that what they hear is provisional and contingent: the result of a complex series of compromises in which survivors determine what will be tellable

---

[5] The qualifier "willing recounter" is, of course, important. Otherwise, the moral obligation might be not to pursue conversation, and understanding, further. Similarly, the obligations are not all on the side of the listener. In many instances, the recounter might devoutly wish that the part be taken as the whole, and left at that.

by them and, at the same moment, hearable by their listeners—in this case, the students themselves.

One might imagine that all this second-order reflection on process would distance students from what survivors actually say, but, as suggested above, I believe the opposite is true. Rather than receiving testimony as a finished text, they enter into it as an active, sometimes painstakingly active, endeavor. Knowing that, as listeners, they are directly implicated in that endeavor implicates them further. At the very least, their experience is analogous to the difference between visiting an art gallery and watching a painter actually paint. As with most young people (and older people for that matter), they are drawn to the opportunity to see someone actually *making* something, to the excitement of knowing that the thing being made is important, and to the exquisite responsibility of knowing that they, authentically, are part of it.

In the end, then, I hope my students are both chastened and encouraged by their immersion in Leon's recounting and that of other survivors as well. Listening is hard work when everything points to more, even including the negation of speech and sound themselves. Listening well is always hard work—to survivors, and not only to survivors.

Still, when Leon and others actually join us in class, I hope that my students will be encouraged to their own participation in knowing: above all, to a more spirited engagement than the images of simply giving testimony, or simply receiving it, usually suggest.


## REFERENCES

Donat, A. (1978). *The Holocaust kingdom*. New York: Holocaust Library.

Greenspan, H. (1998). *On listening to Holocaust survivors: Recounting and life history*. Westport, CT: Praeger.

Greenspan, H. (1999). Listening to Holocaust survivors: Interpreting a repeated story. *Shofar, 17*, 4.

Langer, L. (1978). *The age of atrocity: Death in modern literature*. Boston: Beacon Press.

Speigelman, A. (1986). *Maus*. New York: Pantheon.

Wells, L. (1978). *The death brigade*. New York: Holocaust Library.

Wiesel, E. (1960). *Night*. (S. Rodway, Trans.). New York: Hill & Wang.

# 7

# TEACHING INTERPRETATION

RICHARD OCHBERG

About ten years ago I developed an exercise for teaching my undergraduate psychotherapy students something about interpretation. I wanted to illustrate how a clinician of my psychodynamic stripe listens closely to the stories that clients tell about their everyday lives—and how we detect in these the repeated intrusion of their troubling preoccupations. Standing in front of a blackboard, I led each class through a close reading of several very short stories written (by a student several years earlier) in response to the first five pictures (cards) of the Thematic Apperception Test (TAT). Working slowly through these stories, we underlined phrases that caught our attention and grouped them into themes. Eventually we grouped the themes into larger configurations that revealed a conflict faced by the narrator: between her desire for companionship and her fear that this desire marked her—in her own eyes as much as anyone else's—as contemptibly dependent. (Let me say immediately that I am not at all sure everyone will agree with my reading: No responsible clinician would presume to render a judgment on such scant evidence. I wanted to illustrate, in miniature, a process—not a conclusion.)

After I had taught this exercise some 30-odd times, I began to believe that I had it down: I knew by heart virtually every question that students raised and my own rejoinders. At that point I decided to write it up, imagining that it might be useful to various colleagues—not just those teaching psychotherapy but also adult development, personality, or courses that connect individual lives and society. (I had, by then, started using this exercise and others similar to it when I taught those courses.) Because I knew my material cold, I imagined that I could knock this off in at most a month. Well, that was four years ago, and I still seem to be puzzling over it. If I have not wholly settled how to teach this exercise I have at least become clearer in my mind about why it is so difficult. Here is how this now seems to me.

When I first designed this exercise, I hoped to provide students with a rough and ready procedure that they could follow on their own. (They would shortly begin inventing fictional clients and interviewing each other. The exercise was intended to help them pay attention to each other's nuances of language.) For this to work, of course, they had to understand not only what I do when I listen or read—they had to be able to do something similar on their own. As long as I was leading everyone through the exercise I could persuade myself that it was successful. (As a matter of fact, students did learn to focus on nuances of language and the preoccupations these reveal—they were less successful at seeing how these were organized into patterns of conflict.) However, once I tried writing it all down so that a reader could do the same thing without me, everything seemed to become vastly more ambiguous.

I began to notice how my interpretation was shaped by dozens of small decisions, governed by a seemingly endless code of rules, variations, and exceptions. (For example, should the interpreter pay attention to a single word, a phrase, a sentence, a story, or an ensemble of stories? Actually, I do all of these—but it is difficult to explain how I choose among them at any given moment.) For many months I attempted to write a detailed rulebook, but the more I tried to spell out everything I do the more convoluted it became. (I actually wrote a "final" draft several years ago—only to discover when I recently reread it that it was utterly incomprehensible even to me.) This led me to reconsider what I really do when I work, and what I imagine might be the point of teaching this approach. To put this in a familiar phrase, I rediscovered the hermeneutic circle—and its implications for teaching.

Originally, I tried to present a way of building up an interpretation from the bottom. Start with vivid phrases whose importance is obvious to everyone. Combine similar phrases into clusters; these show that the narrator has a recurrent preoccupation. Organize the clusters into polar distinctions and show how the favored end of one distinction entails the negative pole of another one: This reveals the narrator's conflict.

The difficulty, as every interpreter knows, is that no one could actually follow this recipe, at least in this up-from-the-bottom form. It may be possible to start with phrases that capture every reader's attention; it may even be possible to group similar phrases together. (Even this step requires that we see what might count as "the same sort of thing," and to do this we need more than the text itself; we need an organizing theory.) By the time we arrive at the later steps in an interpretation—organizing the clusters into a larger configuration—we have moved far beyond what is "apparent to any observer." Instead, we must be guided by some larger conception of the meaning that the narrator might be trying to make. This is not entirely discoverable in the text itself; instead it depends on the assumptions about meaning that we bring to it

Now I would like to add one more layer to this familiar idea. Not only is an interpretation shaped by our "fore-understanding" of what the text might mean, it is also shaped by the use to which we anticipate putting it. Perhaps the best way to illustrate this is by way of my own research.

I am interested in how people understand themselves and their position in the larger society—and how this understanding may be constrained by the forms of public talk that society puts at their disposal. When I listen to an informant or read an interview transcript I ask myself, How might I use this to explore the discourse of gender, the moral contours of habitus, or the prospects for awakening sociological imagination and political activism?—and I do so from the beginning. I cannot emphasize this too strongly. I do not first interpret a text and only then cast about for some larger way of using it Instead, the way that I pay attention to the text is shaped, from the start, by my anticipation of conversations that I might join.

Naturally, to do this I must be familiar with the conversations that are going on in our community. For example, when this narrator tells us, through her TAT stories, that she has grave doubts about her self-sufficiency, a bell must go off in my mind. I must say to myself, "You know, you might use this case to join the debate about selfhood." Her comments might remind me of something Geertz said: "The Western conception of the person as a bounded, unique, more or less integrated motivational and cognitive universe, a dynamic center of awareness, emotion, judgment, and action organized into a distinctive whole and set contrastively both against other such wholes and against a social and natural background is, however incorrigible it may seem to us, a rather peculiar idea within the context of the world's cultures" (1976/1979, p. 229).

Of course, Geertz is hardly alone: Many writers—especially those with an interest in cultural variation—have expressed similar doubts about the universality of Western "self"-experience. Nor is this critique limited to anthropologists. Feminists have argued that a whole constellation of related terms (such as *individuality, autonomy,* and so on) take for granted the values that men deem admirable while deprecating those of women (Gilligan, 1982; Heilbrun, 1988; Keller, 1983; Miller, 1976).

If I am familiar with this widespread critique I may say to myself not only, "What is this narrator trying to say?" but also, "How might I use her in order to join a conversation that currently preoccupies much of my community?" Naturally, I hope that in reading her this way I am not distorting her meaning—I certainly want to capture what matters to her. At the same time, I am going to pay attention to her selectively, focusing on those aspects of her account that allow me to address whatever issues seem urgent not just to her but to our larger, communal conversation.

This brings me to a question that may trouble some readers: Is this approach useful only to clinicians or can it also speak to researchers? Here, I want to say two things, and I hope they do not appear contradictory. Originally, I developed this exercise to teach students to think as therapists do. I wanted them to notice how this narrator criticizes herself—perhaps unreasonably. Unreasonable self-criticism is, of course, a central idea in the psychodynamic understanding of unhappiness; the procedure I follow is calculated to bring her self-criticism to light. Throughout this chapter I will point out how I read these stories in the way that I do because of the particular theory of self-misunderstanding that I bring to them. I take this connection between interests and interpretive strategies quite seriously. There are many ways of reading any text; we choose a particular strategy because it lets us see what matters to us. This is one of the most important lessons students can learn. Instead of imagining that there is any single, universally valid procedure, they see that all readings are shaped by what we hope to notice in a text or the sensibility of its author.

Having said this, I would be sorry if any reader dismissed this exercise as being of interest only to clinicians. The main idea is that people may find fault with themselves instead of—more reasonably—their situation. This view of self-misunderstanding is by no means limited to psychotherapy. The larger sociological idea is that prevailing forms of public talk—notably including academic talk—may abet such unreasonable self-criticism. It is the job of interpretation (among other jobs, naturally) to show how repressive discourse works—and thereby rob it of its unwarranted authority. In this respect, the aims of psychodynamic therapy and critical social theory have much in common. However, I am getting very far ahead of myself.

When I first designed this exercise, I had no intention of leading my students into this discussion of hermeneutics and critical social theory. All that I hoped to do was to teach them a procedure that they might apply, in my absence, to their own work. I am, therefore, going to start by presenting this exercise as I actually taught it to my class of would-be therapists. Eventually I will suggest how one might use it to illustrate much larger ideas in the critique of public discourse.

## THE EXERCISE

### Phase One: Reading for Individual Images

I start by asking students to read the first story and underline whatever phrases capture their attention.

Story 1: The boy looking at the violin is so frustrated that he's given up practicing. He feels like he'd rather be doing anything else in the world, and he's thinking about other kids playing outside; playing basketball and riding bikes in the afternoon sun. He's so completely frustrated that he's going to cry a little, but will then pick up his violin and continue to practice. He'll be teary eyed, but glad that he continued to play because, even though he still makes too many mistakes, he loves music.

Usually there is fairly high consensus in the class over this story. Almost everyone underlines the phrases describing emotion (frustrated, teary eyed, cry a little), action (given up, continue to play), and relationships (other kids playing outside).

Although most students underline nearly everything that I consider noteworthy, there is one interesting exception: Hardly anyone underscores the phrase, "afternoon sun." (Those who do usually explain that there is no sun in the picture. This is an important point: Anything that is not in the picture itself must come from the author's imagination.) I, however, have other reasons for noticing this image. It fits with a great many others that crop up in the next few stories (of course, the students have no way of knowing this). It also conveys a certain mood; a more orthodox psychoanalyst might call it an "oral" image. I do not make much of this just yet, but I ask students to remember this phrase for later.

I then ask whether they have any impressions of the person who wrote the story. In particular, does the author seem to be an active, assertive person or more the quiet, contemplative type? At this point the vote usually divides about evenly. I then ask them to compare this story to the one written by a second narrator.

Story 1 (second narrator): The little boy is tired of practicing his violin lessons. He never really liked the violin anyways; it was his parents' idea to take lessons. "How can I get out of this?" he thinks to himself. He doesn't want to get his parents angry and he hates the violin. The boy decides to keep playing but will purposefully perform terribly in hopes that his parents will suggest that he stop.

The difference between this narration and the first one seems obvious to almost everyone. The story written by the second author sounds much more vigorous. The emotions are stronger: The boy hates the violin. Relationships are pictured as a contest of wills: His parents might get angry. Action has a more decisive tone: The boy decides, he purposefully performs terribly, he tries to get out of a bad situation.

Occasionally someone points out that the boy in the first story chooses to do what he really wants, while the boy in the second version ends up obeying his parents. From this angle, the first story seems to depict a more effective character. This leads to an interesting discussion about how one reads a story for clues to temperament. The boy in the second story sounds more willful, even if his ability to act is more constrained. In contrast, the first narrator describes a world of feelings ("teary eyed," "cry a little") rather than a world of action. Even the phrase, "warm afternoon sun" goes along with a somewhat languid, passive style. It would not surprise us if this narrator were somewhat lonely (other kids are playing somewhere else) and perhaps a bit sad. I should add that although these impressions are on my mind, I would not try to defend them with such minimal evidence. However, I may return to these ideas as the evidence builds.

## Phase Two: Clusters and Distinctions

The next step is to move from individual phrases to larger clusters. I ask students to read Stories 2 and 3 (written by the original narrator), underline whatever images strike them, and propose groups of phrases that describe similar moods, desires, styles of action, and so on. Most students catch on fairly quickly; they usually agree about what the main clusters are.

> Story 2: The woman carrying the books in the field feels cold and empty. She has often thought about people like the ones in the background. She has been watching the man, attracted by the strength and warmth of his body; she feels very different from him, but wishes in a way that she could take on his body and spirit. She is perplexed by her revulsion for the woman, and thinks that she looks very sad. She will walk the rest of the way home feeling lonely. No one will be home to greet her, and she won't be able to concentrate on her reading because she will daydream about the people she saw earlier.

> Story 3: The woman with her head on her arm has just awakened and it is early in the morning. She is looking out the window at the birds in the trees and thinks that she'd like to just sit here all day. Her body feels relaxed and warm, and she wiggles her toes in her big cotton socks. She imagines that someone is watching her and admiring her, and she daydreams about how she and this person will have tea and toast for breakfast. In fact, there is no one else in the house and soon she will go downstairs and have a steaming cup of tea and write a letter to a friend.

The clearest and most important cluster (at least in the first three stories) contains images of sadness and loneliness; everyone notices these.

A second cluster contains images of daydreaming about other people. This is a striking group, yet it presents us with a bit of a problem. Students often suggest that it is a variation on the theme of loneliness: These protagonists are daydreaming about people who are far away or who do not really exist. Although this is true for some of the images, the daydreamer in Story

3 sounds more content than lonely. Well, perhaps we will find some way to make sense of this later.

There is a third cluster that seems important to me, although students rarely notice it until I point it out; this is the contrast between "coldness' and "warmth." Everyone notices the phrase, "cold and empty," it usually gets included under "loneliness." Although there is indeed a strong connection between "cold" and "lonely" in this text, I propose, at least for the moment, that we consider "warm" and "cold" to be opposite ends of a distinct cluster. I do this for two reasons. First, the warm end of this group contains a number of images that are easily overlooked but that convey a subtle sense of mood. (I have in mind such phrases as "big cotton socks" and "steaming cup of tea.") Recognizing the emotional tone of such images is part of what I am trying to teach. Second, when we get further down the road I plan to use this imagery of temperature to tease apart two different alternatives to loneliness.

This is often a good time to draw students into a larger discussion about how we are proceeding. The idea is to dispel both the illusion that there is any single best approach and the skeptical conclusion that our procedure is wholly whimsical. In particular, it may be useful to comment on these questions:

*1. How Do We Decide Which Images Belong in a Cluster?*

Usually, this discussion starts with some uncertainty about the warm/cold cluster. I explain that a cluster should be broad enough to include whatever images convey a similar mood, concern, or purpose. For example, a cluster that included only "tea and toast" and "steaming tea" would be too narrow. Instead, I recommend that the "warm" pole of this cluster include all of the phrases that suggest cozy contentment. I think it includes "big cotton socks" and "tea and toast," even if they do not mention warmth explicitly; it may even include images of drowsy contentment (Incidentally, by emphasizing the mood conjured up by a phrase, I mean to rule out those images that do not really belong. For example, when we get to the fourth story some students propose the phrase, "everything under the sun." My own feeling is that this phrase does not conjure up the same mood and therefore does not belong in this cluster.)

On the other hand, a cluster should be narrow enough to capture distinctly whatever makes it compelling to the narrator. "Lonely" and "contemptible" are distinct issues (though as we will see, this narrator sees them as related); it would not be useful to combine them prematurely into a single, global cluster of "negative thoughts." If I were speaking to a more advanced class, I might point out that no hard and fast rule allows us to predict in advance which clusters will be useful. Instead, the clusters emerge—and may change—as we work along. In this case, our interest in "cozy contentment" is driven, in part, by the way that it reverses what our narrator has previously said about cold, empty sadness. We could not possibly have predicted this. An unusually astute student might notice that this procedure differs sharply from content coding—where the categories are determined in advance—this too might be worth discussing.

### 2. What Do We Do With Phrases That Do Not Seem to Fit Anywhere?

There are two phrases that everyone notices: "she is perplexed by her revulsion for the woman," and, "she wants to take on his body and spirit." For the moment, these striking phrases do not fit into any cluster; therefore, we need to hold onto them and see what emerges next.

To anticipate a similar problem that lies ahead, when we get to Story 4 everyone notices that the man is repulsed by the woman's infidelity. However, this idea stands alone; there is nothing like it anywhere else. On the other hand, Story 4 gives us a second reason that the man is repulsed: The woman whines that she still loves him. This phrase goes along with the theme of sadness and revulsion in Story 2. Because infidelity is unrelated to anything else, and because we are given a way to understand the man's revulsion without the woman's infidelity, I am inclined to drop infidelity from further consideration. This is, admittedly, a debatable call.

### Continuing to Read for Clusters: Stories 4 and 5

Only at this point do I ask students to read the last two stories. If we are on the right track, these should provide additional images that belong in the clusters we have already identified; if this does not happen we should worry that we have gone astray. By now, most students find this fairly easy:

> Story 4: The man leaning away from the woman feels repulsed by her as he has just guessed at her infidelity. She whines that she still loves him, which makes him sick to his stomach. All he wants to do is get out of the apartment, away from the woman. He will speak to her very little, gather his few belongings and leave quickly. He'll walk in the warm night, taking deep breaths. In a way he feels relieved now, and he sits in a park looking at the sky. He won't return her calls and he'll never see her again.

> Story 5: The woman in the doorway has just gotten up from the kitchen table. An acquaintance of hers has just been let in by her daughter. She doesn't know her very well and it is late, but she likes the visitor and offers her a drink. The visitor explains that she has just been driving around and remembered that the woman lived here. They sit for hours talking about everything under the sun, until the hostess feels herself about to doze off. The visitor says she was glad she came by, and the

hostess agrees. The hostess closes the door with contentment; the two had really been on the same wavelength; it felt like they had known each other for years; she knew they'd be friends.

As it turns out, Stories 4 and 5 abound in images of loneliness versus companionship, and of warmth. (There is no further mention of daydreaming.) Of course, the most vivid phrases come in Story 4: the woman "whines," the man is "sick to his stomach." These, combined with the striking but previously isolated phrases from Story 2 suggest a new cluster; we might call it, "admiration for men" versus "contempt for women."

(A curious aside: It is only at this point that students ask whether these stories were written by a man or a woman. I ask their opinion; most favor a female author on the grounds that events seem to be described from the perspective of the female characters. "But would a woman really say such disparaging things about her female characters?" I ask. "Oh, yes," they say—and it is the women in the class who seem best able to explain this.)

## Phase Three: From Clusters to Psychodynamic Conflict

So far, we have organized a score of vivid phrases into a handful of contrasts. These take us a long way toward an interpretation, but they are not yet the interpretation itself. The next step is to see how these contrasts relate to each other, and how this relationship explains whatever is puzzling or troubling in these stories. To do this, we first have to decide what the problem is.

My candidate for a problem is this narrator's contempt for women (presumably including herself); this seems related in some way to their loneliness. Why does she feel this way? (Here again, there may be an interesting discussion. Some students may propose that this narrator's problem is that she feels lonely. This may indeed be a problem for her, but if so, it is not the sort that a psychotherapist could help alleviate. If our narrator is lonely she needs to find more friends; if she despises herself for feeling lonely she may need to change her way of thinking. Only the second possibility is a problem for psychotherapy.)

We also have to see what sort of explanation we want—and how our reading of a text is shaped by the interests we bring to it. Our choice of an explanation is not entirely determined by what is "in the text"—that is, phrases that we can underline with a yellow marker. Instead, or at least in addition, our choice of an explanation depends on our understanding of both lives and interpretations.

More specifically: I bring to this reading a theory of psychological disturbance—and the help that interpretation can offer—framed in terms of conflict. (I should add that I do so whether I am speaking as a therapist or a researcher; though naturally, I emphasize the therapeutic point when

I am teaching this class.) To say that our informants have conflicts means that a way of thinking or acting that seems to them desirable from one perspective seems thoroughly undesirable from another. Therefore, they seem to be always on the verge of saying (to us and to themselves) one sort of thing, then rebuking themselves and protesting (though perhaps too much), "Of course that is not what I really mean." Not every problem can be framed in terms of conflict, but when this model fits it can offer a powerful insight. Among other things, conflict explains why some people remain troubled even when their situation apparently improves. This is what distinguishes "neurotic unhappiness" from the "ordinary kind."

This view of self-censorship, not just of action but of desire itself, is what gives psychodynamic interpretation its form. Our job—whether we are engaged in individual psychotherapy or the critique of public discourse—is to bring the habit of self-censorship to light so that people can recognize what they are doing and perhaps decide to do otherwise. (Of course, I am simplifying greatly how difficult this is.) We read with an eye to conflict not because we believe that this is the whole truth about our informants, but because this is the portion of their self-misunderstanding that a good interpretation might transform.

I usually approach the idea of a conflict by asking the class two questions, whose answers point in opposite directions. The first is, "What is the world like for this narrator when life is good?" Most students find this easy: The world is good when it is cozy and secure, and above all, when it is filled with companionship. By contrast, the world is a horrible place when it seems cold, empty, and above all, lonely. I then ask, "What is this narrator herself like when she seems good (worthy, admirable)?" This is a tougher question for most students—they have trouble distinguishing it from the previous one. (It often helps to put the matter in the negative, "What is she like when she seems worthless to herself?") Invariably someone in the class comes up with the answer, "She seems worthless to herself (contemptible, repulsive, sickening) when she is clingy, whiny, dependent."

From here it is fairly simple to point out that these two answers direct the narrator toward mutually incompatible lines of action. If she pursues what she wants (or perhaps, if she tries too desperately to escape the cold loneliness that she dreads), she risks turning herself into the kind of person that she herself finds repulsive. In more formal terms, her desires are at odds with her ego ideal: that is why she has not just a problem but a conflict

Ordinarily this is where I stop for the day. (I may emphasize how a conflict differs from a problem—and what students need to do if they are going to create fictional clients who have conflicts of their own.) However, this account of our narrator is still quite superficial; we have not yet touched on some of the most interesting things that could be said about her. In particular, we have said nothing yet about the very strong counter-evidence:

evidence that our narrator has, at times, quite positive feelings about women—including, presumably, herself.

## Phase Four: Bringing in the Counter-Evidence

It may occur to some students that the conflict we have just sketched appears to come and go. Our narrator says quite harsh things about women in Stories 2 and 4, but she paints a much more benign picture in Stories 3 and 5. What are we to make of this? Can she possibly have a conflict only some of the time? Actually, this is not out of the question. After all, most people—even those who are fragile in some way—behave reasonably most of the time. Their perceptions of situations and emotional reactions are, for the most part, unexceptional. It is only occasionally, when some private button is pushed, that they fly off the handle. Perhaps our narrator is like this too: perhaps she is overwhelmed by neediness and shame only when she feels abandoned by some attractive man. This is possible, but we should not conclude too quickly that it is the case.

Our theories of personality (and our everyday experience of people) suggest that if this narrator really is as insecure as we suspect we may detect this even in her happier moments. Even when things seem to be going well she may feel that the world, or something in herself, is about to come unglued. We might find some hint of this even in those stories that appear cozy and companionable. So it is to these happy stories that we now turn, with a deliberately skeptical eye. (In the interests of brevity I am going to confine this discussion to Story 3, which is the more blatantly defensive; many of the same points could be made about Story 5.)

### Why We Might Be Skeptical of Story 3

The first point is that this story is wildly at odds with what most people see in this picture (a figure seated on the floor, slumped over against a narrow cot). Our narrator tells a story of cozy contentment; more usually, "This picture lends itself to stories involving depression, dejection, and suicide," (Stein, 1955, p. 5; see also Rapaport, Gill, & Schafer, 1978). Should we conclude that this narrator is one of those optimistic sorts who insist on seeing every near-empty glass as partly full? Not likely: Her previous story, in response to TAT picture 2, was exceptionally bleak. Why then does she not tell a sad story here, where it would be more appropriate?

With this question in mind we might notice that Story 3 reverses the previous one. In Story 2, a woman watches a man and is attracted to him; here, a woman is being watched and admired herself. Story 2 describes a cold, sad, lonely, and repulsive woman; in Story 3 a woman is warm, happy, and admirable and has friends. This point-for-point reversal seems highly suggestive. In short, we might suspect that Story 3 is a defense.

It seems reasonable to suppose that as our narrator examines TAT picture 3, the theme of extreme sadness intrudes despite her best efforts. After all, most people see the figure in Card 3 as sad and lonely; then too, this theme is already very much on our narrator's mind. However, this theme now feels intolerable to her—perhaps because the picture is too bleak, perhaps because she is horrified by what she admitted in her previous story—therefore she does whatever she can to disavow it. Her third story forestalls what she feels herself on the brink of saying about this picture and repairs what she has already said about the previous one. It is as if our narrator is saying (to us? to herself?) "I don't really believe that a solitary woman is necessarily as cold, sad, and repulsive as I just told you." This, I think, is more plausible than to conclude that she—unlike virtually everyone else—really does see in Card 3 a picture of cozy contentment.

Of course, it is one thing to say that we readers have our doubts about these stories of cozy women; the more pointed question is whether our narrator is doubtful of them herself. If she is unable to convince herself then even her best attempts at a solution may end up letting her down. With this in mind we might notice what happens next: No sooner has Story 3 repaired the damage done by its predecessor than Story 4 bursts forth with an even harsher denunciation of a whiny woman who makes a man "sick to his stomach." We begin to see that these stories oscillate: each one seems driven as much by its predecessor as by the picture before her. Story 2 is unreasonably bleak, Story 3 unreasonably cozy, Story 4 is, again, unreasonably harsh. This pattern of oscillating misperceptions (at least, compared to what most people see in these pictures) is exactly what we would expect if our narrator is trying desperately—but with only intermittent success—to keep her private demons at bay. (Incidentally, I think that Story 5 continues this pattern. Once again, our narrator tells an unusual story—most people think the woman in this picture is peering anxiously into a room, perhaps because she has heard an unexpected noise. I think that Story 5, as with Story 3, repairs the scathing denunciation of lonely women.)

Our suspicion—that this narrator is trying mightily but with imperfect success to disavow her bleak thoughts—would be even stronger if we found that contempt for women slips past the benign veneer of Story 3 itself. With this in mind we might examine it more closely. I have suggested that Story 3 attempts to reclaim, for women, the happy virtues that Story 2 ascribes only to men. However, Story 3 makes a substantially weaker claim. The man in Story 2 is watched and admired by a real woman—in marked contrast, the woman in Story 3 only imagines that someone is watching and admiring her: She is having a daydream. In case we missed the point, the line rubs our nose in the fictitiousness of her experience, "In fact, there is no one else in the house . . ." To my ears, this line makes the woman in the story seem more pitiful than content; this seems interesting. The narrator might have supplied her protagonist with a real admirer—but no, even in this made-up world only imaginary companions comfort her. It suggests that the narrator has a hard time believing her own optimistic fictions.

Finally, we might consider how the story ends. The protagonist is going to get up, go downstairs, and write a letter to a friend. This is certainly an improvement: She is back in the world of real people instead of imaginary companions. Still, we cannot help noticing that the friend is far away: This reminds us of the boy in Story 1, daydreaming of playmates outside.

Now, I think we must be careful not to exaggerate our narrator's distress. These stories are by no means wholly bleak. (The stories told by victims of abuse, for example, are often much more malevolent and unrealistic.) Our narrator does not view the world as uniformly cold and empty, nor does she see women as wholly sad and contemptible. She is quite capable of imagining companionship (though we might notice that these companions are always other women—never men).

Nevertheless, even the optimistic stories sound unconvincing; they protest too much, and too ineffectually. They tell us of happy, companionable women where most narrators see sadness or anxiety. They attempt to rescue their protagonists, but they offer only the companionship of imaginary admirers or distant friends. In the end, I remain skeptical of the cozy solution—and I suspect that the narrator is, too.

### Why Is the Narrator Doubtful of Cozy Women?

In this last section I want to consider why our narrator might have her doubts about cozy women. This will be the most speculative part of this reading—therefore, I want to offer a word of explanation. Throughout this chapter I have said that an interpretation is driven not just by the evidence but by how it might contribute to some larger conversation. For example, in the discussion earlier I noted that we read an account looking for conflict because this allows us to focus on whatever help we can offer as psychodynamic therapists. Now I want to suggest that—if we are not only therapists but psychosocial theorists—we also read with an eye toward a particular type of social critique. How does public discourse lead individuals to misconstrue themselves, to their detriment? More particularly (in this case) how does the discourse of gender lead women to misunderstand, to their own disparagement, what one might reasonably mean by "selfhood?"

### The Feminist Critique of Selfhood

In her book, *Toward a New Psychology of Women*, Miller (1976) suggests that we should regard skeptically a variety of terms related to autonomous selfhood. This warning is addressed to women as much as men, to popular self-understanding as much as academic theory. The more familiar idea is that men may regard women in terms of ideas that do indeed capture men's experience but that misapprehend women's. If so, women may appear to the men in their lives—or even to academic theorists, who ought to know better—as immature, immoral, or weak. Miller is hardly alone: For some time now feminist critics have pointed out how saturated with such pejorative assumptions is our allegedly gender-blind psychology (Gilligan, 1982; Heilbrun, 1988; Keller, 1983). However, it is not only men who misconstrue women—women may do so themselves. With this in mind let us return to our narrator and see whether her doubts about cozy women tell us any more about the public discourse of "selfhood"—and its danger to women's self-understanding. The narrator of these stories is an informal theorist of personality; her question is, "Why are women more vulnerable to loneliness than men?" (More exactly, her question may be, "What is the difference between the way that men and women avoid loneliness—and what does this difference imply about their 'selves?' " I suggest that we look for an answer in the imagery of warmth and coldness.

As we have heard, this narrator uses images of warmth and coldness throughout her stories—she links these terms to each of her other significant dichotomies. Lonely, sad, contemptible women are cold; admirable men are warm; even the little boy in Story 1 imagines that other, happier kids are playing outside "in the warm sun." Of course, cozy women are also warm—in this regard they are similar to men—but somehow they do not quite seem as admirable. Perhaps their warmth is of a different sort.

According to our narrator, the man in Story 2 has a strong, warm body—which is what makes him attractive. The woman wishes she could "take on his body and spirit." (This does not mean that she wants to have sex with him; instead, she wants to partake of his vitality.) In contrast, the cozy women do not seem to be warm in themselves; they are warmed up by steaming tea and big cotton socks. Now I would like to suggest that this difference—between having a warm spirit and being warmed up by a hot cup of tea—tells us not just what this narrator believes about men's and women's bodies but about their "selves."

If I am right about this interpretation (and once again, let me admit that it is speculative), then everything our narrator says about the "warmth" and "coldness" of men and women is a kind of private code. Instead of "cold," read "sad and repulsive"; instead of "warm," read "happy and admirable"; instead of "body," read "self." Finally, let us see if this translation lets us answer our earlier question: Is there a difference (according to our narrator) in how men and women avoid loneliness—and why does one way seem to her better than the other?

Perhaps we can simplify things by asking: What is the opposite of loneliness? Our narrator appears to offer two answers: companionship and self-reliance. Men (who seem to her to have some inner source of warm vitality) can rejoice in their solitary self-sufficiency—as did the man in Story 4. Women (who must be warmed up by something or someone outside themselves) can only avoid loneliness through companionship.

Of course, one might ask, Why is solitary self-sufficiency any more admirable than companionship? The answer is—well, there is no good answer. Our narrator has, apparently, bought into a widely shared notion of self-sufficiency that has no particular merit. She might have decided that feeling lonely is the natural, appropriate reaction to solitude—just as hunger is the natural reaction to an absence of food—and that companionship is the most plausible solution. Were she to think this way, loneliness—perhaps we should call it "aloneness"—would describe an unfortunate situation rather than a character flaw. In this case there would be no reason to denigrate women who feel lonely when they are alone. (Further, the man in Story 4, who resolves a dispute with a lover by disappearing into the night, might seem immature rather than admirable.) On the other hand, if self-sufficiency is the "mature" antidote, then loneliness is a contemptible weakness—one that is hardly improved by hot tea, imaginary admirers, or even real neighbors.

Now the point is that our narrator is not really free to choose between these alternatives—the choice has already been made for her by our prevailing discourse. In the real world of her daily life (not the world of ironical anthropologists and skeptical feminists), self-sufficiency is "obviously" better than companionship. It is hardly surprising that our narrator falls in with this assumption. How could she fail to take seriously the cultural (and androcentric) injunction that one should be self-sufficient? And if self-sufficiency does not satisfy her, this seems to damn not only how she lives but who she is. Everything that Geertz attributes—with ironic exaggeration—to Western (and male) selfhood, this narrator takes seriously. If she does not find in herself an "integrated . . . universe, a dynamic center of awareness, emotion, judgment, and action . . . set contrastively . . . against other such wholes," then perhaps she does not have enough of a "self." This may be why she seems to herself "revolting" and "sickening." Unlike Miller or Geertz (and so many other critics) our narrator takes the injunction to be "self-sufficient" at face value. By doing so—and showing us the cost of doing so—she illustrates what is wrong with a widely shared but insufficiently examined public idea.


CONCLUSION

Throughout this chapter I have tried to indicate how one might use this interpretation to join a number of larger conversations. In this last section I would like to consider some of these ideas more directly. In the back of my mind is the hope that interpretation might be taught, not just as an adjunct to traditional courses—principles of psychotherapy or social psychology—but as a course in its own right. The aim of such a course would be to introduce students to some of the ways that meaning has been studied in the social disciplines—and why we believe that meaning matters. (It might also suggest to more advanced students some directions for their own research.)

Exercises such as this one, that teach students a variety of interpretive procedures, would have a place in such a course. However, there is a danger that students might regard these procedures in the same atheoretical spirit that they regard, say, statistics. Students are unlikely to appreciate—unless we emphasize the point—that the procedures we adopt are inseparable from the aspects of meaning we are able to observe. Seeing how this is so may be the most important lesson that such a course could teach.

I want to begin by explaining why a common approach to studying "meaning" seems to me insufficient. In the last few years there has been an enormous blossoming of research that draws its raw material from the stories people tell about themselves in open-ended interviews. This approach, it is often said, allows informants to tell their stories in their own words and thereby reveal whatever is distinctive in their perspective. However, I am not persuaded that interviewing, by itself, brings this about. Consider a classic example:

The Jackroller (Shaw, 1930) presents, in his own words, the life story of a juvenile delinquent. In an introduction to a later edition Becker (1966) explains, "This perspective differs from that of some other social scientists in assigning major importance to the interpretations people place on their experience." Becker, of course, is pointing to the fundamental promise of interpretation—but does The Jackroller actually deliver on this promise? If we really grasped this young man's perspective we would understand not just the events in his life but "the interpretation [he] places on his experience." For example, we might recognize a common thread in his experience of his family, his teachers, and the police—not because they all acted similarly but because he construes them similarly. We might reach such an understanding by examining closely how he describes each of them, just as we did with the TAT stories. Yet although the raw material for such an analysis is at hand—we have the jackroller's own words—these words are never actually analyzed. We are never shown, for example, which distinctions organize his construction of experience, what he emphasizes and suppresses, how he uses a particular genre of narration to organize his life story in one way rather than another, and so on. Without something of this sort, we are left to conclude that anyone who lived through the same events would have told much the same story. That is: We understand only what happened to this young man—we do not understand anything distinctive about "the interpretation he placed on his experience."

The problem that I am trying to describe is, I suspect, familiar to most instructors. In order to notice the interpretation of an experience—that is, its meaning—we must be able to separate what happened from what our informant made of what happened. However, this distinction is often elusive. Here, I am reminded of a moment in my own tortuous progress, many years ago, in a course on the history of art.

As I recall that long semester, each week I wrote an essay about some painting in the Fogg. "That would be a picture of a boat: You can see it right there, next to the fish." Naturally I said this in more flowery language but it did not really help. Back would come my grade—some version of a C—and my instructor's cryptic comment, "Tell me about the construction of the painting, not its subject matter." This went on until the day I stumbled upon a Delacroix (a Turkish rider on a rearing horse) and noticed—first in disbelief and then with the growing, astonished pleasure of having cracked a particularly fiendish code—that the whole thing was a pinwheel of symmetrical colors. Here was a dab of pink and yes, sure enough, here was a dab of pink on the other side. This paper won me a B+, and nothing has been the same since.

I mention this distant episode because I believe that something similar must happen for students of interpretation. Just as I eventually came to see that a painting is its organization (not just its subject matter), so a student must come to see that a narrative works because of how it says something—not just what it says. But how is anyone supposed to notice this? This brings us to the utility of studying methods. To paraphrase Wittgenstein (1958), the best way to see what we mean by the "meaning" of text may be to examine what we do when we explain it to someone else. By teaching students what interpreters do, we may help them notice what we think meaning is.

However, there are a number of dangers in this approach. One is that by focusing on texts—TAT stories, interview transcripts, and so on—we may lose the connection between how meaning is made in the artificial setting of research and how it is made—and matters—in real life. In addition, by focusing on methods we may mislead students into setting aside precisely that habit of critical reflection that interpretation is supposed to encourage. Students might believe that although there are differences in how individuals (or cultures) construe experience, the fundamental procedures of interpretation are universal. No matter what particular system of meanings we are trying to understand, we are bound to pay attention to such things as plot, genre, audience response, and so on. These aspects of interpretation—a student might mistakenly conclude—are universally valid. Neither of these dangers seems to me insuperable, as long as we address them in our teaching. We need to link the meaning we discover in personal narratives to meaning in daily life, and we need to link our interpretive procedures to larger public interests. Here are some examples.

One of the central questions to which we are repeatedly drawn is: How can we feel that our lives have been meaningful? How can we avoid feeling that our choices have been capricious (and perhaps not our own at all), that we have let ourselves down—that, in the end, our lives have not really amounted to much? No doubt there are many answers to this, but surely part of an answer is that we regard our lives as meaningful if we detect in them the steadfast pursuit of some enduring commitment. That is why interpreters pay so much attention to how narrators construct continuity in what they might otherwise regard as the discordant twists and turns of their own history (Cohler, 1988; Linde, 1993; Mishler, 1992). To put the same idea in the negative, we might examine why and at what cost narrators exaggerate the discontinuities in their history (Rosenwald & Wiersma, 1983). We focus on the construction of plot because we have an interest in how narrators persuade themselves and others that they have acted agentically (or how they deny doing so)—and plot allows us to see this (Ochberg, 1996).

However, this Promethean view of meaningfulness—in both stories and lives—now seems to many of us excessively individualistic. These days we hear—especially from feminists but not exclusively so—that we matter to ourselves (perhaps we are ourselves) by way of how we are engaged with others. That is why we are starting to pay more attention to how stories may be co-authored, how any individual story makes connections with others (Gergen & Gergen, 1988), or how it evokes a response from an audience (Fish, 1980; Harding, 1992).

Then again, this interpersonal perspective may have its limitations— it may be an overly benign view of communion. Some narrators may have excellent reasons to doubt the good will of their audiences—therefore we need interpretive strategies that bring to light the deliberate evasiveness of their stories (Ochberg, 2000). Furthermore, some narrators may be prevented from telling a particular type of story by the genres favored in their community. Therefore, interpreters must pay attention to how communal standards make some narratives appear indecent or incoherent (Gergen, 1992). We also want to notice how narrators occasionally recognize the constraints that their community places on self-understanding, and thereby revise their life stories—and their lives (Ochberg, 1992; Ochberg & Comeau, 2001).

In short, our approach to an interpretation is determined by what we want to see. We are always asking ourselves (or assuming that we already know), "In what particular ways does meaning matter—and therefore, how should we pay attention in order to notice this?" This brings me to my last point. There is no universal consensus about what matters. Instead, our view of what matters—and therefore, how we should pay attention to meaning—varies from one community and one historical moment to another. To see how this is so is to restore interpretation to history.

For example (and here I am sketching connections in very broad strokes), it may be that cultural differences in meaning matter to us now because of our recently acquired embarrassment about colonialism. That is why our current approach to interpretation highlights the problem of cross-cultural understanding instead of searching for putative universals. Social censorship matters to us now partly because of our not-so-distant experience with totalitarianism. This may be one reason that many interpreters pay as much attention to what narrators seem unable to say as to what they do put into words. Feminism (among other perspectives) emphasizes our interconnectedness. That is one reason why many interpreters insist that we pay attention to the interpersonal aspects of meaning—in preference to those approaches that link autobiography to the individualistic self (Olney, 1980).

Were we to lead students into such a conversation, some of them might learn something much more important than any procedure for interpretation (including, of course, the one I have sketched here). They might see that there is an intimate connection between the ways that we pay attention and what we are able to notice. In turn, what we choose to notice—and ignore—is shaped by our ever-changing conception of what matters. Finally, these are not just rarefied debates among ivory tower academics; they have implications for the way we live. For example, when Margaret Thatcher said, infamously, "There is no society," she was not joining an academic argument over methodological individualism; she was justifying a political assault on what she regarded as the excesses of the welfare state. To show students these connections—between how we are prepared to listen and live—is, I think, the largest contribution that interpretation might make to a liberal education.

## REFERENCES

Becker, H. (1966). Introduction. In C. Shaw, *The jackroller* (pp. v–xviii). Chicago: University of Chicago Press.

Cohler, B. (1988). The human studies and the life history: The Social Service Review lecture. *Social Service Review, 62*(4), 552–575.

Fish, S. (1980). *Is there a text in this class? The authority of interpretive communities.* Cambridge, MA: Harvard University Press.

Geertz, C. (1976/1979). From the native's point of view: On the nature of anthropological understanding. In P. Rabinow & W. Sullivan (Eds.), *Interpretive social science* (pp. 225–241). Berkeley: University of California Press.

Gergen, K., & Gergen, M. (1988). Narrative and the self as relationship. In L. Berkowitz (Ed.), *Advances in experimental social psychology* (Vol. 21). San Diego, CA: Academic Press.

Gergen, M. (1992). Life stories: Pieces of a dream. In G. Rosenwald & R. Ochberg (Eds.), *Storied lives: The cultural politics of self-understanding* (pp. 127–144). New Haven, CT: Yale University Press.

Gilligan, C. (1982). *In a different voice*. Cambridge, MA: Harvard University Press.

Harding, S. (1992). The afterlife of stories: Genesis of a man of God. In G. Rosenwald & R. Ochberg (Eds.), *Storied lives: The cultural politics of self-understanding* (pp. 60–75). New Haven, CT: Yale University Press.

Heilbrun, C. G. (1988). *Writing a woman's life*. New York: Norton.

Keller, E. (1983). Gender and science. In S. Harding & M. Hantikka (Eds.), *Discovering reality: Feminist perspectives on epistemology, metaphysics, methodology, and philosophy of science* (pp. 187–206). Dordrecht, Holland: D. Reidel.

Linde, C. (1993). *Life stories: The creation of coherence*. New York: Oxford University Press.

Miller, J. (1976). *Toward a new psychology of women*. Boston: Beacon Press.

Mishler, E. (1992). Work, identity, and narrative: An artist–craftsman's story. In G. Rosenwald & R. Ochberg (Eds.), *Storied lives: The cultural politics of self-understanding* (pp. 21–40). New Haven, CT: Yale University Press.

Ochberg, R. (1992). Social insight and psychological liberation. In G. Rosenwald & R. Ochberg (Eds.), *Storied lives: The cultural politics of self-understanding* (pp. 214–230). New Haven, CT: Yale University Press.

Ochberg, R. (1996). Life stories and storied lives. In A. Lieblich & R. Josselson (Eds.), *Exploring identity and gender: The narrative study of lives* (Vol. 2, pp. 113–144). Thousand Oaks, CA: Sage.

Ochberg, R. (2000). On being part of the audience. In S. Moch & M. Gates (Eds.), *The researcher experience in qualitative research* (pp. 109–123). Thousand Oaks, CA: Sage.

Ochberg, R., & Comeau, B. (2001). Moving up and the problem of explaining an "unreasonable" ambition. In D. McAdams, R. Josselson, & A. Lieblich (Eds.), *Turns in the road: Narrative studies of lives in transition* (pp. 121–149). Washington, DC: American Psychological Association.

Olney, J. (1980). *Autobiography: Essays theoretical and critical*. Princeton, NJ: Princeton University Press.

Rapaport, D., Gill, M., & Schafer, R. (1978). *Diagnostic psychological testing*. New York: International Universities Press.

Rosenwald, G., & Wiersma, J. (1983). Women, career changes, and the new self. *Psychiatry, 46,* 213–229.

Shaw, C. (1930). *The jackroller.* Chicago: University of Chicago Press.

Stein, M. (1955). *The thematic apperception test.* Cambridge, MA: Addison-Wesley.

Wittgenstein, (1958). *The blue and brown books: Preliminary studies for the 'philosophical investigations.'* New York: Harper and Brothers.

# 8

## TASK, PROCESS, AND DISCOMFORT IN THE INTERPRETATION OF LIFE HISTORIES

GEORGE C. ROSENWALD

How the history of the academic study of lives will be recorded—whether we will look back on a narrative turn in the social sciences or on a passing narrative fad—depends in part on how this discipline is conceived and passed on.

There is more than one plausible approach to the study of lives. Each appeals to a distinct curiosity and calls for distinct methods and skills. In the first section of this chapter, I shall define one such curiosity, widely prevalent among college students (but not only among them), yet rarely legitimized in the mainstream curricula of academic psychology, which a disciplined study of life history is apt to satisfy. In the second section, I lay out the logic governing such an approach and the personal skills and attitudes it requires. I begin the final section by specifying and exemplifying difficulties that many students (and hence their instructors) experience as they engage this kind of study. I suggest that these troubles reflect contradictory cultural values mediated to these students throughout their educational and other socialization. I conclude with some tentative suggestions for instructors as to how they might help students cope with these difficulties. My point will be that even if we do everything "right," it will not be smooth sailing.

### THE TASK

The scholars working in this field today are not the first to appreciate the relevance of life history narratives to the concerns of their disciplines. But they are the first to face growing, interested, at times eager, audiences in classrooms.

The few academic psychologists who were engaged in the study of lives in the first half of the 20th century pursued somewhat different agendas. One author might have looked at individual lives as records of the social process by which a new member is added to the group (Dollard, 1935). Another might have paid special attention to the configuration of qualities that gave an individual the stamp of uniqueness (Allport, 1937). A third might have sought to decipher an individual's dominant life theme or master sentiment (Binswanger, 1944–1945/1958). A fourth might have explored how biological, psychoanalytic, and social perspectives contribute to our understanding of an individual life course (White, 1952).

But on one point they tended to agree. The relationship between a person's life and the verbal account he or she gave of it was regarded as relatively unproblematic: The account was simply a convenient report of the life; one could, so to speak, discern the life through the report. Today, this relationship is no longer regarded as quite so transparent. Linguists, historians, and literary theorists have subjected the genres of narrative and autobiography to close examination and ask whether it makes sense to speak of a life story's truth or whether one can clearly (or even unclearly) distinguish between a writer's fiction and his or her autobiography.

These debates and the proliferation of life history studies in other social sciences have somewhat increased the prestige of this sort of "qualitative research" in psychology. However, this loosening of the traditional methodological strictures has not prevented the assimilation of this new study into the old philosophy and agenda of research. For instance, Runyan sees the study of lives as the fertile ground for a synthesis of "soft" psychology, bringing together the findings of personality, developmental, and social psychology (1997). In this keystone function, the study of lives could challenge mainstream researchers to bend various uncoordinated investigations to a common and converging purpose. The study of lives would then consolidate the traditional scientific program of academic psychology.

In this orientation, the life history would head the canon of personality assessment methods both in practice and research. Just as the medical history is an indispensable element in the physician's and the medical researcher's workups—along with the physical examination and laboratory tests—so the life history would become a standard, if not the paramount, instrument for the adequate description and evaluation of any individual—along with tests, questionnaires, ratings, behavioral observations, and so on.

When the life history is assimilated into the traditional scientific study of personality, as is often done today, personal narratives are coded in accordance with certain classificatory schemes; the coded items are tallied for each individual in a designated group; and the groups are then compared statistically. Because this manner of dealing with life history materials conforms to established scientific procedures for analyzing quantitative data, it involves no *special* pedagogic strategy or problems.[1] The problems it does raise are technical, not unlike those associated with questionnaire construction or test standardization.

Useful as this approach may be to social researchers, it is not what attracts most college students to a course on the study of lives. Adolescents and young people on the threshold of adult responsibility frequently experience acute perplexity about particular lives—not only their own, but those of significant others. They want to scrutinize a single life history in detail so as to comprehend how early experiences gave shape to later developments and how different facets of a life cohere. In this day, when interest in cultural diversity runs high, many also want to go beyond the mere observation of normative differences and ask how the culture "gets into" the individual. This complex interest often represents more than idle curiosity; it may rather be stimulated by the prospect of having to make choices and commitments based on one's understanding of oneself and others.

Today's mainstream psychology curriculum does not prepare students well for such a task. This academic neglect is not an oversight, of course. The majority of academic psychologists have long believed that questions about particular lives do not fall within their jurisdiction and are, if anything, distractions from the agenda of science. Even the hopeful possibility that a public widely sophisticated about individual lives might make for an enhancement of social relations avails little against the pressures of limited scholarly resources and the weight of academic tradition. Also, the mainstream senses what I shall try to make plain—that the satisfaction of these students' interests calls for a substantial shift in the philosophical presuppositions of psychological inquiry.

If we now turn from the statistical comparison of coded autobiographical accounts to the study of individual life narratives, we face the further distinction between *comprehensive* and *focal* approaches.

## THE PROCESS

Irving Alexander is a genial and persuasive proponent of the comprehensive approach. He and his students ask two questions about any individual whose life they wish to examine: (a) What is this person like? and (b) How did he or she become this kind of person? This approach has its modern

---

[1] Even though the authors of such studies transform life-historical narratives into quantitative results, they often claim to present qualitative research. This terminological inflation may be evidence for the growing, if ambivalent, esteem in which qualitative research is held today.

origin in Murray's (1938), White's (1952), and Tomkins's (1987) research and teaching.

As a device for orienting oneself to the study of a life, Alexander's two questions would almost surely receive the approval of all the early life history scholars and of many others today. All of them approach lives with complex, partly implicit templates reflecting their interests and their descriptive and analytic categories. These templates can be applied to any person but are of course filled in distinctively, even uniquely, for each individual studied. It is the general nature of the templates applied in this approach, the open-ended questions posed, and the comprehensive life-historical research demanded by these and similar questions that give the comprehensive approach its name.

The *focal* approach to the study of lives has a quasi-clinical, specifically a psychoanalytic origin. It is quasi-clinical because it borrows insights from the study of normal development as well as from the treatment of mental and emotional disorders and applies these to individuals who are considered relatively free of disturbance. Typically, the focus of this approach is on an aspect of the individual's life that appears puzzling to common sense—paradoxical, exaggerated, irrational, inconsistent. The first exemplar of a focal study is surely Freud's monograph on Leonardo da Vinci (1910/1957). Much debated as to its conclusions, because it was based on flawed historical materials, this monograph nevertheless remains the most widely emulated methodological model for the contemporary psychobiographer. Freud did not ask the two questions cited above; rather, he took up certain contradictions and oddities in Leonardo's life that had been puzzling previous biographers and art historians and attempted to solve these.

I do not offer the distinction between these two approaches in order to set one above the other. Nor would I even suggest that the approaches have nothing in common; indeed, they overlap in certain phases of the interpretive process. My purpose is rather to show that each satisfies a somewhat different investigatory interest, emphasizes different skills, and offers different learning opportunities and challenges.

Because, in my own teaching, I have favored the focal over the comprehensive approach, I will discuss it more fully. But because both approaches have their appropriate uses, I want to clarify my choice by sketching some characteristics of each before I take up the pedagogic problems.

The comprehensive approach to the study of a life history stands in the same relation to the mastery of psychological theory as does conversation in a foreign language to the mastery of that language. The student learns how theoretical terms are used and how they aid the conceptualization of a life. There simply is no better way to learn this. Especially because many concepts have been absorbed into colloquial discourse and thereby lost some of their points and edges, it is helpful to acquaint students with their original explanatory or interpretive power.

The comprehensive approach is open-ended in two senses. One, a given biographical account can be interpreted in more than one theoretical language. One can ask a class: "How would Freud (or Jung or Erikson or Allport) describe this individual, and what developmental process would each ascribe to this person?" Two, there is no natural stopping point to a comprehensive description or developmental account. Students can go into as much or as little descriptive detail and provide as thorough or shallow a developmental account as the given biographical material, the chosen theory, and their own sophistication allow. This makes the approach more flexible than the focal one. But even though it sets no limit to ingenuity, it also cannot prevent vacuous descriptions and (re)constructions.

As implied, the crucial aspect of such a project is not the ability to translate biographical elements point-for-point into theoretical vocabulary ("Her daydream reflects *achievement motivation* but her pervasive naiveté is a sign of *repression*"); rather, what matters is the degree of organization and coherence achieved. The most useful descriptions are those which show relationships among synchronous domains of life, such as occupational habits, interpersonal style, political attitudes, or esthetic values and those which bring out nonobvious continuities and discontinuities among diachronic elements, say, the child's erstwhile relationship to parents and the later relationship to others in positions of authority. When a comprehensive project is carried out successfully, the student is apt to come away with the sense of having achieved some *mastery of theory*.

*Focal* projects, by contrast, presuppose a degree of practical acquaintance with theory and derive their value from the satisfaction of a circumscribed, case-based curiosity. It is, therefore, astonishingly easy to interest students in a seemingly isolated puzzling phenomenon or pattern within a given life story. Because such puzzles occur in the course of our normal daily interactions with others, the focal approach may be said to satisfy a common human curiosity. It is a curiosity about *particular* phenomena.

For example, students can develop a lively interest in why Emily Dickinson, a poet of extraordinary gifts and considerable social advantages, should have become so reclusive in her later years that she often declined to sit in the same room with visitors to her home, preferring instead to converse with them from an adjoining room through a half-open door. Students do not expect to get a satisfying answer to this question by consulting the scientific research literature on shyness, and they do not suppose that an answer to this question can be applied confidently to any or all other shy individuals. It is nevertheless the sort of question that, for reasons already mentioned, many students want to become more adept at answering for themselves. They seem to derive special satisfaction from psychobiographic projects if they are allowed to select the personage as well as the focal problem they will explore. Making sense of another person's problems in living may seem to them like "know[ing] one's own story while that story is still unfolding" (Alexander, 1990, p. 6). Whereas the interest in comprehensive projects is predominantly theory-driven, focal projects derive their allure from a more elementary experience-driven curiosity.[2]

Because focal tasks require students to offer answers to specific questions, they are finite in scope. Once the student has proposed an adequate explanation of Dickinson's shyness and has presented the pertinent biographic evidence, there is no need to go further. (This is not to deny that other scholars could, in time, improve on a given interpretation.) In comparison with a comprehensive task, this is an advantage insofar as student and teacher alike will be able to determine whether the student has arrived at a solution to the problem, regardless of how adequate this solution may be judged. But this same finitude is a disadvantage if the project was poorly conceived from the outset—say, insufficient biographical records from which to seek an answer to the focal question—and the student turns away from psychobiography with a sense of frustration. Simply put, the focal approach can be more demanding as well as more satisfying than the comprehensive. Whereas the comprehensive approach leads to a *sense of general (theoretical) competence*, the focal leads to a *sense of case-specific discovery*.

What I have called an adequate answer is nothing like the solution to an arithmetic problem. It is more similar to the *interpretation* that a literary critic or a historian offers in dealing with a puzzling text or sequence of past events. Interpretations are never true or false; they are accounts that seek to normalize or rationalize anomalous or incomprehensible texts or chronicles. In the case of psychobiography, this is done with the aid of theoretical terms that warrant the refiguration of the apparently isolated biographical *anomaly* as an integral element in the *comprehensible* background of the whole life story—often with the result that even what seemed unremarkable to begin with is now seen in a new and sharper light.

An interpretation is an argument for regarding the life story, as it was given, in a new and clearer way. What, in general, constitutes a *good* argument of this sort is a question beyond the limits of this chapter. It should be emphasized, however, that even satisfying interpretations are never satisfying for all times or audiences. They can be satisfying only

---

[2] A mixed model may be used as well. Here students are asked to answer a few predetermined questions on the basis of biographical material, for instance, "what is M's implicit belief about the nature of men and women, and how did he acquire it?" or "how has W's life been influenced by the way her father typically coped with stress and anxiety?" For a discussion of how several lives can be studied focally and yet without statistical aggregation, see Rosenwald (1988).

within the theoretical and cultural context in which they were offered. New contexts require new interpretations.

This puts students in an odd predicament. They must *argue* for formulations, knowing that while there are no right and wrong ones, there are certainly implausible, unsatisfying ones, and knowing also that even a successful interpretation is perishable. The comprehensive approach makes students' work easier. Because the rhetorical burden on students is lighter, the impermanence and relativity of the results are more easily tolerated.

A focal formulation is structured. Problematic life patterns, such as Dickinson's shyness, almost always express more than one disposition. Moreover, each such disposition, activated by contemporaneous conditions, has its own developmental history. Accordingly, when one begins with remote experiences of childhood, one must make visible the turning points and transformational phases along the path to the puzzling adult pattern. The links in such a chained argument must not only cohere in a *theoretically* sound fashion; they must also be supported by sufficient life-historical detail to convey *biographical* plausibility in the case under study.

Because an interpretation seeks simplicity and economy, evidence must be weighed as to relevance. A given biographical item may be one of few buttressing a claim central to the argument or one of many supporting a subsidiary claim and contributing little to the overall argument. For example, Wyatt and Willcox, in their methodologically exemplary psychobiography of Sir Henry Clinton, a British general during the American Revolutionary War, seek to illuminate this gifted military leader's pattern of self-defeat (Wyatt & Willcox, 1959). They claim that he was guilt-ridden or, as psychoanalytic writers often say, "wrecked by success." In addition to many telling biographical details that lend powerful support to their formulation—for instance, Clinton's pattern of proposing ingenious military stratagems to his superiors but in such an insensitive, abrasive manner that they would be sure to reject these—the authors also cite Clinton's extreme and unassuageable grief over the death of his wife as evidence for a susceptibility to guilt feelings. But this is one of their less valuable data because, even though it points to guilt feelings, these are not about ambition! The interpretive argument would have lost none of its persuasive power if this item had been omitted. Such considerations of relevance and probative weight can help an instructor guide students as they seek to refine and polish their arguments.

The issue of relevance has an ethical dimension as well. In scientific research, it is expected that investigators not deliberately manipulate the outcome of an investigation. In life-historical research, a comparable requirement operates. As shown, biographical data differ in relevance to a given interpretative proposal. But relevance does not mean corroboration! A biographical datum may be relevant to a formulation because it contradicts it. Discrepancies and inconsistencies in the life-historical record may complicate an interpretation or reduce its power. Students must learn that, although they are not accountable for inconsistencies of which they are ignorant, the systematic suppression or selection of data is not acceptable. Moreover, they should come to appreciate that facts that at first appear to undermine an interpretive proposal may, when seen in the proper light, add specificity and subtlety to the formulation.

## DISCOMFORT IN INTERPRETATION

I have discussed the psychobiographical task and its phenomenology in an impersonal, ahistorical fashion, without direct consideration of what instructors will encounter when they bring this discipline to students. In the remainder of this chapter I shall take up the discussion of some pedagogic difficulties in the classroom, and I shall suggest what factors, originating *outside* the classroom, might be responsible for these difficulties.

Instructors and students may enter their relationship with genuine enthusiasm. For reasons already mentioned, the focal approach to the psychological study of lives often appeals to students in a more immediate way than do other topics in psychology; such study, they know, may not be a requirement for career success, but it will feed an interest of a more private nature.

However, the enthusiasm is, in many cases, short-lived. Although many students are able to immerse themselves in the discipline, some cannot bring themselves to do what they must to progress in it. They may be thought to suffer from a sort of allergy; like an allergic animal lover, they want to draw close to the object of interest, but recoil every time they attempt it.

To begin with, many undergraduates have thoroughly internalized mainstream psychology's consensus that only scientific procedures can deliver what is worthy of being called knowledge; no other method even appears quite rational to them. Therefore, some are ready at times to abandon psychobiographic interpretation, taking refuge in the resignatory bromide that a certain puzzling or unusual life pattern may be "just one of those things" or "could be biological." Better no explanation, they seem to think, than one that is too "far-fetched," leaving open the question which interpretations they would consider acceptable and which exotic. As already mentioned, some of their mainstream instructors will agree that Dickinson's shyness, as a specific instance, cannot be dealt with scientifically. In short, the affinity of the psychobiographic enterprise to the humanities is alarming to some students.

But the institutional obstacles are not only attitudinal or ideological. There is a second "allergy" that exerts inhibiting effects in the domain of *psychological theory* and in that of *interpretive method*. I shall illustrate the theoretical aspect with an example drawn from a course on the "Psychological Study of Lives" that I have taught for many years. The term project in this class requires each student to identify some conspicuous puzzling pattern of action in the life of an historical personage and to offer a life-historical interpretation, that is, a psychologically and historically informed account of the individual's life that would render the perplexing phenomenon comprehensible.

Some years ago, a student in this class addressed the following question in his term paper: How can we understand that Adolf Hitler, who, in his youth, had artistic ambitions and presumably some aesthetic sensibility, could conceive of exterminating an entire people and, what is more, sell this plan to the members of an otherwise highly cultured nation? The answer the student came up with after his biographical research was that Hitler lacked good role models, had an unhappy childhood, suspected a Jewish doctor of having aggravated his mother's final illness, and spent his youth in the anti-Semitic atmosphere of Vienna.

At first glance, this answer seemed plausible enough, raising few objections from his fellow students in the class. Viewed more closely, however, such an answer is apt to disappoint anyone wishing to make sense of the *paradox* featured in the question and to do so in a manner that reflects this specific life history. Indeed, one might expect someone capable of asking this question to be shocked by the flatness of the answer. Moreover, it is hard to see how such an impersonal, all-purpose answer to such a sophisticated and individually focused question—or a series of similar answers to similar questions—could keep students' interest in psychobiography alive. One gets the sense that something important has been avoided here, and this avoidance is what I mean when I speak of an "allergy."

Characteristically, this student did not refer to any passions, fantasies, or personally meaningful perceptions on Hitler's part. Only his early environment is described. This hesitance about an inner life is widespread among students and expresses what appears as a profound discomfort with the notion of powerful impulses and yearnings. Accordingly, they tend to see Dickinson, too, as a victim of losses or privations rather than as acting on any powerful urges, longings, intentions, or fears—implying a type of psychological immobility quite unthinkable in the life of a great poet.

Students seem especially uneasy about motivations that are not obviously socially acceptable. They are not simply reluctant, however, to deal with such concepts; they actively resist them at times in a manner suggesting the mobilization of an implicit, perhaps unarticulated ethical value. This becomes especially evident when they are faced with patterns of self-stagnation or self-subversion. They tend to reduce these as well as any other irrational behavior patterns to something that was done to the person. Very rarely do they seem to notice that people can be greedy or generous, full of hate or lust, builders or schemers, provocateurs or harmonizers, fanatics or hypocrites, prosecutors or penitents—or several of these at once.

John Dollard urged students of life history to attend to the "projectile character" of human behavior, by which he meant the self-generated, insistent, at times blindly uncompromising manner in which personal motives and styles press for actualization (1935, p. 20). This side of the coin is widely ignored by students in favor of the shaping of lives by external forces and circumstances.

They think of a human research participant as someone to whom other people happen, but not someone who happens to others. This one-sidedness is all the more remarkable because, in their lives outside the classroom, these students lead vigorous, expressive, sensuous, if not exactly individualized, lives and are certainly not unfamiliar with the trials and conflicts normal for their age. Therefore, if Hemingway's machismo and Malcolm X's charisma appear to many of them chiefly as scars inflicted by others, an explanation is called for. Students often seem to have been estranged from their own inner experience and thence cannot draw on this resource so as to apply it analogically to the interpretation of other people's lives.

A word of warning is in place here. Although the instructor encounters the obstacles I am discussing in the classroom and, more specifically, in the oral and written utterances of students, it must be remembered that such impediments to the learning process do not originate in individual students but represent cultural values mediated through these students. I shall shortly expand on this point. Keeping this cultural mediation in mind helps in two ways. It alleviates the instructor's frustration with the students as individuals, allowing him or her to see students as barred from the satisfaction of their own interests; in other words, it helps reduce the tendency to blame the products of our socialization. Also, it allows us, albeit only in degrees, to mitigate the pressure of inhibiting values by making them explicit. Such explication can mobilize a process of individual and collective reflection. To be sure, the constraining effect of these values, which receive such wide support in the culture, cannot be easily undone in this fashion.

What, then, are these cultural values? Students' avoidance of their own and others' subjectivity is partly accounted for, I would suggest, by the adaptationist heritage of academic psychology. Since William James, students have been taught that the organism *naturally* tends to conform to the requirements of the surrounding world, especially other people's requirements, in order to satisfy its own requirements in optimal fashion. When this metaphor governs one's view of lives, one's attention is necessarily drawn to the external conditions as the chief source of variation in lives and as the engine and compass of individual living action. It is perhaps not astonishing then that students have difficulty seeing lives in any other way, especially because there is hardly a topic in academic psychology—from development, to individual differences, to social interaction—that is not dominated by the adaptationist metaphor.[3]

Not only does the metaphor locate the control of lives in the external world; it also identifies this control as aiding satisfaction and—if only one adapts *increasingly* well—with progress! The notion that the natural tendency to adapt to the requirements of the world could ever lead to adverse consequences for the quality of one's life is rendered unintelligible at the level of the concept itself. This may explain why students often wish to interpret self-stagnating or self-defeating life patterns as serving growth instead—for instance, when a student suggests that Edgar Allan Poe alienated many potential sponsors and patrons "in order to strengthen his autonomy"—an interpretation that is almost impossible to sustain in the face of the writer's life history.

The thought that even men and women of great merit and renown may sometimes stumble is, I believe, experienced as a personal let-down by many young people who themselves stand on the threshold of adult responsibility and who feel the pressure to succeed at any price.

Consistent with their reluctance to engage others' inner life of passions, many students also seem wary of their own inner cognitive and empathic resources. This is the methodological aspect of the "allergy." It pertains to the *logic* of psychobiography and poses special challenges for the instructor.

Let us say we are interested in understanding why Dickinson eventually avoided human interactions so fastidiously. This would involve two steps. First, we would have to identify the beliefs, motives, and perceptions on which she was acting when she erected barriers between herself and others. That is, we must begin by formulating the reasons she would have given for her avoidance of people if she had been asked and if she had had full self-knowledge. Was she afraid of contact, perhaps of infection? Did she think she was too unattractive to be seen? Was her aloofness a way of protecting people against her lugubrious preoccupations or perhaps herself against the distracting influence other people would exert? Was she too proud to mingle with the hoi polloi? What, in other words, was the *meaning* of her behavior?

Second, we would have to trace this interpreted meaning in her life history to early experiences, cultural norms, and so forth. If she was haughty or fearful, how did she come to feel this way? If she saw other people as dangerous or vulnerable, how did she acquire these stereotypes? What was

---

[3] How this metaphor gained its power initially, at the foundation of American psychology, is a compelling question, not to be treated here, but one which surely requires an examination of the social and economic burgeoning of late 19th- and early 20th-century American society.

the meaning of the outward events that turned her from an earlier sociability to the later seclusiveness?

Both of these phases in a focal project require students to construct the personal meaning of certain events, actions, episodes. How did a particular child interpret a sibling's death? What feelings did it have about its parents' disciplinary style? How much and in what way did an adolescent's personal appearance matter to him or her? How did an individual experience his or her own strong desires and those of others?

In making attributions of motives, feelings, perceptions, and beliefs, one must call on one's intuition and one's experience of life as well as on what one has come to understand about the lives of others in various situations. I encourage students to sniff out the meaning of the behavior, to look for small signs and tell-tale details, to read between the lines, to look for patterns, and so forth. Many of them are afraid to do this. "How can I be sure that anyone else will see this my way?" they ask. I reassure them: "No matter what your research design professors have told you, you need not worry about a flood of idiosyncratic readings. If you think you understand Dickinson's shyness and make your understanding clear to me, then the chances are excellent that I will be helped by your view. Try it!" As it happens, students' apprehensions are usually groundless because they rarely perform any but the most conservative and uncontroversial interpretive leaps.

Even then, they still worry: "How do I know this is right?" I cannot remind them often enough that an interpretive proposal is neither right nor wrong, but more or less successful, given the biographical facts and the particular audience they wish to enlighten. They should strive for coherence, consistency, comprehensiveness, and simplicity in their formulations—not truth. Moreover, it is well to point out to them that the members of a particular culture tend to share a commitment to certain preferred story lines and types of explanation and that this will dispose readers favorably toward students' interpretations..

But students' methodological reflexes seem immune to such reassurances. That these reflexes are anchored in ethical values is suggested by two considerations. One, even though they are offered a blanket reprieve from many of their worries about proof and truth, they decline it. Told that their interpretation need only be plausible, no more, they still commonly insist on being right, nothing less than right. They raise the stakes, it seems, by trying to meet another and, as they see it, higher standard.

Two, when students are asked to respond to model psychobiographic essays assigned in class, it is not uncommon to hear reactions ranging from grumbling skepticism to indignation and disparagement to outright disgust and hostility—especially when unresolved archaic desires or fears of childhood are put forward to account for recalcitrant maladaptive behavior patterns in the adult.

By comparison with the interpretive demands just discussed, psychological research, as students have previously encountered it, appears innocuous to them even when it presents *all* human beings in an unflattering light. Generalizations about *groups* of people and *classes* of events retain an air of impersonality: So long as no one in particular is targeted, no one is hurt. But when psychological principles are applied to real, specific, admired individuals, then deep currents of reluctance are tapped. Doubtless, the selection of *famous* individuals for these projects, made unavoidable by the need for detailed biographical sources, also stimulates the tendency to idealize celebrities. Some students show signs of discomfort and some actually confess to feelings of remorse when they cannot avoid recognizing destructive (or self-destructive) themes in the life of an admired individual—as though they were themselves complicit in an act of destruction. This is not altogether easy to understand because our popular media open many windows on cultural idols' foibles and moral infirmities.

Sometimes students reject complex motivational and developmental interpretations because they are "too complicated." One student declared recently: "I just can't believe that a set of circumstances in a person's childhood could have such far-reaching consequences in adulthood." In the abstract, students acknowledge the complexity and idiosyncrasy or, as they like to say, "uniqueness" of people's lives. But when it comes to specific puzzling cases, their prior education often prompts them to retreat to common-sense formulae, for instance, "insecurity," the failure of certain kinds of learning to have taken place, or "low self-esteem."

The implicit reasoning producing such proposals appears to be

1. X displays a life-long pattern of self-restriction,
2. Research has shown that individuals with low self-esteem tend to display such patterns,
3. Therefore, X may (or must) have suffered from low self-esteem.

They may then argue that an important person in X's life suppressed his or her self-esteem or that the economic, educational, or social environment in which X grew up tended to inhibit X's development. Such a method makes few demands on students' intuitive or empathic grasp of X's lifeworld; rather, it circumvents the "allergy." They need only assign the focal phenomenon to a category familiar from scientific research and follow the logical implication. (The underlying syllogism is actually invalid.) The result of this reasoning is a *causal hypothesis* rather than a *life-historical interpretation;* behavior is addressed without regard to its individually specific meaning.

As stated, these students' quasi-allergic reactions to the psychobiographic task are the products not only of academic socialization and, therefore, widely shared, but reflect the larger context of students' social existence as well as the pressures of the dominant culture.

One, these students are committed to *progress*. They want to be open to the future, open to opportunities. The traces of the life-historical past within the meaning structures of the present seem to them an encumbrance that limits adaptability. Two, they are committed to a *means-end rationality*. If the inner life is partly unconscious and sends out sporadic flashes of irrationality, then one is no longer master in one's house. Three, despite the vaunted sexual revolution, these students are, by and large, severely *puritanical* in their outlook. They want to confine basic drives, such as various erotic and aggressive motives, to a special private place—a gated sanctuary—rather than acknowledge that these drives often crash the gates and trespass on supposedly sober, purposive pursuits.

In brief, students are caught up in a conflict of cultural values. The famed individualism of American culture—its demand that one maximize one's skill and effort to increase one's value as a person—spurs students' quest to achieve maximal understanding of themselves and of other people. But the equally famed cultural regard for practicality in the here-and-now and the distrust of "mere" promise and speculation exert a powerful restraint on students' mobilization of the skills and functions necessary to achieve the goal of individualized human understanding.[4]

What can the instructor do? One, he or she can make the nature of the resistances—and the underlying cultural exigencies—explicit rather than attempt to finesse them. Two, I have learned over the years that abstract philosophical arguments about truth and method are without effect. Many questions about ambiguity, bias, alternative explanations, and the like are much better approached with examples taken from the students' own projects: "Try it, and then we'll talk about it." Concreteness offers no guarantee, but many doubts can be laid to rest when exposed to the light of actuality.

Three, instructors must cleanse themselves of mainstream prejudice. Even great champions of the case-study method occasionally lapse into a defensive style, letting the mainstream nomothete dictate the terms of the debate. "Our methods aren't as bad as you think," they seem to say, "We, too, can generalize and test hypotheses—namely, about the indi-

---

[4]In the experience of one of this chapter's anonymous reviewers, the attitudinal and functional restrictions described in this chapter are more typical of American students than of European and Israeli ones. This observation tends to confirm the cultural mediation thesis for which I have been arguing here.

vidual case!"—as though this kind of knowledge were the only kind worth pursuing.

This sort of conciliatory attitude is not only ineffective; it trades away the best we have to offer, namely, the acknowledgment that there is a cognitive interest, a wish to understand social and psychological phenomena in a way that is not accessible to traditional aggregative, hypothesis-testing, law-framing methods. It is more honest and more effective to differentiate the narrative study of lives from the mainstream psychology that is our own and our students' traditional home base.

So long as we nourish the illusion that the two approaches tend toward identical goals and satisfy the same interest, the competition between them will persist—to the disadvantage of the interpretive approach. Furthermore, given the cultural values to which the parametric–empiricist and the particularist–interpretive approaches appear relevant, this competition will be fought out in the Heaven-and-Hell vocabulary of, as Erikson once put it, "superior and inferior, good and bad, masculine and feminine, free and slave, potent and impotent, beautiful and ugly, fast and slow, tall and small, in a simple alternative, in order to make one battle and one strategy out of a bewildering number of skirmishes" (Erikson, 1959, p. 30).

The battle revolves around young people's exertions to consolidate a workable ego-identity out of the welter of motives, capacities, and ideologies vying for emphasis, elaboration, and loyalty. To the opposing value-pairs mentioned by Erikson, we might add students' implicit evaluation of the two methods as objective and subjective, optimistic and pessimistic, simple and complex, tough-minded and tender-minded. Even though these characterizations reflect a grave misunderstanding of *all* scholarship—scientific and hermeneutic—given the values that the traditions of our culture impress on us, these polarities have the power to evoke deep longings and anxieties in many students, as they seek to define themselves.

I strive to relieve them of an unnecessary and senseless choice by telling them that the narrative approach to the study of a life is not a part of scientific psychology, but rather a humanistic inquiry not unlike history or archaeology. It has not only its own methods and its own goals, but its own measures of excellence. The canons of science are not fit to judge these methods and goals any more than the methods and goals of history or archaeology. I see this as a way to establish the autonomy of the narrative approach and of the interest it satisfies. I know that when I set course for these goals, I invite students on a different journey from the one many expected. A few, therefore, develop mutinous attitudes or jump ship. But for the remainder, the voyage becomes easier once they trust the vessel. If they stay on, they may experience the gladness of an arrival.

# REFERENCES

Alexander, I. E. (1990). *Personology: Method and content in personality assessment and psychobiography*. Durham, NC: Duke University Press.

Allport, G. W. (1937). *Personality: A psychological interpretation*. New York: Holt.

Binswanger, L. (1958). The case of Ellen West. In R. May, E. Angel, & H. F. Ellenberger (Eds.), *Existence: A new dimension in psychiatry and psychology* (pp. 237–364). New York: Basic Books. (Original work published 1944–1945)

Dollard, J. (1935). *Criteria for the life history*. New Haven, CT: Yale University Press.

Erikson, E. H. (1959). Ego-development and historical change. *Psychological Issues*, *1*(1), 18–49.

Freud, S. (1957). Leonardo da Vinci and a memory of his childhood. In *Standard edition of the complete psychological works of Sigmund Freud* (Vol. XI, pp. 57–137). London: Hogarth Press. (Original work published 1910)

Murray, H. A. (1938). *Explorations in personality*. New York: Oxford University Press.

Rosenwald, G. C. (1988). A theory of multiple-case research. *Journal of Personality*, *56*, 239–264.

Runyan, W. McK. (1997). Studying lives: Psychobiography and the conceptual structure of personality psychology. In R. Hogan (Ed.), *Handbook of personality psychology* (pp. 41–69). San Diego, CA: Academic Press.

Tomkins, S. S. (1987). Script theory. In J. Aronoff, A. I. Rabin, & R. A. Zucker (Eds.), *The emergence of personality* (pp. 147–216). New York: Springer.

White, R. W. (1952). *Lives in progress*. New York: Dryden Press.

Wyatt, F., & Willcox, W. (1959). Sir Henry Clinton: A psychological exploration in history. *William and Mary Quarterly*, XVI, 3–26.

# 9

# THE PROTOTYPICAL SCENE: A METHOD FOR GENERATING PSYCHOBIOGRAPHICAL HYPOTHESES

WILLIAM TODD SCHULTZ

In trying to understand lives, the medium is text, or what people write and say, and what others write and say about them. Taking the long view of a life history, persons are first and foremost what they tell us, their life story. Teaching students how to begin making effective sense of a person therefore requires two things: a system for identifying especially important word-based communications and a posture for interpreting those communications. This chapter concerns, chiefly, the former. I want to propose a method for singling out key events in personal narratives that can be introduced early on in classes and serve as an anchor for personological inquiry—something students need more than anything else, in my experience, if we want our efforts to be successful. More specifically, my question is this: From among the numberless scenes recounted by research participants, varying in context, time-frame, affective-tone, and emphasis, can we hope to isolate one—and *only one*—which, in its essentials, encapsulates an entire life history, or at least the core parameters of an individual life story?

This possibility first emerged during an undergraduate honors class I taught on autobiography, fiction, and self-invention. Both individually and in small groups, we looked in that class at the lives of writers Kathryn Harrison, Jack Kerouac, Franz Kafka, and Sylvia Plath. We poured over journal entries, memoirs, letters, diaries, poetry, secondary literature, and

I want to thank members of my Spring 2000 Honors class, "Autobiography, Fiction, and Self-Invention," for their help in formulating these ideas, and for their openness to trying an entirely exploratory course. My thanks, also, to my colleagues in the Society for Personology, to whom this paper was presented in Wellesley, Massachusetts, on June 16, 2001. At various points along the way valuable feedback was offered by Alan Elms (as always), Ruthellen Josselson, Dan McAdams, Irving Alexander, Jim Anderson, John Kotre, Rae Carlson, and an immensely kind and thoughtful anonymous reviewer. I dedicate this chapter to the "fish stick."

autobiographical fiction. Students were fully loaded up with life data and charged with creatively crafting from it some sort of clarifying coherence. Repeatedly, and in a way almost impossible to ignore, a single scene from each life came to assume a kind of supersaliency. Over time we elected to call such scenes "prototypical": In their details we discovered the blueprint of a life (even though their authors did not usually present the scenes in such terms), and, nearly by accident, a method of life illumination. Attention then turned to the identification of similarly prototypical scenes in future instances. We wondered how one could reliably know a prototypical scene when one "sees" it, and if prototypical scenes might provide a promising focus, thereby serving as a guide to the development of psychobiographical hypotheses. In other words, we accorded the concept a central status in our class and continued tinkering with it to the very end, feeling we had serendipitously stumbled upon an idea of great value.

In this chapter I want to share the fruits of our concerted labor—these being, primarily, a handful of prototypical scene indicators. But before doing so, an immediate reference case for the kind of scene the class isolated might be useful. On several different occasions the writer Truman Capote told a story about his childhood which seems, for various reasons, deserving of prototypical status. It happened when he was 2 years old, a fact calling into question the memory's authenticity. Perhaps the event was told to Capote, perhaps he recalled it somehow (if it happened when he was 3 or 4, say, rather than 2), or perhaps he made it up—there is no way to say for sure. As Capote's friend, the writer John Knowles, described it:

> Just after I met him, Truman began telling me his life story. This terrible, tragic story. The central tragedy, as he saw it, in his life is a scene. Truman is two years old. He wakes up in an utterly strange room, empty. He yells, but he's locked in there. He's petrified, doesn't know where he is—which is in some dumpy hotel in the Deep South—and his parents have gone out to get drunk and dance. They have locked this tiny little boy in his room. That was his image of terror, and I think it was his way of symbolizing the insecurity of his youth—this image of that kind of abandonment. (quoted in Plimpton, 1997, p. 26)

Capote recounts the same scene to interviewer Gerald Grobel: "It was a certain period in my life. I was only about two years old, but I was very aware of being locked in this hotel room. My mother was a very young girl. We were living in this hotel in New Orleans. She had no one to leave me with. She had no money and she had nothing to do with my father. She would leave me locked in this hotel room when she went out in the evening with her beaus and I would become hysterical because I couldn't get out of this room" (1985, p. 48).

This memory assumes a supersaliency because of its singularity, its quality of discreteness. As Knowles explains, the scene of abandonment is Capote's "central" tragedy. It is "nuclear"; it summarizes the life story. There is a need, moreover, to recollect it, as though it were especially explanatory. It also has the earmarks of developmental trauma. Capote recalls it with terror. He remembers becoming hysterical (as any 2-year-old would, no doubt). And the scene underscores an obvious life-theme: abandonment fear and subsequent efforts to defend against that fear. As Capote himself would later declare, "Because of my childhood, because I always had the sense of being abandoned, certain things have fantastic effects on me, beyond what someone else might feel. . . . Every morning I wake up and in about two minutes I'm weeping. . . . I'm so unhappy. I just have to come to terms with something. There is something wrong. I don't know what it is" (quoted in Clarke, 1988, p. 498).

Abandonment themes showed up in Capote's fiction, too. His most famous short story, "Miriam," concerns a mysteriously motherless little girl who enters then promptly destroys the life of a 61-year-old widow, Mrs. H. T. Miller (Capote, 1969). As the story unfolds, Miriam makes the widow want her. The widow is pathetically powerless to say no. She ends up helpless, under Miriam's thumb, and quite possibly mad. Is Miriam-qua-Capote the motherless castoff come home to exact revenge, to drive the capricious and crazy-making mother into abject insanity? It seems likely.

One other feature of Capote's memory, and of prototypical scenes in general, deserves notice: Neither can be said to possess literal truth. Such scenes are part—or maybe more than part—invention.[1] They get told and retold not only because they really happened, but because of what they represent—the life story writ-small, so to speak. In one condensed package, they symbolize the leitmotif of a life. Their truth is less important than their representativeness.

The Capote example already exposes a number of potential prototypical scene indicators. What I plan to do next is focus on these signals more explicitly, beginning with previous efforts to assemble similar systems of identification, particularly those of Alexander (1988, 1990) and Singer and Salovey (1993). I follow up the analysis of signals with detailed illustrations of the application of prototypical scenes to individual lives—writers Kathryn Harrison, Jack Kerouac, and Sylvia Plath—mostly in order to highlight the concept's usefulness.

---

[1] This fact guarantees the concept's nonreductionistic character. Prototypical scenes are partly veridical memories—bottom-up events, that is—and partly adult constructions, or top-down embellishments.

# USING PROTOTYPICAL SCENE INDICATORS TO TEACH NARRATIVE METHODS

As I envision it, the prototypical scene facilitates the teaching of narrative methods in several respects. My students (all undergraduates) tend to respond to a class like psychobiography in one of two ways: They are either thrilled by its interpretive nature and the creative demands it makes, or they are overwhelmed or confused by the richness and heterogeneity of the biographical record. They do not know where or how to start, or what is important or unimportant within a life's raw data. First defining then helping students track down scenes that may be prototypical, in the process setting other life-episodes aside, increases the signal-to-noise ratio; the scene can be focused on and worked with in relative isolation initially, giving students something specific to "grasp" and examine. It suggests possible meanings that then give rise to hypotheses worth testing out on life materials. In the best of cases, the prototypical scene becomes a road map. With its lessons in mind, students stand a better chance of making effective sense of a life.

On two or three occasions students have expressed some irritation at what they perceive to be psychobiography's looseness of method and the puzzling multiplicity of interpretations offered for particular life events (for instance, why van Gogh cut off his ear, or factors leading to Picasso's invention of Cubism or Pollock's turn to drip painting). At least in part, the prototypical scene responds to such concerns. As I show later, it provides a method, a set of criteria. It also narrows the field of meaning by training attention on discrete events. If standards can be introduced for the identification of prototypical scenes, and if such scenes can be carefully thought-through, then worries about an apparent lack of method and the correlated sense of lostness in the midst of life materials ought to reduce significantly. Prototypical scenes provide focus and suggest paths to pursue. Their effect should be calming.

One last point is also worth considering. Steeped as most students are in the postmodern tradition, they occasionally try advancing the argument that all interpretations of a life are equal, in effect embracing an ideology of undecidability. We cannot really know anything for sure, they say, so what is the point of trying? What can be gained? My view is that this attitude needs to be contested. Some interpretations *are* better than others, and some meanings more pronounced, more cogent (Runyan's 1982 paper on van Gogh makes this point effectively). Because, in an ideal sense, prototypical scenes possess such unique significance and lead to particularly effective understandings of lives, they reinstate the real possibility of knowing. They repay our efforts. Students can be made to see that, and when they do, they should feel empowered and hopeful, rather than daunted.

The notion that it might be possible to systematically extract uniquely revealing fragments from life-writings began with Irving Alexander's work on "principal identifiers of salience" (Alexander, 1988, 1990). These immensely useful identifiers—which I include early on in all my narrative-based courses—make up a "set of pointers" for homing in on psychologically important information. I present each in turn, with occasional examples of my own (additional examples of each identifier have been provided by both Elms, 1994, and of course by Alexander, 1988, 1990).

## Primacy

I suggest to students that what comes first sometimes tells us more than anything else, as in the tradition of attaching extra importance to earliest memories, first loves, first traumas, and so on, under the assumption that people do not start stories haphazardly. I often bring in texts and ask the class to speculate about their openings, then keep these speculations in mind as additional life material is introduced. For instance, Nabokov begins his autobiography *Speak, Memory* with an account of a suspiciously hypothetical "chronophobe" (Nabokov himself?) unnerved by the image of a brand-new baby carriage glimpsed in home movies made a few weeks before his birth. It stands on the porch "with the smug, encroaching air of a coffin" (1966, p. 19). He goes on: "Over and over again my mind has made colossal efforts to distinguish the faintest of personal glimmers in the impersonal darkness on both sides of my life," the two black voids, fore and aft (p. 20).

Interestingly, Nabokov's relationship to time is a central focus of Brian Boyd's (1990) mammoth biography. As Boyd sees it, "One of the central themes of Nabokov's work has always been that Time, if we could return to it endlessly, might disclose evidence of a richness and design obscured by the crowdedness of passing mortal time" (p. 467). For Nabokov, art and the creative imagination make transcendence possible. By discovering the ultimate artfulness behind things—the particulars and patterns of the world, including fate—we merge with creative forces "beyond death" and form a "new relation to time," which Nabokov described as a "prison" (p. 319). Along with personality and the closed circle of mortal knowledge, Boyd identifies time as the "third constraint upon consciousness" in Nabokov's metaphysics. This time constraint can be surmounted, however, for as Nabokov blithely declares: "I confess I do not believe in time. I like to fold my magic carpet, after use, in such a way as to superimpose one part of the pattern upon another" (Nabokov, 1966, p. 139). Nabokov the practicing lepidopterist found his "highest enjoyment of timelessness" when standing among rare butterflies: "This is ecstasy, and behind the ecstasy is something else, which is hard to explain" (p. 139).

Here, then, is an example of how lingering over beginnings can suggest life themes or enduring concerns.

## Uniqueness

Sometimes research participants preface statements by declaring their uniqueness or else speak in language that clearly departs from a usual mode of expression (Alexander, 1988, 1990). Other times, material stands out because of its patent oddity. Students seem to grasp this idea intuitively. For instance, Leonardo was not in the habit of telling stories about his childhood, so when he described a fantasy of a "vulture" visiting him in his cradle and thrusting its tail into his mouth, Freud took notice, making the fantasy a central feature of his psychobiography of the great painter (with disastrous results, in this case, because of a mistranslation—the bird was not a vulture, but a kite; see Elms, 1994).

My class found a nice illustration of uniqueness in Kafka's painfully dense *Letter to His Father*. How he begins the anecdote is especially telling:

> There is only one episode in the early years of which I have a direct memory. You [Kafka's father] may remember it, too. One night I kept on whimpering for water, not, I am certain, because I was thirsty, but probably partly to be annoying, partly to amuse myself. After several vigorous threats had failed to have any effect, you took me out of bed, carried me out onto the pavlatche, and left me there alone for a while in my nightshirt, outside the shut door. . . . I dare say I was quite obedient afterwards at that period, but it did me inner harm. What was for me a matter of course, that senseless asking for water, and the extraordinary terror of being carried outside were two things that I, my nature being what it was, could never properly connect with each other. Even years afterwards I suffered from the tormenting fancy that the huge man, my father, the ultimate authority, would come almost for no reason at all and take me out of bed in the night. . . . (1976, p. 17)

Kafka earmarks the incident for us by highlighting its uniqueness. It is the only memory he retains from his early years. That being the case, we are justified in wondering why. In the next paragraph, he traces the "sense of nothingness" often dominating him to this action by his father, the ultimate authority. Because nothingness, absurdity, and the inscrutability of causality between events all combine to form a part of the definition of "Kafkaesque," Kafka's aside is anything but inconsequential. And when one recalls that much of Kafka's fiction takes as its subject the bewildering actions of authorities guided by incomprehensible laws, this memory of being carried out onto the pavlatche retrospectively predicts a major theme in Kafka's art. For these reasons and others, Kafka's memory strikes me as at least potentially prototypical. At minimum, it encapsulates a life theme.

And though—for reasons I discuss later—saliency cues do not always succeed in identifying what I think of as prototypical scenes, this example shows that they sometimes *might*, under the right circumstances.

I would add one additional possibility to the saliency cue of uniqueness, this being that sometimes life events stand out for their unrepeatedness regardless of whether or not subjects draw attention to them in speech or writing. I am thinking of an event in the life of Picasso. At age 16 while living in the isolated mountain village of Horta de Ebro, Picasso would have occasion to observe the macabre nocturnal autopsy of an old woman and her granddaughter, both killed by lightning. A cut was made with a saw from the top of the young girl's scalp down to her neck in order to expose the brain, in effect severing one half of the face from the other (Mailer, 1995, p. 24). Armed with such evidence, some have argued—most notably Picasso biographer Patrick O'Brian—that Picasso's split heads and double profiles, so plentiful in his mid- and later painting, can be traced to what Mailer calls the "pickled horror" of witnessing this crude dissection. Unique experiences call for unique responses, and Picasso's fractured faces certainly are unique—and uniquely horrifying.

## Frequency

Another term for this "pointer" might be repetition, a textual element students should be told to watch for carefully. When research participants frequently retell the same story, sometimes in almost identical language, that act marks the episode as peculiarly unfinished and psychologically compelling. In Freudian terms, we repeat what we have not mastered. Repetition, therefore, denotes unresolved conflict. And unresolved conflict is always of paramount importance to personologists. Because he told it time and again, Capote's memory of being locked in a hotel room is a good example of repetition. So is Alan Elms's excellent account of Allport's fateful meeting with Freud, an event of such "pungent significance" that Allport would go on to invent a theory refuting the entire Freudian system, especially Freud's notion of the infantile motives for adult behavior (see Elms, 1994).

## Negation

If one can entertain the likelihood of a truth by eliminating its negative component, then what we conspicuously disavow might suggest psychological significance (Alexander, 1988, 1990). "When the subject tells you who she or he isn't," as Elms explains, "you should pay at least as much attention" as when a subject tells you who he or she is (1994, p. 246). In his prison letter to Lord Alfred Douglas—the man who, according to most interpreters, precipitated Oscar Wilde's descent into ruin—Wilde repeatedly assures

Douglas that he does not blame him (Wilde, 1996). Many regard this particular disavowal as the confirmation of its opposite: blame.

## Emphasis

This cue includes "obvious forms of accent or underlining in oral or written communication" (Alexander, 1990, p. 17). Alexander names three types: overemphasis (attention focused on something typically considered commonplace); underemphasis (little attention paid to something important); and misplaced emphasis (excessive attention paid to aspects of a situation that seem clearly less significant than others). *Omission*, another of Alexander's saliency cues, is emphasis's antithesis. Elms (1994) calls omission the "Sherlock Holmes rule." Sometimes we should ask more questions when a dog does not bark than when it does. An example might be a research participant's failure to identify a particular family member in an autobiographical essay including detailed references to all other members of the family unit. Another possibility is the omission of an expected affective response (this according to certain culturally established norms of behavior). In his autobiography *Boy*, Roald Dahl (1984) describes his father's death with such neutrality and relative under-elaboration that one cannot help but wonder what he may be holding back.

## Error, Incompletion, and Isolation

These conclude the list of potential saliency cues. I combine them here because they possess a kind of family resemblance. Errors include all forms of "mischievement"—verbal slips, distortions, miscommunications, and ostensible accidents. Such "bunglings" can reveal hidden motives or conflicts. Incompletion occurs when "an expository sequence begins, follows a course, but ends before closure is reached" (Alexander, 1990, p. 23). A topic is introduced then abruptly terminated without explanation. Isolation is called by Elms (1994) the "Come Again?" criterion (p. 247). That is, if we find ourselves asking of autobiographical writings, "What is this all about?" or "What is she talking about here?," then we may be dealing with important material. In one sense, isolation is non sequitor speech—the seemingly irrelevant association or aside. Here Kafka's letter provides yet another example. While talking about his shyness and its eventual manifestations, he parenthetically interjects the lines "Up to now I have intentionally passed over in silence relatively little in this letter, but now and later I shall have to keep silent about some things that are still too hard for me to confess—to you and to myself. . . . It is not easy to find a middle way" (1976, p. 73). He then immediately returns to his prior line of thought. Obviously what Kafka keeps silent about is of tremendous importance.

Isolations in material bespeak mysteries. They leave one happily puzzled and wanting to know more.

Before outlining the core criteria of prototypical scenes which, again, do not always overlap Alexander's saliency pointers, Singer and Salovey's (1993) concept of self-defining memory—a close cousin of the prototypical scene—also warrants consideration. Self-defining memories, of which there may be various subtypes, are just that—self-defining. They are "very familiar, clear, and important memories that [have] been recalled and thought about many times" (Moffitt & Singer, 1994, p. 26). They also facilitate self-understanding, and "might be the type of memory told to a friend to convey important information powerfully" (p. 26). Self-defining memories evoke strong feelings too, either positive, negative, or a combination of both.

In their book *The Remembered Self*, Singer and Salovey (1993) draw on extrapsychological sources—poetry, novels, autobiography, and biography—to delineate various specific features indicative of memories rising to self-defining status. These include: *affective intensity* (memories that often seize one suddenly and with passionate feeling), *vividness* (memories that appear in consciousness with the perspicuity of an actual experience, creating the illusion of being in another place and reality), *repetition* (memories that are omnipresent and therefore readily accessible), and *likelihood of linkage* (the tendency for some memories to "magnify" themes or affects). Finally, self-defining memories either *preserve enduring concerns* or organize themselves around *unresolved conflicts*.

Now to the matter of conceptual comparison. As I see it, all self-defining memories are salient or "vivid"; they stand out. The same can be said of prototypical scenes. On the other hand, salient psychological episodes are not always self-defining, nor are they necessarily prototypical. They are uniquely important—that much is axiomatic—but not so important as to become constellating. In similar fashion, self-defining memories, though closer in form and function to prototypical scenes than any given salient psychological episode, still are not always and inevitably prototypical. This is so chiefly because self-defining memories are a plurality—there may be many of them in any life, some positive, some negative, some suggesting change, some continuity—whereas, as I want to argue, prototypical scenes are by definition singular. Each life contains only one. If we just can find the prototypical scene, exhume it from beneath the scattered events, memories, and episodes in which it is embedded, and then interpret its meaning, we may learn more about a life than hitherto seemed possible.[2]

---

[2] Prototypical scenes also resemble Tomkins's (1987) notion of the nuclear script, except that scripts are sets of scenes—not single events. Also, in nuclear scripts, something very good turns very bad; prototypical scenes do not necessarily recapitulate this sequence. Rather, they depict something neutral turning bad—a violation of expectation, perhaps—or else something bad simply staying bad.

So with that kind of Holy Grail-like odyssey in mind, I turn now to the indicators of prototypical scenes, each of which suggested itself after focused examination of the lives and work of a handful of writers, three of whom I discuss in much more detail later (namely, Harrison, Kerouac, and Plath).

First are cues that overlap those already mentioned by Singer and Salovey (1993) and Alexander (1988, 1990)—these are *specificity, incongruity,* and *interpenetration.* A striking richness of detail is often met with in prototypical scenes. They are not recalled generically, as concepts lacking content; they are recalled with precision, apparent certainty, and exactitude. Colors are common, props find specific representation, the subject knows who was present and who was not, and the setting—the location where the event took place—is foregrounded with confidence. In most cases dialogue also occurs. The actors are "quoted," and when the scene gets retold, their lines do not vary or else vary only slightly. On meeting Freud the young Gordon Allport reacted to Freud's initial reticence by sharing an anecdote about a dirt-phobic boy Allport had observed on the train ride over. Freud's unsurprising punch line is given by Allport numerous times—in print, on film, and on audiotape—but the words hardly change: "Was that little boy you?" or "And was that little boy you?" Likewise, the boy's description remains the same in each telling: he is "excessively clean and well-starched," as is his mother (see Elms, 1994, pp. 72–73). These scenes have a certain frozen quality to them. To the subject, they stand out—agates in a bag of rocks. And with each new rehearsal, the details are freshly implanted.

Salient psychological episodes stand in isolation from surrounding speech. In much the same way, prototypical scenes seem incongruous. They are interruptions in an otherwise smooth flow of text; they land, as it were, lumpily on the page. Kafka's pavlatche memory is a good example, and so is Kerouac's memory of being slapped by his brother Gerard (described later). Kerouac even places the recollection in parentheses, deliberately setting it off from events surrounding it. Alexander (1988, 1990) draws attention to the quality of "fit." When episodes lack "fit," we need to ask why, and to bracket such episodes for future close inspection. Freud was right: It is a mistake to regard anything in mental life as haphazard, trivial, or accidental. Incongruities are not simple afterthoughts.

Aside from their specificity and incongruity, prototypical scenes draw attention to themselves by virtue of their obvious repetition. They interpenetrate. As with Sylvia Plath's memory of her first visit to her father's grave, one finds the same scene carefully described and considered in poetry, fiction, journals, diaries, letters, and so on. The scene intrudes. It comes unbidden. That fact partially accounts for its incongruity—prototypical scenes elbow their way into texts like slips of the tongue or fragments of recurrent dreams.

They will not be denied representation. Their resulting ubiquity—not mere repetition, but psychologically important repetition—owes its tenacity to strong motive forces. These scenes have an emotionally unfinished quality. Overdetermined and subtly allegorical, they evolve into especially potent signifiers successfully condensing an astonishing range of core (and probably unconscious) life history elements. To neuroticize prototypical scenes would be a bad idea. On the other hand, they do possess a degree of compulsivity. As with negative self-defining memories (Singer & Salovey, 1993), their pull on subjects may connote attempted mastery of the unconscious trends they so effectively bring together.

Along similar lines, prototypical scenes depict *conflict*. In every instance identified thus far, relational turbulence plays some part, and the characters included are typically family (Capote's mother, Kafka's father, Kerouac's brother, Harrison's mother and father, Plath's mother and father). Because of its almost complete predictability, this fact must be more than accidental. Indeed, what could be more insistent or more summative of life patterns than a memory focused on primary relationships? The conflict, moreover, is sustained. One notices an absence of overcoming. In *The Bell Jar*, Plath follows the visit to her father's grave with her first very serious and intentionally lethal suicide attempt (then finally succeeds outside the fiction); with his last work, the unfinished *Answered Prayers*, Capote creates an alter-ego—P. B. Jones—still crippled by abandonment fear, and in the habit of abandoning before himself being abandoned (see Schultz, 2001); and as mentioned already, Kafka never escaped his father's grave shadow. As he writes in the aforementioned letter: "I was not, or, to put it most optimistically, was not yet, free. My writing was all about you; all I did there, after all, was to bemoan what I could not bemoan upon your breast. It was an intentionally long-drawn-out leave-taking. . . . In my childhood it ruled my life as a premonition, later as a hope, and still later often as despair, and it dictated—it may be said, yet again in your shape—my few small decisions" (1976, p. 87). Family conflict not overcome points to a scene that is potentially prototypical.

So specificity, incongruity, interpenetration, and family conflict all serve as excellent cues. Next in line is *developmental gravity*. Prototypical scenes find in childhood or young adulthood their temporal setting. Again, this jibes with a long tradition of considering childhood events particularly formative and psychologically influential well into maturity. Capote, Kafka, and Kerouac were all very small children in their prototypical memories; Plath, Harrison, and even Allport were in mid- to late-adolescence. In each instance, what Erikson called developmental crises or "decisive encounters" seem recognizable. Capote's centered on trust, on the question of whether caretakers could be counted on to be reliably supportive; Kafka was shamed in the face of his mild attempt at self-assertion; and Plath went to Otto's grave in pursuit of identity. *The Bell Jar* is one long identity crisis. Its female minor characters all represent stereotypically feminine role choices for girls growing up in the 1950s. Rather than being promiscuous, a virginal southern farm girl, or a hat designer, Plath musters just enough courage to call herself a poet. The response—one she got in life, too, especially from her mother—was bewilderment.

The last major pointer is this: Prototypical scenes *creatively rehearse throwness*. By "throwness" I do not mean what Heidegger had in mind when proposing the term, but rather the experience of being "thrown into" a situation or quandary requiring an accounting via self-examination. Prototypical scenes are violations of the status quo, disruptions of what is normally taken-for-granted. Kafka was carried out onto the pavlatche, Capote was locked in a room, Kerouac (as shown later) was slapped by his brother, Harrison (also shown later) was taken to a gynecologist for deflowering. In most cases a highly significant figure does something to the subject, something initially inscrutable and/or even cruel, and the subject is left to make what sense he or she can of the episode. Passive dissonance forms part of the picture—such scenes seem to be determined by the bizarre action of another—yet freedom, as Kafka glimpsed, lies in the retelling. The narration of protypical scenes is an undeniably creative act. The safest approach, as mentioned before, is to call them both truths and lies. The literal reality of the scene carries obvious weight, but so does the fictional component provided retrospectively by the subject. We cannot know when these scenes first appeared in their authors' mental landscape. Most likely they took gradual shape until, at last, assuming their now frozen form born of infinite rehearsal. One cannot altogether rule out the possibility that they did not happen at all, that they possess zero literal reality, but I find that option remote at best. Memory is a construction and can be fallible. Still, the fact that pseudomemories exist does not entitle us to regard all memories as fanciful. Capote says he was locked in a hotel room at age two. Remote memories such as his are exceedingly rare (see Fivush, Pipe, Murachver, & Reese, 1997). If the event really happened when Capote was, say, four, then his creative retelling serves to heighten the trauma in psychologically interesting ways. These scenes are early occurrences, but their construction—the shape they take—is an adult achievement. In that way they are simultaneously past and present, and probably predictive of future conflicts and life-themes, as well.

In summary, prototypical scenes are specific, incongruous interpenetrations of developmental gravity, marked by family conflict and a need to creatively rehearse throwness. This set of pointers is core. Students can be reminded to stay watchful for them and allow them to guide their navigations through the inevitably accreting mound of biographical fact. At the same time, I would not necessarily exclude from the list those cues found in the work of Singer and Salovey (1993) and Alexander (1988, 1990), in particular affective intensity and placement. Prototypical scenes can be affectively intense, and as we shall see, their placement in relation to surrounding episodes often reveals their deeper meaning.

With the above identifiers now in place, I want to show how they might be employed in examinations of individual instances. Once pinpointed, do prototypical scenes really illumine lives as uniquely as advertised?

## KATHRYN HARRISON

Kathryn Harrison's visit to a gynecologist's office at age 15 when, as she says, "my mother made me get my first diaphragm," represents an exemplary prototypical scene (1991, p. 179). First of all, the scene interpenetrates. Harrison includes it in her autobiographical novel *Thicker Than Water* and in her memoir about her consensual affair with her father, *The Kiss*. It also (a) possesses an abundance of specifics (e.g., dialogue, and colors of gray, blue, and green), (b) concerns a mother–daughter conflict (with father lurking sinisterly off-center), and (c) depicts an experience of being thrown into a situation through the bizarre action of an other. Placement—one of Alexander's pointers—also marks the scene off. In *Thicker Than Water*, the incident seems deliberately bookmarked by memories of sex. Harrison speaks of "being fucked" for the first time, and thinking of her mother, of the "whole brilliant unknown territory of sex traversed in somnambulence." She says she "drove men to violence so that perhaps they could awaken me" (p. 178). Then the scene appears:

> [My mother] drove us to the gynecologist's gray-walled office on the fifteenth floor of a skyscraper in West Los Angeles. Through the tinted windows and the summer smog, the city below looked cool and elusive, half-hidden under a blue shroud. Toward the ocean, where the pall lifted, I could see traffic crawling on the tiny distant freeway.
>
> My mother was in the examining room when the doctor broke my hymen so he could fit me properly for the device. He used a series of graduated green plastic phalli. First a tiny, little boy-sized one, then larger and larger ones, until he withdrew one whose shaft had been discolored by a smear of blood. My mother leaned against the wall, watching. She stood just to the left of a poster that revealed the most intimate, cellular level of human communion, one triumphant sperm breaking through the egg's thin, eager wall.
>
> I writhed on the table as the doctor swabbed my genitals with disinfectant. Then, after producing the correct size of diaphragm and instructing me on its insertion, the doctor left the room, taking my mother with him, so that I might climb painfully down from the table and try to put it in correctly by myself.

> . . . It sprang out of my grasp, skidding along the floor, twice before
> I got it in. . . . But I didn't use it. I thought of it as hers. She was the
> one who had wanted it. (pp. 179–180)

Harrison follows this with more about her sexual history, recalling "all the boys who fucked me, some reaching for me with love on their faces, some with anger, one disgustedly." She says she continued to think of her mother every time and of "the constant message of my childhood. Do not make the mistakes your mother did. Do not get involved with the Wrong Boy" (p. 180).

This one scene contains a wealth of compressed meaning. There is the culpability of the misguided mother. There is the doctor-father the mother leaves with (Harrison's father is also a doctor, but has a PhD). There are the alien green, weirdly unnatural phalli and the large one bloodily withdrawn. Might these symbolize Harrison's later, also "unnatural" affair with her father—the supremely "Wrong Boy"—likewise engineered by a mother who "drove" her to it? In a recounting of that affair in her memoir *The Kiss*, Harrison gives us the same scene, with placement again suggestive of importance. Thoughts of mother and sex precede the scene, and Harrison repeats—in exactly the same words—the message of her childhood, "Don't make the mistakes your mother made" (1998, p. 41). This time the doctor seems reluctant to use the green plastic penises—of a color that "exists nowhere in nature"—and asks the mother if that is what she wants. Yes, she says. Harrison reaches the inevitable conclusion: "This doctor deflowers me in front of my mother" (p. 43). The very next scene has Harrison talking to her father on the phone in preparation for his visit, a visit culminating in a highly sexual kiss at the airport that commences the affair.

A few other details drawn from the memoir refer back to the gynecologist scene. First, Harrison expresses shock at discovering her father's uncircumcised penis, which she "can't help but find alien, unclean"—just like the alien-appearing green phalli. Second, she connects a later suicide attempt by overdose to the gynecologist visit, saying "I think I took [the pills] so that my body would die along with what else was murdered that day—girlhood, hope, any notion of being safe anywhere, with anyone" (p. 186).

For Harrison, then, this scene embeds a life history of loss of innocence and descent into unnatural sex. It is an indictment of the mother, signaling an immensely conflicted relationship. It recurs in locations within a larger narrative that serve to increase its significance. Its developmental gravity is clear—the experience leaves Harrison with a sense of being unsafe anywhere, with anyone. And its emotional tone is one of anguished dyscontrol, with Harrison passively submitting to a "thrownness" precipitated by a well-meaning, but disturbingly oblivious, parent. Freud (1918/1996) once said that a full understanding of any single life might allow for a full understanding of human mental life in general. A similar possibility applies to the prototypical scene. Understanding it may actually allow us to understand the "myth" that is its author.

Harrison's was the first prototypical scene identified in the class. As such, its emergence as a possibly generalizable notion met with considerable excitement. I asked the class (in small groups) to brainstorm criteria sets and deliberately avoided imposing any of my own nascent ideas. They enjoyed the enterprise, articulating a set of roughly 12 markers (many resembling Alexander's saliency cues, which we had already discussed at length). We then trimmed the list down, settling on eight cues that seemed especially promising. These became a rough template we planned to apply to future cases (we eventually dropped a few more cues along the way). The class already had grasped the idea's usefulness; once we had agreed on the centrality of the gynecologist scene, they immediately—and spontaneously—noticed how it illuminated additional features of Harrison's life and writing (for instance, we spent some time examining contexts in which Harrison foregrounded the color green). They saw the scene, in other words, as a particularly valuable clue, and as an organizing structure with which to make connections.

Conceptual questions also arose. Students wondered whether the prototypical scene really was so singular. Why just one prototypical scene? Why not a handful? They asked, too, whether the scene might change over time. Could one prototypical scene gradually give way to another? Once constructed by its author, did the scene remain fixed, or was it relatively plastic or, at least, modifiable? All these questions—each fascinating in its own way—became "teachable moments." They led to a consideration of the nature of personality and the scriptedness of identity. Answers were not quickly forthcoming, but even so, the class seemed to recognize that this was an idea in progress, and rather than shutting the conversation down, that recognition generated added excitement. As I said before, the class felt "on to something," and looked forward to working with the idea more as the semester continued.


## JACK KEROUAC

The name Jack Kerouac usually calls to mind blissed-out rucksack wanderers shouting frosty haikus from mountaintops or getting drunk in jazz-inflected San Francisco bars. Yet when one looks more closely into the writings—the novels and recently published sets of letters, and the intimate journal reproduction *Some of the Dharma*—it is hard to discount a far more dominant theme: grief. Kerouac pictured his life unfolding in the complex shadow of a saintly and probably highly idealized brother named Gerard, who died at age 9 when Jack was 4 years old. Kerouac's *Visions of Gerard* densely explores Gerard's loss, and holds the key to Kerouac's entire "Duluoz Legend," the myth of Kerouac's life (see Schultz, 1996). As Kerouac says there, "For the first four years of my life, while he lived, I was not Ti Jean Duluoz, I was Gerard, the world was his face, the flower of his face. . . . I would deliver no more obloquies and curse at my damned earth, but obsecrations only, could I resolve in me to keep his fixed-in memory face free from running off from me" (1991, pp. 1–2). Much of Kerouac's writing, in fact, served the aim of resuscitating Gerard—loving the image back into some kind of life—for as Kerouac also declares, "the whole reason why I ever wrote at all and drew breath to bite in vain with pen of ink, great gad with indefensible Usable pencil, because of Gerard, the idealism, Gerard the religious hero—'*Write in honor of his death*' (as one would say, write for the love of God)" (p. 112). But Kerouac could not shake the idea that he somehow had betrayed Gerard by not dying himself, at one point writing in a long confessional letter to Neal Cassady, a probable brother substitute, "Judas is me, Jesus is Gerard. What have I gone and done, and what hath God wrought?" (1995, p. 282).

In light of Gerard's importance to Kerouac, plus Kerouac's obvious ambivalence toward Gerard's hallowed image, one might expect to find a prototypical scene centering on just this conflicted relationship. The best candidate, in my view, revolves around a slap that calls to mind Judas's kiss, yet a slap delivered, not by Jack, but by Gerard. Here is how Kerouac tells it in *Visions of Gerard*:

> "Always be careful not to hurt anyone," [Gerard advises Jack], "never get mad if you can help it—I gave you a slap in the face the other day but I didn't know it when I did it"—
>
> (That'd been one of the last days when he felt good enough to get up and play with his erector set, a gray exciting morning for all-day work, gladly he'd at the breakfast crumb-swept newspapers of the table begun to raise his first important girder when I importunately rushed up tho gleefully to join in the watching but knocked the whole thing over scattering screws and bolts all over and upsetting the delicate traps, inadvertently and with that eternal perdurable mistakenness we all know, he slapped my face yelling "Decolle donc!" (Get away!) and must have instantly regretted it, no doubt that in a few minutes his remorse was greater than my disappointed regret—). (1991, p. 104)

In a famous letter to Neal Cassady Kerouac repeats the same scene, this time with small but significant additions and alterations:

> Just before he died he slapped me in the face. It is the last thing I remember before he died. It was a gray morning, my sister was going to school, breakfast was being removed from the table. Gerard sat at his erector set before the most magnificent structure of his brief career. . . . But I had to come along and grab at his little arrangements, . . .

disturbing him so suddenly that with understandable rage he impulsively tightened inside and his hand shot out and slapped me in the face. "Get away from here!" he cried. . . . I don't know what happened from there. Bill Burroughs claims according to his amateur psychoanalysis of me in 1945 that I resented the slap in the face and wished Gerard would die, and he died a few days later. (1995, p. 259)

So the scene interpenetrates, thus lending it an unfinished, emotionally tugging quality. It is specifically rendered. Among other details, the color gray recurs, as does the blurted reaction from Gerard, "Get away from here!" The scene possesses a striking incongruity owing chiefly to Kerouac's puzzling use of parentheses. And it depicts a state of thrownness, with Kerouac left to make sense of this final—and fraught—memory of his brother. One might add that the memory is unique in the terms outlined by Alexander (1988, 1990). Kerouac makes a point of telling us that it is the last thing he recalls before Gerard dies.

In *Visions of Gerard* the scene is preceded by thoughts of death, explicit declarations such as "death is the only decent subject, because it marks the end of illusion and delusion" and "the whole world has no reality, it's only imaginary, and what are we to do?—Nothing—*nothing*—*nothing*" (1991, p. 103). Gerard's loss has become the engine behind Jack's art and his quest for meaning that led, eventually, to Buddhism and the mind-created nature of everything (in the book, Gerard is portrayed as a kind of Jesus/Buddha hybrid, as though Jack hopes to find in him a validating condensation of Catholicism and Zen). Notable is the weird use of parentheses referred to above. Do they suggest a textual denial, an emotional distancing? Perhaps Kerouac failed at the time to appreciate the episode's decisiveness, something he seems far more understanding of in the letter to Cassady.

The letter places Gerard's actual death just after the scene, with Jack eagerly exclaiming to his yet uninformed father, "Gerard is dead! Gerard is dead!" This heightens the slap's significance. It may really have been the last thing Jack recalls about his relationship with Gerard. That makes rehearsal of the scene even more necessary, because conflict requires resolution. Searching for some way to minimize his brother's culpability, Kerouac obliquely concludes: "If Gerard died it only meant he went to Canada, and God knows what else I knew about death and what I'm trying to hide this minute" (p. 260). The last isolated comment—"what I'm trying to hide this minute"—elicits a "come again?" reaction (Elms, 1994). It tells us Burroughs was probably right. At some level Jack wished for Gerard's death, and when he got what he "wanted," he could not live with himself.

This particular scene's emergence as "prototypical" came about in a slightly different fashion. Here I instructed the class to watch for such scenes in Kerouac's life and work. A single student seized on this one example, advancing an argument for its singularity. I saw the promise in the idea and encouraged additional conversation. Other scenes also had been mentioned as candidates, but after mulling over the alternatives, and extending the slap scene's apparent meaning to related features of Kerouac's biography and his literary preoccupations—characters, themes, and motives—we came gradually to regard it as uniquely constellating; the class naturally reached agreement on it. I took this opportunity to point out the iterative nature of the psychobiographical process. We talked about how, once an idea begins to form, it then takes its cue from surrounding life history features; a goodness-of-fit is sought between the emerging hypothesis and the facts it hopes to make effective sense of. The facts lead to additional tinkering, and the additional tinkering slowly comes to better account for the facts. Flying in the face of preexisting ideas about the nature of the scientific enterprise, this was a slightly new idea for many class members. Nonetheless, it served as a nice example of narrative method. We allowed our understanding to evolve in "real time," thereby modeling, almost inadvertently, how psychobiographers go about their research.

## SYLVIA PLATH

The poet Sylvia Plath lost her father, Otto, when she was barely 8 years old. His death must have been particularly confusing because of the fact that it was avoidable. Out of fear of a cancer diagnosis, Otto Plath ignored a leg wound that eventually grew more and more disabling. A doctor finally diagnosed diabetes—yet the news came too late. Otto died from the disease. There was the sense, in addition, that he gave up the fight, that he crumbled, achieving a suicide by indirection (suicidologist Shneidman calls this "subintentioned death," 1996, p. 63). As Kerouac did with Gerard, Plath claims responsibility for the loss. In her journals she writes: "I have lost a father and his love early; feel angry at [mother] because of this and feel she feels I killed him" (1982/1993, p. 278). About her psychotherapy she says: "Facing dark and terrible things: those dreams of deformity and death [her father's gangrenous leg had been amputated before he died]. If I really think I killed and castrated my father may all my dreams of deformed and tortured people be my guilty visions of him or fears of punishment for me? And how to lay them? To stop them operating through the rest of my life?" (p. 299).

Otto was Sylvia's unlaid ghost. She tells herself cryptically, "Must do justice to my father's grave" (p. 300). Her prototypical scene represents an effort to do just that. In her journals, her poetry, and her autobiographical novel *The Bell Jar*, Plath describes a visit to the cemetery where her father is buried. First is the journal account, registered on March 9, 1959—three years before Plath's suicide of February 1962:

> Went to my father's grave, a very depressing sight. Three graveyards separated by streets, all made within the last fifty years or so, ugly crude block stones, headstones together, as if the dead were sleeping head to head in a poorhouse. In the third yard. . . . I found the flat stone, Otto E. Plath: 1885–1940, right beside the path, where it would be walked over. Felt cheated. My temptation to dig him up. To prove he existed and really was dead. How far gone would he be? No trees, no peace, his headstone jammed up against the body on the other side. Left shortly. It is good to have the place in mind. . . . (1982/1993, p. 298)

Eleven days later Plath records finishing her poem "Electra on Azalea Path," about her father's death, and "this charity ward, this poorhouse, where the dead/ Crowd foot to foot, head to head. . ." (1981, p. 116). She begins, "The day you died I went into the dirt,/ Into the lightless hibernaculum,/" and so underscores the 20-year "wintering" her father's loss occasioned, "as if you [Otto] had never existed, as if I came/ God-fathered into the world from my mother's belly" (p. 116). The image, as does Gerard's, refuses to rest: "I lay dreaming your epic, image by image./ Nobody died or withered on that stage./ Everything took place in a durable whiteness./ The day I woke, I woke up on Churchyard Hill./ I found your name, I found your bones and all/ Enlisted in a cramped necropolis,/ Your speckled stone askew by an iron fence" (pp. 116–117). Plath borrows "the stilts of an old tragedy," comparing Otto to Agamemnon—the latter murdered by his wife, Clytemnestra, in retaliation for Agamemnon's sacrifice of their daughter, Iphigenia—but then wavers, apparently finding the myth unsatisfactory: "The truth is, one late October [Plath was born October 27], at my birth-cry/ A scorpion stung its head, an ill-starred thing;/ My mother dreamed you face down in the sea" (p. 117).

The poem concludes with the sort of searing psychological imagery so characteristic of Plath: "I brought my love to bear, and then you died./ It was the gangrene ate you to the bone/ My mother said; you died like any man./ How shall I age into that state of mind?/ I am the ghost of an infamous suicide,/ My own blue razor rusting in my throat./ O pardon the one who knocks for pardon at/ Your gate, father—your hound-bitch, daughter, friend./ It was my love did us both to death" (p. 117).

This poem "makes meaning" through creative rehearsal. If Plath is subdued in her journal account, here she is inflamed. Suicide is one obvious subtext. The "wintering" referred to in the wake of her father's death was only "good for twenty years"—at 20, Plath made her first suicide attempt (described faithfully in *The Bell Jar*). When Plath writes "I am the ghost of an infamous suicide," she seems to be speaking of two "suicides" at once:

her own failed attempt at 20 (which actually became a newspaper story) and her father's subintentioned death by diabetes.

The poem also assigns blame. In this case, as many children do, Plath accepts responsibility—"it was my love did us both to death." Yet by including the myth she manages to blame her mother, as well. And the symbolism does not stop there. For if Plath is Electra, then she will help to kill her own mother. Here the poem's title contains a concealed clue. It is hard to read "Azalea Path" and not think "Aurelia Plath" (Plath's mother's name). Electra is "on" Azalea Path/Aurelia Plath. The poem is "on" or "about" the mother, whom the author is "on" in the sense of "on top of" or "stamping on" (Plath would write other poems like "Medusa" in which she clearly "tramples" the mother image).

So by reimagining the graveyard scene the poem recapitulates each central conflict of Plath's short life: father loss, mother hate, murderous feelings, suicide, and self-blame/self-loathing. Prototypical scenes compress a host of life-history features. This one from Plath is absolutely exemplary.

As I said, the scene appears yet again in Plath's novel *The Bell Jar*, placed between a half-hearted, passive suicide gesture and the sudden thought "I knew just how to go about it," followed immediately by Plath's first genuine suicide attempt by overdose (of her mother's medicines, fittingly enough). That is, directly after describing the visit to her father's grave, Plath's alter-ego Esther Greenwood tries to kill herself. This justifies our asking, What role does the father and the graveyard visit play in the suicide attempt? Why did Plath structure the episodes this way? Focusing in on the prototypical scene alerts us to possible subtexts.

As written in *The Bell Jar*, the scene includes moments of insight not apparent from previous iterations. By this time, Plath may have made some headway in self-understanding. The passage begins with Esther/Sylvia searching for the graveyard but finding it difficult to locate. She imagines entering the Catholic church, and going to some Boston priest with suicide on her mind, asking, "O Father, help me" (p. 135).

She recalls how her mother had not allowed her to attend Otto's funeral, and how his death had always seemed "unreal" to her: "I had a great yearning, lately, to pay my father back for all the years of neglect, and start tending his grave. I had always been my father's favorite, and it seemed fitting I should take on a mourning my mother had never bothered with" (p. 135). Whether Plath noticed the irony of this first line I do not know, but when she speaks of paying her father back, it reads like "getting even with him," not "making up with him." Did she resent his abandonment through death? It seems likely.

At last she finds the gravestone, described almost exactly as it is in the poem: "Then I remembered that I had never cried for my father's death.

My mother hadn't cried either. . . . I laid my face to the smooth face of the marble and howled my loss into the cold salt rain" (pp. 136–137).

Whereas the mood of the poem is anger or angry confession, the mood in the novel is grief and mourning. There is a release, a sense of doing what she should have done before. Mourning will allow her to move on. But again, it is not so simple, because what she moves on to, in the novel and in life, is suicide. As noted, the sentence quoted just above is followed by the recognition "I knew just how to go about it": she swallows her mother's pills directly after returning home. This contiguity finds a motive in Plath's most famous poem, "Daddy." She writes, in intentionally primitive rhyme: "I was ten when they buried you./ At twenty I tried to die/ And get back, back, back to you/ I thought even the bones would do/ But they pulled me out of the sack,/ And they stuck me together with glue./" (1981, p. 224). Killing herself to join her father serves at least two aims, both possibly unconscious: one, she is punished for "killing" her father in the first place, by "loving him to death," and two, she leaves her mother alone in her selfish grieflessness, preferring death with a dead father to life with a live mother, who in "Medusa" she calls an "eely tentacle," squeezing the breath from her (p. 224).

Plath's prototypical scene contains nearly all the elements outlined previously—specificity, interpenetration, family conflict, developmental gravity, and thrownness in the sense that the death is something that happened to Plath too, something she must make sense of before consolidating her own identity. The scene even appears a little incongruous, beginning jarringly with a quote from Esther—"Which way is the graveyard?"—and ending with "I knew just how to go about it." The "it" is suicide, of course, but also something a little more nebulous. Plath moved forward by going back. As her final poems make clear, the thrill of dying or coming close to it allowed her to rise, like Lazarus. She needed to kill something in order to be free.

Plath's was the last life we looked at in our class. By this time, we had discussed the prototypical scene at length. Now broader questions began to emerge, and they became, in a fruitful way, more critical, more skeptical. These gave rise to some valuable discussions.

Class members introduced the cross-cultural dimension. What about cultures that do not conceptualize identity in Western terms? Some cultures have a more relational model of self. Anthropological research shows that the concept of self does indeed vary cross-culturally. Could we expect to locate prototypical scenes cross-culturally? Is the idea universal?

Or, on a different note, because we are all to some degree multiple selves, with multiple roles in life, does each role or each identity require its own prototypical scene? Can one scene validly represent all these differing self-presentations?

Finally, students wondered about lives that seemed to include an abrupt reformulation of self. In cases where subjects radically redefined who they were, how could an earlier prototypical scene adequately capture this new identity? Would the new identity not require a new prototypical scene? Likewise, for lives in progress, such as those of the students in the class—lives that were unfinished and relatively undefined—at what point or, more chronologically, at what age is it possible to begin the process of evaluating candidate scenes in terms of their potential prototypicality?

All such questions identified ways in which the concept needed a certain amount of reconsideration. They nicely problematized the idea. I chose, in this case, not to seek any sort of premature foreclosure on earlier formulations and certainly not to dismiss these insightful qualifications, but rather to reaffirm the initially provisional nature of novel observations, and the need to continue asking difficult questions as a means of moving the idea in a direction most useful. I reminded the class, yet again, that this was a concept in its early stages. Much work remained to be done. And they seemed appreciative of that acknowledgement, and maybe gained a renewed sense for how such ideas come into being and, only slowly and thoughtfully, reach a sort of finished form.


## CONCLUSION

In classes centered on lives apprehended through text, what students want more than anything else is a way to situate themselves within the endless proliferation of biographical fact. The idea of "interpretive free-play" usually leaves them unmoored and directionless. That can be a problem, because it encourages giving up, or else what I consider a kind of synonym for giving up—the sense of uninterpretability. Students need to understand the advantages of adopting a narrative approach; they need to experience its intrinsic value as a means of engaging stories, any life's basic datum. The prototypical scene gives them something specific to work with. They might explore the scene individually or in small groups, teasing out its possible meanings. From there, meanings that have been generated can be compared, with significant agreements noted and applauded, and disagreements either struggled through in an attempt to reach consensus, or set aside for future consideration. With the prototypical scene in mind, students may then step back into the flow of life data—yet this time armed with expectations, leads, hunches, and hypotheses. In the never-ending iterative process, some inspirations pay off and some come up empty, just as it happens when other, more conventional methods are employed. This is the so-called hermeneutical circle: We work from part to whole, then back to part, allowing each to inform the other until we find a "goodness-of-fit" between our evolving understanding and the story of a life.

For reasons we ought to take seriously and not dismiss as mere naiveté, students want from psychobiography some sort of conclusion, an answer, however tentative. I am always happy to see this. Their impulse is correct. If the life begins and ends in incoherence, if every single interpretation gets qualified into oblivion, we risk mutiny or, worse, surrender. My feeling is that the use of concepts such as saliency cues, self-defining memories, and prototypical scenes steers students in the direction of finding cogent coherences. The facts converge on such saliencies, in effect demonstrating their power. What had been mere coincidence or accidental intertextuality now possesses undeniable meaning, and this meaning is an answer, an outcome students take pride in generating.

So in the end, identifying prototypical scenes serves a twin function: They confirm what we feel we already know about a life's myth—a very useful function, one might add—and they send us off in directions not previously taken. Is it asking too much of subjects to require, or expect to find in their work, one shining encapsulation of a life's parameters? Obviously, I do not think so. Or to put it differently, much will be gained and little lost by encouraging students to search out scenes that seem uniquely revealing. Narrative aims at self-mythology. In telling our story, we hope to lend it coherence, generativity, and a kind of helpful simplicity of aim and purpose. In some ways the prototypical scene is the principle of parsimony in action. It draws webs of meaning together into one concise package, providing a handy touch point we can return to when a need arises to quickly remind ourselves who we are. Because they leave behind relatively thorough records of thought and communication, creative writers may be especially prone to producing prototypical scenes or to increasing the likelihood of their identification, but that fact alone does not make the concept artifactual. There is nothing to suggest that those less gifted do not feel the same need. At any rate, future research should resolve the question.

As concept and as method, the prototypical scene offers a promising orientation for life writers. By keeping its identifiers in mind and staying on the look out for its often incongruous appearance in biographical material, we increase our chances of striking personological pay dirt. Narrative always reveals itself, but before we can ask the right questions or develop the right interpretations, we need to single out those features worth pondering. Salient psychological moments, self-defining memories, and prototypical scenes start us on our way. They clear out a path and in so doing reveal a possible destination.

# REFERENCES

Alexander, I. (1988). "Personality, psychological assessment, and psychobiography." *Journal of Personality*, 56(1), 265–294.

Alexander, I. (1990). *Personology: Method and content in personality assessment and psychobiography*. Durham, NC: Duke University Press.

Boyd, B. (1990). *Vladimir Nabokov: The Russian years*. Princeton, NJ: Princeton University Press.

Capote, T. (1969). *Trilogy*. New York: Macmillan.

Capote, T. (1988). *Answered prayers*. New York: Plume.

Clarke, G. (1988). *Truman Capote: A biography*. New York: Simon & Schuster.

Dahl, R. (1984). *Boy*. New York: Farrar, Straus, & Giroux.

Elms, A. (1994). *Uncovering lives: The uneasy alliance of biography and psychology*. London: Oxford University Press.

Fivush, R., Pipe, M., Murachver, T., & Reese, E. (1997). "Events spoken and unspoken: Implications of language and memory development for the recovered memory debate." In M. Conway (Ed.), *Recovered memories, false memories* (pp. 34–62). London: Oxford University Press.

Freud, S. (1996). *Three case histories*. New York: Touchstone. (Originally published 1918)

Grobel, L. (1985). *Conversations with Capote*. New York: NAL Books.

Harrison, K. (1991). *Thicker than water*. New York: Avon.

Harrison, K. (1998). *The kiss*. New York: Avon.

Kafka, F. (1976). *Letter to his father*. New York: Schocken Books.

Kerouac, J. (1991). *Visions of Gerard*. New York: Viking.

Kerouac, J. (1995). *Selected letters: 1940–1956*. New York: Viking.

Kerouac, J. (1999). *Some of The Dharma*. New York: Penguin.

Mailer, N. (1995). *Portrait of Picasso as a young man*. New York: Warner Books.

Moffitt, K., & Singer, J. (1994). "Continuity in the life story: Self-defining memories, affect, and approach-avoidance personal strivings. *Journal of Personality*, 62(1), 21–43.

Nabokov, V. (1966). *Speak, memory*. New York: Putnam's.

Plath, S. (1981). *The bell jar*. New York: Bantam Books. (Original work published 1971)

Plath, S. (1981). *The collected poems*. New York: Harper & Row.

Plath, S. (1993). *The journals of Sylvia Plath*. New York: Avon. (Original work published 1982)

Plimpton, G. (1997). *Truman Capote: In which various friends, enemies, acquaintances, and detractors recall his turbulent career*. New York: Talese-Doubleday.

Runyan, W. (1982). *Life histories and psychobiography*. New York: Oxford.

Schultz, W. T. (1996). An "*Orpheus Complex*" in two writers-of-loss. *Biography: An Interdisciplinary Quarterly, 19*(4), 371–393.

Schultz, W. T. (2001). "Why Truman Capote fried the fancier fish in *answered prayers*." Manuscript under review.

Shneidman, E. (1996). *The suicidal mind.* New York: Oxford.

Singer, J., & Salovey, P. (1993). *The remembered self: Emotion and memory in personality.* New York: Free Press.

Tomkins, S. (1987). Script theory. In J. Arnoff, A. I. Rabin, & R. Zucker (Eds.), *The emergence of personality.* New York: Springer.

Wilde, O. (1996). *De Profundis.* London: Dover.

# 10

# A PSYCHOLOGICAL PERSPECTIVE ON THE RELATIONSHIP OF WILLIAM AND HENRY JAMES

JAMES WILLIAM ANDERSON

*When I heard about this volume on the teaching of the narrative study for lives, an idea flashed through my mind. The idea was suggested to me by a feature in my WordPerfect 5.1 program called "Reveal Codes." At the press of a keystroke, I can see the hidden information that underlies the neat blocks of type that appear on my screen. It shows me what I have done in the way of formatting the text: for example, providing a header on each page and justifying the right margin.*

*I thought of creating a paper that could be used for teaching students about psychobiography, one of the approaches used in the narrative study of lives. The strategy I use in this paper is as follows. I provide a short psychobiographical essay—on William and Henry James—and interweave with it an explanation of the hidden thinking that underlies the essay. I reveal many of the questions I considered as I constructed my account of the relationship of these two brothers. As with the material brought up by "Reveal Codes," this information helped shape the final psychobiographical essay but does not appear visibly in it. My goal is to help students understand psychobiography better by acquainting them with many of the central issues an author faces, such as the structuring of an essay, the use of theory, and the role of empathy and countertransference. My commentary is in italics; the essay on the Jameses is in regular type.*

*My purpose in conceiving the psychobiographical essay on the Jameses was to present my perspective on the psychological dynamics of their relationship. There are various styles of psychobiography. One legitimate style takes a concrete approach. Psychobiographers using this approach discuss the data, outline the psychological theories they are using, and show how the theories apply to the material (see, for example, Carlson, 1988; Demos, 1982; Waite, 1977). In this essay, I used a different approach, a narrative approach, that is similar to the style of Edel (1953–1972), Manuel (1968), and Cody (1971). I tried to tell a story that would carry the reader along. My understanding was influenced by psychological perspectives, but I avoided technical terms, made use of language that is readily understandable, and relied, as much as possible, on the words of the subjects. In this essay I built up my picture of their relationship by examining three telling episodes involving William and Henry.*

*The first episode has to do with Henry's decision to buy a house; the episode does not involve a decisive event in the lives of the Jameses, but it enabled me to introduce certain key aspects of their interactional style.*

\* \* \*

The home in which Henry James had already been living, as a renter, for a year, suddenly came up for sale in 1899. Living alone and settled into life as an American expatriate, the celebrated, 56-year-old novelist concluded that the home, called Lamb House and located in Rye, 50 miles southeast of London, suited his needs perfectly.

He wrote at once to his brother William, who had made as much of a name for himself in psychology as Henry had made for himself in fiction. Fifteen months older than Henry and a professor at Harvard, William resided in Cambridge with his wife, Alice, and their children.

Henry wished William were nearer "that I might consult with you a little" about the transaction. The opportunity, he explained, "fixes me, in security, *ideal* suitability & safety for life, in a blessed little *home* . . . & of which nothing could possibly exceed the congruity with my needs, actual & future, my purse & my desires." "The only thing," he quickly noted, was that he did not have the asked-for $10,000, but he had an idea about how to borrow what he needed. "I'm so *outside* of every business contrivance & proceeding," he noted, "that, were you at hand I should ask you for a wrinkle or two on this head" (Skrupskelis & Berkeley, 1994, pp. 66–67).

William and Alice replied immediately with a fusillade of three letters in two days. William said he had no doubt that it was wise to purchase the house, but he counseled Henry at length about offering less than the asking price and searching for the best interest rate. He just barely mentioned, "I rejoice heartily with you in this windfall of a chance" (Skrupskelis & Berkeley, 1994, p. 69).

Henry answered that he had "drawn upon myself & my project a colder blast than I could apprehend." He discussed in detail why the terms of purchase made sense and added, "surely at my age, with full possession of one's facts & one's *data*, & with no burden of precipitate or foolish acquisition . . . compromising one's past, one may ask to be quietly trusted." After lamenting that "[m]y joy has shrivelled under your very lucid warnings," he explained why William's advice had had such an impact on him:

My misfortune . . . is that, as an individual of imagination (& "nerves")
all compact, . . . I am temporarily accessible, in an extreme degree, to
"suggestion"—from *any* quarter that supervenes, or intervenes . . . &
that, though all the while, in the background, my own judgment waits
in limited—partial—eclipse, absolutely certain to reappear, the other
influence launches me on a sea—a torment—of sickening nervosity, in
which work, attention, sleep, alas peace, perish for the time & in which
I can only wait for them to come back, as they do, after a while, with
a bound. (Skrupskelis & Berkeley, 1994, pp. 71–75)

\*   \*   \*

*The passage just quoted illustrates the value of showing the reader, at crucial
moments, the subject's exact words. We have Henry's perceptive psychological
observation of himself: He reports that he is extremely suggestible and that a piece
of advice can throw him into "a torment" of "sickening nervosity" in which he
loses all sense of peace. If a picture is worth a thousand words, the actual words
used by a subject are also worth a thousand times their number because they
provide a picture of the subject. It would take pages to describe what the reader
can sense from this passage, such as Henry's anxiety, his scrupulosity, and his
desire to explain himself while at the same time not offending his brother.*

*The first question I faced as I planned the psychobiographical essay was:
On what sources will I rely? As several commentators have pointed out (see
Alexander, 1990, pp. 11–13; Anderson, 1981b, pp. 246–251; Elms, 1994,
pp. 21–25; Runyan, 1982, pp. 202–206), psychobiography relies on primary
material, such as letters and diaries, that enable one to get access to the subject's
psychological world. William and Henry James spent most of their adulthoods
separated by the Atlantic Ocean, and they largely carried on their relationship
through correspondence; hence I had the opportunity of grounding my study of
them in the very words that they wrote to and received from each other.*

*Although my essay is based largely on a close reading of their correspondence,
psychobiography also benefits from the author's immersion in the lives of the
subject. Over the years I have gone through all the major biographical studies of
the James family, read the large majority of the works of the two brothers, poured
through their published letters, and spent many weeks studying the unpublished
James Papers, which are archived in the Houghton Library at Harvard University.
Although students preparing a psychobiographical essay cannot be expected to
spend years exploring their subjects' lives, the lesson is that the more they can
learn about their subjects the better.*

\*   \*   \*

"It has filled this home with grief," William wrote back, "to find that
our letters about the purchase 'rubbed you the wrong way.' " Because Henry

had worked out all the details, William went on, "there is nothing more to be said than 'bravo' to the undertaking." He added in his defense, "when one is asked for counsel—& I tho't you were asking for that—what is more appropriate than to show all the lions in the path?" He concluded with an apology and a quotation from Tennyson, "So both Alice and I beg your pardon profoundly for giving you so bad a night, with our petty store of maxims preaching down a daughter's heart" (Skrupskelis & Berkeley, 1994, p. 76).

As Henry wrote his next letter, he soon found himself crying. The least he deserved, he felt, was a modest home such as Lamb House. He noted that many of his fellow authors, "the literary fry," live in "splendour." And yet "I feel that I may strike the world as still, at 56, with my long labour & my genius, reckless, presumptuous & unwarranted in curling up . . . in a poor little $10,000 shelter." As a result, "I do feel the bitterness of humiliation, the iron enters into my soul, & (I blush to confess it,) I weep!" (Skrupskelis & Berkeley, 1994, pp. 78–79)

He noted that William might well ask why he had seemed to appeal in a "consultative way." "It was the impulse to *fraternize* . . . with you, over the pleasure of my purchase, & to see you glow with pride in *my* pride of possession &c" (Skrupskelis & Berkeley, 1994, p. 79).

William acknowledged Henry's "long and heart-melting letter" and pointed out that

> the tears were not all on your side, Alice having shed some on receiving
> your first reply and needing all the example of my well known fortitude
> to keep her from shedding many more and cursing God and dying, that
> very night. (Skrupskelis & Berkeley, 1994, p. 80)

A relatively small matter could leave both brothers in pain, with Henry weeping and William forced to draw on his "well known fortitude." To understand how this could occur, we have to consider what it was like for the two of them to grow up in the odd and challenging environment of the James family.

*   *   *

*I chose this first episode involving Henry's interest in buying a house because it enabled me to introduce the reader to some of the patterns in their relationship: for example, how Henry appears to ask for advice but then does not want it, how William likes to lecture him, and how Henry himself makes it clear he is "suggestible" and is prey to "sickening nervosity."*

*With hope that I had whetted the reader's curiosity, I next wanted to provide a concise analysis of the developmental history of William and Henry and of their relationship. I thought that this analysis, if it makes sense of the various patterns that emerged in their discussions about Henry's purchase of the house, would gain some credibility in the reader's eyes.*

*   *   *

Their mother, Mary James, an anxious woman, was overwhelmed by the burden of taking care of five energetic and needful children who had been born within seven years. She pressured her children to cause as slight a stir as possible. The attention that she could pay to them was limited, except when they were physically ill; then her interest quickened. All of them, not surprisingly, had frequent psychosomatic illnesses in childhood and throughout their lives. There is evidence, too, that they all felt neglected and devalued at times and lacked inner stability, security, and self-confidence.

*   *   *

*Here again I have had a choice to make: Would I document every assertion I present, or would I offer a summary? Only the latter course was possible if I did not want the essay to mushroom to the size of a book. This first paragraph would have taken 50 times as much space if I had offered all my evidence and all my reasoning. The points made here, in fact, are the main conclusions of a full-length essay (Anderson, 1979b) I wrote on Mary James and her style of parenting.*

*   *   *

Mary James probably received little help from her husband in taking care of their children while they were young because he was preoccupied with his own problems. Henry James Sr. had a depressive breakdown when William was two years old and Henry was just one. "A conviction of inner defilement so sheer took possession of me," James Sr. later recalled, "that death seemed better than life" (W. James, 1884, p. 56). He found relief through a religious conversion and spent the rest of his life developing and expounding his theological ideas. Although a spirited and vital man with a picturesque writing style, he had little capacity to nourish his children's growth. He was constantly struggling to keep his self-abasement and his fears of disaster at bay.

Henry, the second child, became the mother's favorite and earned the nickname in the family of "the Angel." He was able to discern what she wanted and to comply. One benefit is that he received more affection from her than did the rest of the children. He also developed the extraordinary psychological acuity that he later displayed in his fiction. But he was left without a stable sense of what was important to him. He became the person whom he described in the letter, a person who is influenced by "suggestion," whose "own judgment" goes temporarily into "eclipse," and who sinks into "a sea . . . of sickening nervosity." What he wanted from William was admiration and support. When he told William about the opportunity to buy Lamb House, he hoped to see him "glow with pride." He encountered, instead, a barrage of well-meant advice.

William is sometimes viewed as the strong, undauntable elder brother who for no good reason failed to act more empathically toward his troubled siblings. But he was no less psychologically fragile than they; he merely hid it better. As he commented in one of his letters to Henry, "The fact is that my nervous system is utter trash, and always was so. It has been a hard burden to bear all these years, the more so as I have seemed to others perfectly well . . ." (Skrupskelis & Berkeley, 1994, pp. 153–154). William probably tried to keep his emotional pain to himself because, when he expressed it in his family, his mother made it clear that she preferred him to keep quiet. For example, during his twenties, while he was going through a prolonged period of depression and psychosomatic illness, his mother complained to Henry about William, "The trouble with him is he *must express* every fluctuation of feeling, and especially every unfavorable symptom, without reference to the effect upon those about him." She held up Henry to William as an example of how William should be. One time, after William made a sarcastic remark about Henry's "angelic patience," she replied sharply, "*Of course,* his 'angelic patience' shows forth, as you say, but happily that side of his character is always in relief, and does not need great occasions (as it does with some of us) to bring it to view" (M. James, 1874).[1] Henry's method of adjustment was to be agreeable and circumspect; William resented Henry's style and must have felt that it made things harder for himself.

\* \* \*

*A string of declarations, I felt, would come across as too dry to the reader. In the previous and following paragraph, I provided several choice quotations, not so much as proof but rather as illustrations of my points.*

\* \* \*

William found his own way of coping with the family atmosphere and shoring up his self-image by cleaving to his role as the older and superior

---

[1]Quoted by permission of the Houghton Library, Harvard University, shelf mark bMS Am 1093.1 (53).

*Figure 10.1* The two brothers in about the year 1900; William has his hand on Henry's shoulder. By permission of the Houghton Library, Harvard University: self mark pfMS Am 1094, Box 2.

child. Henry recalled that, as far back as when they were little boys, William incontrovertibly asserted the difference between them. Henry offered his company to William, who replied, "I play with boys who curse and swear!" "I had sadly to recognize," Henry observed, "that I didn't, that I couldn't pretend to have come to that yet . . ." (H. James, 1913, p. 259).

A photograph of William and Henry, from about the year 1900, illustrates how they had come to embody their ways of relating to each other. It shows (see Figure 10.1) William putting his arm around Henry as if he were taking care of and supporting him. Henry leans his head toward William in such a way that he looks like the younger, smaller brother, although in fact he was two or three inches taller than William.

* * *

*Because psychological approaches seek to get at the inner world of the subject, psychobiographers make use of unorthodox kinds of evidence. There is this one example in my essay; I consider how a photograph helps show us the way in which the two brothers related to each other. Commentators (such as Anderson, 1981a, 472–474; Edel, 1982, pp. 22–43; and Gay, 1985, pp. 187–205) have discussed various types of evidence that can be psychologically meaningful, such as dreams, Freudian slips, jokes, doodles, and artistic and literary productions.*

* * *

William, similar to Henry, developed his familial role into his voice as a writer. William became the teacher and advice-giver *par excellence*, an elder brother to the nation. What is *The Principles of Psychology* but a textbook that relates everything students should know about psychology? Probably the purest example of his approach is his "Talks to Students" (W. James, 1899), in which, speaking from the podium of the psychology professor, he instructs his listeners on how to find more happiness and significance in their lives.

And even most of his philosophical works are books of lectures in which he saw himself as trumping early thinkers by providing a new approach to many classic conundrums. After *A Pluralistic Universe* was published, he wrote Henry that the book was "making a success." He went on:

> I dont mean *sales*, as yet, but everyone to whom I have sent the volume seems immediately to have *read* it(!) and they mostly write such vehement protestations against it, that I feel sure that it is *original*, and that the puddle is being stirred and the toads forced to jump about. (Skrupskelis & Berkeley, 1994, p. 389)

William and Henry each unconsciously evolved a strategy that enabled him to survive childhood relatively intact. Their siblings—two younger brothers and a sister, were not so fortunate and had lives dominated by emotional distress. But the strategies to which the two elder brothers adhered were carried out at the expense of each other. Henry's angelic behavior gave him the favored place—over William—in their mother's affections. And William maintained his status as being older and wiser by continually, if subtly, denigrating Henry.

\*   \*   \*

We now arrive at one of the most debated topics in psychobiography, the use of psychological theory (see Anderson, 1981a, pp. 467–470; Coles, 1975, pp. 179–210; Loewenberg, 1988; Runyan, 1997, 54–56; Stannard, 1980, pp. 85–116). The danger comes when one starts with a deeply held theoretical notion and then does violence to the subject by forcing the subject to fit that notion. (Just one of a myriad of examples is the attempt by Ernest Jones [1913] to make the evidence concerning Andrea del Sarto conform to his conceit that that artist suffered from "repressed homosexual tendencies" [p. 35]).

The approach I tried to take was to immerse myself in the material about the lives of the James brothers. I hoped that psychological theory would enrich my understanding of them; it would enable me to see aspects of their relationship that otherwise I might have overlooked. I sought to start with the evidence, not with theories.

As a psychoanalyst, I am most familiar with, and rely mostly on, psychoanalytic theory. But I would argue that it is the approach that is most suited to examining the inner lives of individuals. Far from being the reductionistic dogma suggested by some textbook accounts of Freud's ideas, modern psychoanalysis seems to me to provide a complicated and diverse body of theoretical understandings that gets at many of the deeper, largely unconscious patterns which shape people's lives (see Greenberg and Mitchell, 1983, and Summers, 1994, for summaries of late 20th-century developments in psychoanalysis and Loewenberg, 1996, on the application of some of these theoretical approaches to psychobiography). For example, the ideas of Heinz Kohut (1971) about "mirroring" helped draw my attention to what Henry wanted from William, that is, an understanding, admiring response. As another example, Donald W. Winnicott (1965) and Alice Miller (1981) talk about "compliance." Some children, these psychoanalysts note, have trouble developing a reliable sense of self and learning what their own needs are because they organize their lives around trying to please a parent who seeks such a response.

\*   \*   \*

Both of the Jameses, no doubt, also found sustenance through their writing, although it is hard to specify just what function it played for each of them. William once made an intriguing comment that bears on this question. Henry had spoken of his servant's alcoholism. William, in his reply to Henry, speculated that this man got "in drink the excitement of the ideal which you & I find in literary composition." "If we didn't write," William added, "we should probably take to drink" (Skrupskelis & Berkeley, 1994, p. 182).

He seems to be saying that he and Henry had found, through writing, an alternative to what otherwise would have been a mundane, dispiriting existence. I also wonder about a further implication, that it was their shared childhood that had left them with this need for escape. Immediately after making his comment about drink, William thought of the only other surviving person who had grown up in the James family, their brother, Bob, who did not have writing as an outlet and who had turned to the bottle for refuge.

\* \* \*

*Having started with an episode that is of little importance in itself, the exchange over Henry's purchase of Lamb House, and having presented my basic analysis of the relationship between the two brothers, I wanted next to apply it to something that mattered in the lives of the two brothers, and I turned to William's critique of Henry's writing.*

\* \* \*

No episode in the relationship of William and Henry has received more attention than their exchange over Henry's "third manner." This style, in which he wrote his later works, had a great influence on later writers and has occasioned much debate among literary critics. It is characterized by long, sometimes puzzling, sentences; considerable use of nuance and implication; and an attempt to infect the reader with the atmosphere of the works.

William wrote his brother in 1905 that *The Golden Bowl* "put me as most of your recenter long stories have put me, in a very puzzled state of mind." One concern the prudish William had was that the "problem" of the novel was an adulterous relationship. The focus of William's comments, however, was on Henry's style:

> [T]he method of narration of interminable elaboration of suggestive reference ... goes agin the grain of all my own impulses in writing; and yet in spite of it all, there is a brilliancy and cleanness of effect, and in this book especially a high toned social atmosphere that are unique and extraordinary. Your methods & my ideals seem the reverse, the one of the other—and yet I have to admit your extreme success in this book. But why won't you, just to please Brother, sit down and write a new book, with no twilight or mustiness in the plot, with great vigor and decisiveness in the action, no fencing in the dialogue, no psychological commentaries, and absolute straightness in the style? Publish it in my name, I will acknowledge it, and give you half the proceeds. Seriously, I wish you *would*, for you *can*; and I should think it would tempt you, to embark on a "fourth manner." (Skrupskelis & Berkeley, 1994, p. 301)

Before turning to Henry's reply, we should also consider William's reaction half a year later to *The American Scene*, Henry's book of impressions of a trip to the United States. William declared that the book "in its peculiar way seems to me *supremely great.*" He went on:

> You know how opposed your whole "third manner" of execution is to the literary ideals which animate my crude and Orson-like breast, mine being to say a thing in one sentence as straight and explicit as it can be made, and then to drop it for ever; yours being to avoid naming it straight, but by dint of breathing and sighing all round and round it, to arouse in the reader who may have had a similar perception already (Heaven help him if he hasn't!) the illusion of a solid object, made . . . wholly out of impa[l]pable materials, air, and the prismatic interferences of light, ingeniously focused by mirrors upon empty space. (Skrupskelis & Berkeley, 1994, pp. 337–338)

\*   \*   \*

*The function on which psychobiography rests is the biographer's empathy (see Anderson, 1981a, pp. 464–465; H. Kohut, 1985; T. Kohut, 1986; Szaluta, 1999, pp. 148–159; and Young-Bruehl, 1998, pp. 17–25). The first and most essential step in understanding subjects is to be able to put oneself in their shoes. Biographers must use their imagination to feel, as if on a trial basis, what the subjects feel. Dealing with William's reaction to Henry's writing required me to identify with the frustration, confusion, and impatience William felt as he read Henry's later works. Although I gradually have developed an appreciation for Henry's style, I was able to remember and to rely on the emotions I had when I first read* The Ambassadors. *More recently, I taught a continuing-education seminar on Henry James, and I saw how the students were charmed by his early works, such as* Washington Square *and* The Europeans, *but confused and exasperated when they came across works written in the "third manner." I was able, I believe, to picture the emotions on the basis of which William wrote his critique. His literal reaction to the work, of course, played only a small part in his motivation. As I considered William's critique of his brother's writing, I also had to find in myself aspects of my psychological makeup that enabled me to empathize with the other factors that influenced William, such as his desire to maintain his authority over his younger sibling and his impulse to show off his ability to create a stunning description.*

\*   \*   \*

That William's criticisms stung Henry is apparent, because the mild-mannered younger brother answered with more venom than in any other letter that he wrote William:

I mean (in response to what you write me of your having read the *Golden B.*) to try to produce some uncanny form of thing, in fiction, that will gratify you, as Brother—but let me say, dear William, that I shall greatly be humiliated if you *do* like it, & thereby lump it, in your affection, with things, of the current age, that I have heard you express admiration for & that I would sooner descend to a dishonoured grave than have written.

Henry then further denigrated the kind of simplistic, artless novel that he saw William as preferring:

Still, I *will* write you your book, on that two-and two-make-four system on which all the awful truck that surrounds us is produced & then descend to my dishonoured grave—taking up the art of the slate pencil instead of, longer, the art of the brush. . . .

It was late at night, and Henry meant to stop writing but could not resist going on:

I'm always sorry when I hear of your reading anything of mine, & always hope you won't—you seem to me so constitutionally unable to "enjoy" it, & so condemned to look at it from a point of view remotely alien to mine in writing it, & to the conditions out of which, *as* mine, it has inevitably sprung.

Henry pointed out that it is just "the things that alone for me constitute the *interest* of the doing of the novel" that William wants him to "sacrifice." "It shows," he concluded, "how far apart & to what different ends we have had to work out, (very naturally & properly!) our respective intellectual lives" (Skrupskelis & Berkeley, 1994, p. 305).

It may seem surprising that William's comment injured Henry so severely. He acknowledged the "brilliancy" of the "effect" Henry created with his style as well as his "extreme success" in the book. His criticism was no more than what many contemporary critics pointed out, that Henry did not tell his story straightforwardly with "vigor and decisiveness in the action." What most troubled Henry, I think, is that he sensed William disrespected his basic way of being. William resented Henry's submissive, indirect approach to the world and his attention to feeling and psychological subtlety.

Henry had also lost patience with William's stance of always knowing better and preaching down to everyone; here was William telling the widely acknowledged master of fiction how a novel should be written.

Henry, moreover, lacked a center; he had trouble feeling convinced of what he thought was right. As he noted in another letter to William, the whole question of personal preferences seemed to him "imponderable." He explained that he was at a loss "to say very much what I *do* like—or too utterly don't" (Skrupskelis & Berkeley, 1994, p. 261). He had taken a daring risk in experimenting with an innovative style and needed confirmation from others, especially his brother. Here was William, who was the person closest to him and someone who understood and could describe what he was attempting, telling him in no uncertain terms that he should abandon his experiment.

* * *

*In studying the relationship between two people, it becomes essential to empathize with both of them. One could easily take the side of just one of them, as I think often happens (see, for example, Zeligs's (1967) double study of Alger Hiss and Whittaker Chambers, in which his empathy for Hiss is far stronger). Once I interviewed Leon Edel, whose five-volume biography of Henry James is one of the great achievements in American letters. His understanding of Henry is astonishing, but he could not do the same with William and paints him as a villain. I asked him about how they both often became ill when they were together, and he misperceived my question and thought I was asking only about Henry. It was as if Edel, because he was so identified with Henry, could not allow for the possibility that William was also hurt at times by Henry. (For a published version of this interview, see Anderson, 1979a.)*

*With Henry, as with William, I tried to find parts of myself and my experience that accord with the parts of Henry that came into play here. Few people, of course, would have trouble identifying with Henry's basic position here, because he is the one who is hurt. Who cannot remember being lorded over by an older person who acts like a know-it-all?*

*The central factor in Henry's pain, though, was subtler. It seems to me that he had a desire to do something different and daring. Such a risk brings with it intense feelings of wanting to be supported and encouraged—and dismay when one meets with obstacles and incomprehension. I searched for experiences I had had along these lines, for example, when I sought to write a psychobiographical dissertation (on William James, as it happens), something rarely done in a department of psychology. I can remember the intensity of the emotions I felt during that period. And I can imagine how much greater they would be if it were my sibling who flung out disapproval and censure.*

* * *

Although Henry put up a spirited defense, everything he has told us about how suggestible he is and how he lacks a center implies that he would not have been able to escape from William's devastating critique. I wonder whether William's unyielding, nonacceptance of the "third manner" might help answer one of the puzzles in Henry James scholarship. Henry went through one of the most fertile and productive periods in literary history when he wrote the three novels of the "third manner," as well as stories and other works, in just five years. He lived another 11 years and continued able to write, as shown by his churning out stories, travel writings, and memoirs, but he never completed another novel after *The Golden Bowl*. Is it far-fetched to conclude that William could have had such an effect on Henry? I offer this possibility as a speculation. There is a third episode in which William's advice undeniably had dire consequences for Henry, and hence it seems plausible that William's influence could have been great enough to have cut short Henry's career as a novelist.

\*   \*   \*

*One reason for writing psychobiography is because one can sometimes use psychological evidence to deal with questions that have evaded solution when other approaches have been used (see, for example, Runyan (1981), "Why Did Van Gogh Cut off his Ear?," and Anderson (1987), "Why Did William James Abandon Art?") But psychology rarely offers a definitive, incontrovertible answer. That is why, in this case, I made a point of underlining that my answer is "speculative."*

*Let me also comment further on the narrative strategy behind this psychobiographical essay. I hoped to carry the reader along with me as I tried to illuminate the relationship between the two brothers and offered a significant interpretation, that William's critique of his brother's style deeply affected Henry. I wanted next to do two things. First, I sought to show additional evidence of William's influence on Henry and of Henry's "suggestible" nature. Second, I wanted to look at another important event that I thought could be better understood in the light of the analysis of the relationship between the brothers that I had developed in this essay. The final episode involves Henry's nervous breakdown of 1909–1910.*

\*   \*   \*

The episode seems to begin innocently with William, in 1904, sending Henry a book about a new dietary fad. The author, Horace Fletcher, advised people to masticate their food thoroughly and exhaustively; the secret of digestive health was to chew each morsel 100 times. William added his strongest endorsement of this crackpot approach to eating: "Every word is true about it. . . . It may make a great revolution in your whole economy . . . , and I advise you to give it your most respectful attention" (Skrupskelis & Berkeley, 1994, p. 255).

After William's letter arrived, Henry looked forward to receiving the book because William had "mentioned it with such approval." The first evening after it came, he reported, "a mere dip into it made me sit up so straight that I failed, under the consequent excitement, almost entirely of my night's sleep." He decided to give Fletcherism "the most patient and resolute trial," and he added, "I seem to suspect in it secret affinities with my own poor organism . . ." (Skrupskelis & Berkeley, 1994, pp. 261–262). Henry's susceptibility to suggestion, especially from William, was never more in evidence.

Henry underwent a thoroughgoing conversion to Fletcherism. Soon he was commenting, "I continue to found my life on Fletcher. He is immense," and Henry added, as it turned out, ominously, "thanks to which I am getting much less so," that is, he was losing weight (Skrupskelis & Berkeley, 1994, p. 271). William, meanwhile, made a desultory attempt to Fletcherize and soon gave it up.

For years Henry had a tumultuous love affair with this bizarre way of eating. After a period of what he described to William as "too-prolonged & too-consistent Fletcherism," he suffered, in 1909, a nervous breakdown. No doubt, other factors contributed to his collapse, especially his disappointment at the paltry sales of the New York edition of his works, on which he had lavished extravagant hopes. But the form his crisis took was "the condition of more & more sickishly *loathing* food," and he became scared by "rapid & extreme loss of flesh & increase of weakness & emptiness—failure of nourishment" (Skrupskelis & Berkeley, 1994, pp. 409–410). He concluded that "my 6 years of passionate & intimate Fletcherism had, after the first long, & excellent period of benefit, bedevilled my digestion to within an inch of its life." He had become "agitatedly nervous"—much like their sister, he added—"under the depression & discouragement of relapses & sufferings" and his doctor's "bunglements" (Skrupskelis & Berkeley, 1994, p. 416).

At the worst of the crisis, in early 1910, Henry was disheartened and feared for his life. He could neither write nor manage his daily affairs. William's son, Harry, came to England to help care for Henry but could stay only for a short time. "I have a kind of terror of finding myself alone here again with my misery," Henry observed, and he pleaded with William and his wife to cross the Atlantic to be with him. "Here is a wail for you—the voice of my present dejection—and of my infinite yearning," he wrote. "My sense of the matter is that I *can* get better & that I am worth saving for such magnificent work as I want still to do. . . . " He ended the letter by beseeching William: "write some further tender healing, sustaining, reassuring word to your poor demoralized & baffled old Brother" (Skrupskelis & Berkeley, 1994, pp. 413–415).

Henry's autonomy, I would suggest, always had been precarious, as seen in his pattern of compliance with his mother. He felt overwhelmed when his career, on which he so much relied, seemed imperiled, and he tried to take control through the area of eating. William was implicated in the desperate battle that took place within Henry's inner world. The main lines of this internal battle were something like this. Henry tried to shore up his sense of control by looking for an answer in his eating. The consuming of food is the most primal area for such struggles, because it is the area—as early as in infancy—that no outside person can dominate. But at the same time, Henry was relying on William; he was putting into practice a manner of eating that William had advocated for him. Yet Henry also resented being under William's authority. Unconsciously he rebelled; he said, in a sense, "I'm doing what you advised, and I'm showing you how worthless your advice is because it threatens to kill me." But with his spurning of William, he became overwhelmed with loneliness, and he begged William and his wife to take care of him.

*   *   *

*Beyond empathy, the psychobiographer must also use what is sometimes called countertransference, in analogy to the feelings and reactions that therapists have with their patients. These feelings potentially can help therapists understand the inner world of their patients, and similarly they can bring psychobiographers closer to the inner world of their subjects. A consideration of countertransference also helps psychobiographers to try to identify instances in which their own psychological conflicts have interfered with their perception of their subjects. (See Anderson, 1981b, pp. 251–254; Edel, 1984b, pp. 65–92; Erikson, 1975, pp. 113–168; Schepeler, 1990; and Strouse, 1986, pp. 191–195)*

*Starting with Freud's introduction of the term in 1910 (1957, p. 144), countertransference has received intense scrutiny in the psychoanalytic literature (see, for example, Racker (1968) and Tansey & Burke (1989)). There is also a more recent tradition in qualitative research of considering the author's "reflexivity" (see Ellis & Bochner, 2000; Holland, 1977; and Tedlock, 1991). In this latter tradition, attention is paid to how all aspects of the author's background, including socioeconomic status, ethnic and racial identity, and personal factors, influence the author's analysis. The chief difference is that the concept of countertransference points to the most intense, sometimes unconscious feelings that the subject stimulates in the investigator.*

*In encountering Henry's eating disorder, I felt almost a sense of panic—people do die from these disorders—along with an equally distressing feeling of helplessness. I was reminded of a reaction I have had when doing psychotherapy with someone who suffers from an eating disorder. Often I have felt that the patient is dangerously harming herself and I can do nothing about it. That reaction draws my attention to one aspect of the function of the eating disorder; the patient is telling me, as well as others in her life, that this is an area that only she can control. In looking at this episode involving the James brothers, my sense of my countertransference sensitized me to what I think is central to the dynamics, Henry's struggle over control.*

*Countertransference can be a hindrance as easily as a help. The crucial question is: Am I having a reaction that is based on my own psychological sensitivities and preoccupations and not on what my subject has created? With Henry James I had a feeling of being manipulated by him and felt tempted to turn against him and to denounce him. But I could see that my vulnerability to feeling used and manipulated by others had been touched on. I cautioned myself to back off from retaliating and instead to try to understand and to empathize with Henry. (See two collections of papers that emphasize biographers' use of their selves: Baron & Pletsch, 1985, and Moraitis & Pollock, 1987.)*

*I can describe a similar dynamic in my feelings toward William. At times I felt outrage toward him for undermining Henry's bold experiments with a new style of writing. That my feelings were so strong was a signal to me to reflect on what had been touched off in me and to remind myself that there were reasons why William acted as he did, just as there were reasons why Henry reacted as he did.*

\* \* \*

William and his wife, Alice, did come to Henry's aid. They spent a month with Henry at Lamb House. Then William, critically ill with heart disease, went on to the continent to try some medical treatments, while Alice stayed behind to nurse Henry back to health.

William recognized that his brother had had a nervous breakdown connected with Fletcherism. Henry, he saw, had suffered from "a more or less complete anorexia and loathing of the eating-act." William obstinately maintained that Henry's experience did not disprove Fletcher's principles, "but," he noted, "it shows that in some persons there is a danger in making the feeding-act the object of too much conscious attention." He also failed to reach the obvious conclusion that he should have known his brother was one of those people for whom Fletcherism was unsuited and that he had erred in recommending it to him (W. James, 1910).[2]

Although he had emerged from his crisis, Henry traveled to the United States with William and his wife because he did not want to be alone. Just one week after their arrival, on August 26, 1910, William suffered from a fatal heart attack. To a friend, Henry wrote:

> I sit heavily stricken and in darkness—for from far back in dimmest childhood he had been my ideal Elder Brother, and I still, through all the years, saw in him, even as a small timorous boy yet, my protector, my backer, my authority and my pride. (Edel, 1984a, p. 561)

---

[2]Quoted by permission of the Houghton Library, Harvard University, shelf mark bMS Am 1092.9 (815).

Henry's bout with Fletcherism reflects the vicissitudes of his reliance on William. Henry was suggestible and invested William with unquestioned authority. William's psychological understanding of his brother was great enough that he could have understood his vulnerability. But William was fragile in his own way. He needed to buttress his self-esteem constantly by demonstrating his expertise, and he was wedded especially to maintaining his role with his brother as being the one who was older and wiser. Enticed by William's advice, Henry became an adherent to Fletcherism. When Henry became depressed, his distress expressed itself in a particularly dangerous and painful form, through anorexia. But, on the other hand, Henry was so attached to William—as he was to no one else—that he turned, when in despair, to his brother and his brother's wife, and their healing presence enabled him to recover.

*   *   *

*My chief goal in the psychobiographical essay was to provide a convincing analysis of the relationship of the two brothers through the vehicle of a dramatic narrative. The heart of my argument is that the vulnerabilities of the two brothers interacted in such a way that William frequently found himself undermining Henry. William never recovered from Henry's usurpation of his place in the family, while Henry never could escape from William's domination of him. But all the while each of them loved and relied on each other. The last episode deals with the most dangerous example of William's influence and Henry's suggestibility. But I also added Henry's reaction to William's death, because it brings out how reliant he was on, and at times how sustained by, his intimate connection to William.*

*As I tried to show in this paper, the real work took place outside of, but shaped, the psychobiographical essay. The chief activities of a psychobiographer include: narrative strategy; finding and studying materials, such as letters, that can offer access to the inner lives of the subjects; using psychological theory that broadens, rather than reduces, one's perceptions; immersing oneself in the experiences of the subjects; developing empathy for the subjects; and making use of one's countertransference.*

## REFERENCES

Alexander, I. E. (1990). *Personology: Method and content in personality assessment and psychobiography*. Durham, NC: Duke University Press.

Anderson, J. W. (1979a). An interview with Leon Edel on the James Family. *Psychohistory Review, 8*(1–2), 15–22.

Anderson, J. W. (1979b). In search of Mary James. *Psychohistory Review*, 8(1–2), 63–70.

Anderson, J. W. (1981a). The methodology of psychological biography. *Journal of Interdisciplinary History, 11*, 455–474.

Anderson, J. W. (1981b). Psychobiographical methodology: The case of William James. *Review of Personality and Social Psychology, 2*, 245–272.

Anderson, J. W. (1987). Why did William James abandon art? In G. Moraitis & G. H. Pollock (Eds.), *Psychoanalytic studies of biography* (pp. 279–303). Madison, CT: International Universities Press.

Baron, S. H., & Pletsch, C. (Eds.). (1985). *Introspection in biography: The biographer's quest for self-awareness.* Hillsdale, NJ: Analytic Press.

Carlson, R. (1988), Exemplary lives: The use of psychobiography for theory development. *Journal of Personality, 56,* 105–138.

Cody, J. (1971). *After great pain: The inner life of Emily Dickinson.* Cambridge, MA: Harvard University Press.

Coles, R. (1975). *The mind's fate.* Boston: Little, Brown.

Demos, J. (1982). *Entertaining Satan: Witchcraft and the culture of early New England.* New York: Oxford University Press.

Edel, L. (1953–1972). *The life of Henry James* (5 vols.). Philadelphia: Lippincott.

Edel, L. (1982). *Stuff of sleep and dreams.* New York: Harper & Row.

Edel, L. (Ed.). (1984a). *Henry James letters* (Vol. 4). Cambridge, MA: Harvard University Press.

Edel, L. (1984b). *Writing lives: Principia biographica.* New York: Norton.

Ellis, C., & Bochner, A. P. (2000) Autoethnography, personal narrative, reflexivity: Researcher as subject. In N. K. Denzin & Y. S. Lincoln (Eds.), *Handbook of qualitative research* (2nd ed., pp. 733–768). Thousand Oaks, CA: Sage.

Elms, A. C. (1994). *Uncovering lives: The uneasy alliance of biography and psychology.* New York: Oxford University Press.

Erikson, E. H. (1975). *Life history and the historical moment.* New York: Norton.

Freud, S. (1957). The future prospects of psychoanalytic theory. In *Standard edition of the complete psychological works of Sigmund Freud* (Vol. 11, pp. 141–151). London: Hogarth Press. (Original work published 1910)

Gay, P. (1985). *Freud for historians.* New York: Oxford University Press.

Greenberg, J. R., & Mitchell, S. A. (1983). *Object relations in psychoanalytic theory.* Cambridge, MA: Harvard University Press.

Holland, R. (1977). *Self and social context.* London: Macmillan.

James, H. (1913). *A small boy and others.* New York: Scribner's.

James, M. (1874). Letter to William James, 23 January 1874, James Papers, Harvard University, shelf mark bMS Am 1093.1(53).

James, W. (Ed). (1884). *The literary remains of the late Henry James.* New York: Osgood.

James, W. (1899). *Talks to teachers on psychology: And to students on some of life's ideals*. New York: Henry Holt.

James, W. (1910). Letter to Henry Bowditch, 4 June 1910, James Papers, Harvard University, shelf mark bMS Am 1092.9(815).

Jones, E. (1913). The influence of Andrea del Sarto's wife on his art. In E. Jones, *Psycho-myth, psycho-history; Essays in applied psychoanalysis* (Vol. I, pp. 22–38). New York: Hillstone, 1974.

Kohut, H. (1971). *The analysis of the self*. New York: International Universities Press.

Kohut, H. (1985). Self psychology and the science of man. In C. B. Strozier (Ed.), *Self psychology and the humanities: Reflections on a new psychoanalytic approach*. New York: Norton.

Kohut, T. A. (1986). Psychohistory as history. *American Historical Review, 91*, 336–354.

Loewenberg, P. (1988). Psychoanalytic models of history: Freud and after. In W. McK. Runyan (Ed.), *Psychology and historical interpretation* (pp. 126–156). New York: Oxford University Press.

Loewenberg, P. (1996). Psychoanalytic ego psychology and object relations and their uses for the historian. *Psychohistory Review, 25*, 21–46.

Manuel, F. (1968). *A portrait of Isaac Newton*. Cambridge, MA: Harvard University Press.

Miller, A. (1981). *Prisoners of childhood*. New York: Basic Books.

Moraitis, G., & Pollock, G. H. (Eds.). (1987). *Psychoanalytic studies of biography*. Madison, CT: International Universities Press.

Racker, H. (1968). *Transference and countertransference*. New York: International Universities Press.

Runyan, W. McK. (1981). Why did Van Gogh cut off his ear? The problem of alternative explanations in psychobiography. *Journal of Personality and Social Psychology, 40*, 1070–1077.

Runyan, W. McK. (1982). *Life histories and psychobiography: Explorations in theory and method*. New York: Oxford University Press.

Runyan, W. McK. (1997). Studying lives: Psychobiography and the conceptual structure of personality psychology. In R. Hogan, J. Johnson, & S. Briggs (Eds.), *Handbook of personality psychology* (pp. 41–69). San Diego, CA: Academic Press.

Schepeler, E. (1990). The biographer's transference: A chapter in psychobiographical epistemology. *Biography, 13*, 111–129.

Skrupskelis, I. K., & Berkeley, E. M. (Eds.). (1994). *The correspondence of William James* (Vol. 4). Charlottesville: University Press of Virginia.

Stannard, D. E. (1980). *Shrinking history: On Freud and the failure of psychohistory*. New York: Oxford University Press.

Strouse, J. (1986). The real reasons. In W. Zinsser (Ed.), *Extraordinary lives: The art and craft of American biography* (pp. 161–195). New York: American Heritage.

Summers, F. (1994). *Object relations theories and psychopathology*. Hillsdale, NJ: Analytic Press.

Szaluta, J. (1999). *Psychohistory: Theory and practice*. New York: Peter Lang.

Tansey, M. J., & Burke, W. F. (1989). *Understanding countertransference: From projective identification to empathy*. Hillsdale, NJ: Analytic Press, 1989.

Tedlock, B. (1991). From participant observation to the observation of participation: The emergence of narrative ethnography. *Journal of Anthropological Research, 41*, 69–94.

Waite, R. G. L. (1977). *The psychopathic god: Adolf Hitler*. New York: Basic Books.

Winnicott, D. W. (1965). *The maturational processes and the facilitating environment*. New York: International Universities Press.

Young-Bruehl, E. (1998). *Subject to biography*. Cambridge, MA: Harvard University Press.

Zeligs, M. (1967). *Friendship and fratricide: An analysis of Whittaker Chambers and Alger Hiss*. New York: Viking.

# 11

## WRITERS AS READERS
## IN NARRATIVE INQUIRY:
## LEARNING FROM BIOGRAPHY

STEVEN WEILAND

"Learning by doing," it is often said, is the best way to master a new skill. For my students in research methods courses, though they are reluctant to appear indifferent to the history and theory of narrative, it is their own emerging practice that interests them the most. They want to learn how to "do" narrative, often assuming there are well-known and well-defined procedures that will form the backbone of the course. Instead, I propose that narrative research represents a group of problems not only in composing texts but in reading them. Thus, the syllabus includes books that demonstrate possibilities for narrative, work by scholars aware of how storytelling forms operate in the disciplines.

In this, my approach differs from the kinds of "reading" that Amia Lieblich and her colleagues have fruitfully explored in their pedagogically oriented *Narrative Research* (1998). They focus on how primary sources—for example, the results of a life history interview—can be read in order to construct convincing research accounts. As a complement to such efforts, lessons can be learned from reading narratives based in scholarship, in particular those that reflect self-consciousness about their ways and are thus friendly to readers seeking to improve their own practices. Much can be learned from narrative experiments that perhaps even test the very idea that methods can be fully codified for the classroom.

I advise my students to launch their work in narrative inquiry by first becoming good readers in order to cultivate images for themselves of what appealing texts should resemble. In effect, we start at the end of what textbooks often call the "research process," which typically begins, in these conventional accounts, with formulating a "question," and then proceeds to deciding on a "conceptual framework," collecting and interpreting the data, and then "writing it up." An effective writer, I believe, is someone who has learned through curiosity and experience as a reader how to use the resources of language—and the organization or design of a text including any author's relations with readers—to express the intentions, activities, and results of their work.

Students can be invited to read books from many fields, but I think it practical to unify their experiences across disciplines by focusing on biography. Biographical narratives have the feel of the familiar to most readers, making it possible in the classroom to identify those features of a text critical to the telling of a story apart from whatever is intended by a biographer as a contribution to a disciplinary problem or theme. As narrative art of a kind, biography prompts among students challenging questions regarding the form of their commitment to research.

In what follows I focus first on the problem of teaching narrative in the context of general concern about forms of scholarly expression. Although those of us who teach narrative methods can now take for granted their place in science and scholarship, students gain from situating themselves in the continuing debate about their legitimacy and uses. "Learning by doing" in narrative should include attention to how it is that problems of such an approach reach across many fields, often revealing relations between them. I then turn to the role of narrative in guides to "qualitative" research seeking to codify principles and practices of inquiry now increasingly popular in academic work. Though hospitable to narrative of course, work about qualitative methods displays a weakness in the ways that writing is "positioned" in theorizing and teaching. There is insufficient attention to reading, or what can be learned from scholarly work that displays conditions of its own composition. Thus, a section of the chapter, on recent biographies in literary studies, history, and psychology, identifies them as texts that teach, each in their own way, variations in narrative. A brief conclusion reflects this proposal: *Learning as readers*, students can encounter uses of narrative available to them as writers. As Ruthellen Josselson (1999) recognizes, the nature of narrative studies "puts even greater demands on scholars to read widely and deeply, to cast a wide net before determining their idea of the 'field' " (p. xi). This essay suggests some possibilities and rewards for such activity by focusing on biography.

## DILEMMAS OF INTERPRETATION

Is there a scholarly or scientific discipline today without disagreement about its expressive conventions, its vocabulary, and forms of writing? A recent dispute in the *American Psychologist* is representative. Proponents of loyalty to the American Psychological Association (APA) style were opposed by psychologists appealing for work reflecting new ways of thinking across the disciplines and the freedom to use forms that best fit a scholar's interests and style of inquiry. For both sides, the issue is how much choice there should be in scholarly discourse (see Josselson & Lieblich, 1996; Madigan, Johnson, & Linton, 1995). As the movement known as "Rhetoric of Inquiry" demonstrates, the position favoring skepticism of the habits of scholarly and scientific writing is widely shared even if a pedagogy to represent it is still in the making (see Nelson, Megill, & McCloskey, 1987, for the movement's founding and still authoritative statement).

According to anthropologists George Marcus and Michael Fisher (1986), a scholarly "crisis in representation" could be detected in the 1980s. By now the "crisis" has become a part of the normal state of affairs, as writers in many fields recognize the limits of scholarly conventions in representing how we understand experience. Some seek to represent the problem directly in their work, and to explore in theoretical statements strategies for finding more variety or new expressive opportunities in the languages and genres of scholarship.

With guidance from Marcus and Fisher, the influential Clifford Geertz (1988), and others (Denzin, 1997), ethnographers have made problems of language and writing central to inquiry in the social and behavioral sciences. These problems include finding a suitable form of self-consciousness about the activity of writing itself—in particular the need to find new forms, or to adapt traditional ones. Thus, psychologist Jerome Bruner (1990) was one of many theorists of the 1990s to invite fresh attention to "storytelling," across the disciplines. When he named narrative as the form of knowing he favored, after having worked for decades with its "paradigmatic" counterpart or the scientific search for general laws, he recognized especially its role in "folk culture." We find there the ways that people have always gained knowledge and understanding of the world, and represented it in stories (for a useful recent statement of the popular dimensions of narrative see Fulford, 2000).

If narrative is among our most natural activities, then why must its virtues and techniques be taught? Perhaps because in our "postmodernity"—whether welcomed or reviled—human behavior as the primary subject of narrative is seen by many to be no longer easily represented in stories. For Kenneth Gergen (1991), "identity" is now best known in the form of "dilemmas" rather than as a stable product of experience. We are fragmented, conflicted, multiple, and protean and see ourselves as variable and relativist in our actions and beliefs, rather than as consistent actors in the world with a sure grasp of experience.

Although Gergen's view should be complemented by claims for more consistency and durability in human experience (e.g., Smith, 1994), his psychological "postmodernism" represents an accent in scholarship with widespread results for the ways that writers in many fields conceptualize their subjects. Thus, the historian Simon Schama (1991) invited readers to welcome the irony of the title of his book, *Dead Certainties*. He displays there (with "certainty" now dead), the products of his historical imagination, or "unwarranted speculations" as he names them dramatically in the subtitle. Bruner (1990) himself says categorically that "There are no causes to be grasped with certainty where the act of creating meaning is concerned, only acts, expressions, and contexts to be interpreted" (p. 118). Accordingly, narrative itself is an "act of meaning" offering opportunities for representing experience with recognizable authority, and some might say authenticity or a durable sense of identity. As such, it exceeds the capacities of the conventional (and confident) scientific discourse of psychology and its postmodern (and uncertain) critics.

When causality, or any form of relation between social or psychological phenomena, is said to be "certain," it can be represented in writing in ways that reflect well-established habits of scholarly discourse organized around the presentation of evidence and the drawing of conclusions or truth claims. But, as Bruner says in arguing for a narrative psychology based on autobiography, "the 'methodology of causation' can neither capture the social and personal richness of lives in culture nor begin to plumb their historical depth" (p. 137).

Moreover, narratives ask us—as writers and readers—to make claims for knowledge that reflect the difficulties of knowing. By beginning their inquiries with the goal of understanding how "meaning" is made, scholars accept the challenge of "interpreting" experience, including their own as authors and, increasingly, as teachers. But so too is interpretation made of dilemmas, these being the subject now of timely reflection on narrative.


## TEACHING NARRATIVE'S NEW JOURNEY

Ruth Behar, whose *Translated Woman* (1993) is among the most admired of recent works of narrative scholarship, has made it her goal to explain the origins and purposes of the forms she favors. Her reflections on *The Vulnerable Observer* (1996) present "life history" as a peculiarly intimate activity in which the life of the author should be represented in a form that shows how relations between biographical subject and author are in fact primary conditions for the narrative. Narratives of lives depend now on constructing a story that itself represents the problem of making meaning from experience. Many academic authors have welcomed the new opportunities even while recognizing the difficulties in challenging disciplinary traditions.

Where can we go for lessons in teaching narrative? In a recent essay on the problems of ethnographic writing, Behar (1999) brings us into her graduate course on the subject. It gets such attention because writing is a primary resource, if an "unwieldy" one she believes, in research methods. She works on the writing of biographical texts with students from many academic fields.

> [Narrative] continues to be a genre that chronicles strange, often unexpected encounters, and demands an especially attentive listening, looking, feeling, and being there. But the journeys that are taken now, in our postcolonial era, are accountable to history, memory, the emotions, identity, passion, and the soul in ways that never have been before. . . . Ethnographers so thoroughly question their presuppositions now before embarking and wear their hearts so openly on their sleeves that there isn't any place for them to hide. (p. 480)

Behar teaches narrative, as critics of scholarly conventions advise, by minimizing methods. Avoiding rules or (in the popular image) "maps" for inquiry, she uses the writing of narrative itself as a metaphor for the situation of today's scholars. Thus, she tells her students that there is but the memory of what ethnography used to be, a "private club of privileged travelers," and "the blank page of the present."

According to Behar, with every journey taken by an author—apprentice or acclaimed—the form of narrative is reinvented. Thus, she takes the pedagogical position that there are no "explicit criteria" for identifying any experimental narrative as a perfect example of scholarly storytelling. Instead, students (and others) should look for the characteristics of the "arts" of scholarship: "[Writing] must be done with grace, with precision, with an eye for the telling detail, an ear for the insight that comes unexpectedly, with tremendous respect for language . . . and with a love of beauty" (p. 477). An effective teacher can guide students toward improving their narrative work, in these categories and others, by asking that they make of their reading a resource for reflecting on their writing.

As is the case with the inventive biographical narratives that I consider below, Behar's *Translated Woman* itself invites (or demands) attentive reading and teaches by example—in the manner of the ethnographic classroom. Thus, the text opens with an extended narrative in the words of the book's subject, offered without explicit commentary by the scholarly author. The second half of *Translated Woman* is virtually all interpretation, including Behar's effort to bring herself out from the "shadow" of the subject of the life history by confessing her uneasiness about their relations. She anticipates challenges to the accuracy of the subject's story as it is told to her by accepting any "lies" as inevitable parts of the "the fictional or storied nature of the blended text we have been producing together over the years." A biographical principle is at stake for any aspiring or even experienced narrative writer: "There is no true version of a life, after all. There are only stories told about and around a life" (p. 234).

A statement this bold, however, frequently made today in the narrative literature of the social and behavioral sciences, prompts us to ask: "What are the limits of genre innovation in academic inquiry?" This question has special resonance for biography, with the many choices the form offers for the selection and arrangement of the details of any person's life, and the relative significance given them. For Marcus (1994), the conventions of discourse reveal complacency about the relations between most scholars and their subjects. Writing in his field has been "impoverished and far too restrictive." He believes that "We can be sure that our object of study will always exceed its analytic circumscription, especially under conditions of postmodernity." The excess is essential to what Marcus calls "messy texts," or work marked by "its resistance to [the] too-easy assimilation of the phenomenon of interest by any given analytic, ready-made concepts." Such texts are disorderly, Marcus says, because rather than being "fixed" (or certain) in their methods they seek out analytic frameworks in which scholars are "moving and acting within [the landscape] rather than being drawn in from a transcendent and detached viewpoint" (pp. 388, 392). Of course, "messy" is a subjective designation describing a variety of intentions and form—and of demands on readers—and such texts "insist on their own open-endedness, incompleteness, and uncertainty." These are not terms meant to designate strategies for composing a text based in psychology or other disciplines. They refer to the dilemmas of scholarly writing and to the stance any author must take toward the rhetorical demands of his or her subject.


## POSITIONS OF NARRATIVE

When my students read *Translated Woman* they struggle to see the relations between its narrative and more directly interpretive parts. Even as they make connections, they must account for the ways that the text appears to resist coherence of this kind. There is the primacy of the story including Behar's role in getting it, and then there is what we can say about it from many perspectives. I ask the students if the interpretations reveal the meanings of the biographical narrative, or how the gap is managed between the book's different discourses. Where, in other words, does a narrative tell its story? The difficulties of "translation" thus become a major theme, underlining what can be translated from the "language" of narrative to that of a scholar speaking in the voice of a discipline.

Behar herself knows that her course in writing ethnographic narratives offers lessons in "qualitative methods," but she is herself reluctant to structure her teaching around them. Any hint of being rule-bound will threaten what is authentic in today's and tomorrow's most appealing scholarly narratives. In many other classrooms, however, it is precisely the question of such methods—offered typically as an alternative to "scientific study," "statistics," or "positivism"—that shapes consideration of narrative and other seemingly unscientific forms of writing. There is as much variety in teaching qualitative research as there is in the methods themselves (e.g., ethnographic observation, interviewing, using visual materials, doing case studies, etc.). Judging from the amount of textbook publication in qualitative research, there is considerable academic interest in it, reflecting the desires of scholars and students for methodological justification and procedural consistency (for a useful summary see Price, 1999).

Even so, in introducing their comprehensive *Handbook of Qualitative Research*, now a central pedagogical resource in its second edition, Norman Denzin and Yvonna Lincoln (2000) acknowledge that such inquiry is "defined primarily by a series of essential tensions, contradictions, and hesitations [working] back and forth among competing definitions and conceptions of the field" (p. ix). Qualitative research is still an enterprise in the making, particularly in "applied" fields of the social and behavioral sciences, such as gerontology (Gubrium & Sankar, 1997). The instability of qualitative inquiry, or uncertainty about methods, should be one of its permanent attractions for scholarly innovators. Thus, the rush to tame the field in the form of "guides" may have the effect of making it merely into a new form of scholarly convention.

How can the "tensions" in qualitative research be represented in teaching and made part of the experience of students? Not easily, because qualitative research relies on techniques borrowed and adapted from many disciplines, primarily in the social and behavioral sciences but also in the humanities. True mastery of qualitative methods, including narrative, would require expert knowledge in several of these fields, from their characteristic ways of conceptualizing problems through their distinctive genres of representation. But much can be accomplished, including recognition of how the pressures on convention actually operate in particular research efforts, sometimes quite self-consciously in work by authors eager to take part in methodological debate, and sometimes only indirectly in work that "speaks for itself" in matters of formal invention. In narrative, as in other forms of scholarly expression, reflection on methods—whether methods are an explicit part of the text or not—is essential to the distinction between simply doing, and understanding the contexts and consequences (or meanings) of the choices made by an author.

In guiding novice scholars toward recognition of the role of writing in their research, the popular guidebooks rarely get beyond convention. First, there is the habit of virtually all guides to place the work of writing at or near the end of the research "process." Even Denzin and Lincoln, otherwise attentive to the ways that questions of authorship and genre permeate inquiry, favor a familiar position for writing in the order of research—that is, at the end of a sequence of "phases" of the "research process." We can see in this format the habit of gathering data and then "writing up" the research, as if these were discrete acts invariably appearing one after another. Instead, as is reflected in any work of scholarship that is at all self-conscious about its composition, authors find a form as the story to be told unfolds, including drawing on their experiences as readers to provide images of appealing forms, or even sometimes solutions to problems of narrative composition.

Second, however useful the teaching guides to qualitative inquiry have been, they are, similar to most research itself in applied fields, indifferent to the recent history of narrative (and other discursive innovations) in the mainstream disciplines and what that has meant for expressive variety. Anthropology has led the way recently, but history, with literary biography once the academic home of scholarly narrative, is now a location for its revival (for an inventive account, see Goodman, 1998). The cost of isolation from such developments, in psychology as in other fields, is a needlessly narrow idea of what is possible in narrative, and of how scholarship itself develops in a mutuality of fresh discoveries and intentions.

## LESSONS FROM BIOGRAPHY

Given the growth of interest in narrative expression in the behavioral sciences, and the prospects now for the integration of theories, the codification of principles, and the identification of primary research problems and possibilities (see McAdams, 1999, for an authoritative statement), teaching in this field carries substantial, if rewarding, burdens. But in an appealing pedagogical sentiment from philosopher Michael Oakeshott can be found a reminder of the claims of Bruner (and others) about narrative's "natural" place in the ways we think and learn: "As with every other sort of knowledge, learning a technique does not consist in getting rid of pure ignorance, but in reforming knowledge which is already there" (cited in Clandinin & Connelly, 2000, p. 38).

Still, what many students do not now have are experiences as readers that can inspire and inform their work as authors of narrative. Teachers of narrative, desiring to fill such an educational gap, can select among many recent texts. In the ones identified and briefly discussed here we see how

the limits of biographical data prompt different forms of the narrative reconstruction of lives, and how the impact of a biographical subject on a biographer is represented. My goal here is not to propose a new small biographical
canon, but in a kind of minitour of recent and impressive work to encourage
incorporating the reading of any methodologically informative biography
into the teaching of narrative.

## A Complete Unknown

As a literary biographer, Charles Nicholl approaches the life of the
late 19th-century French poet Arthur Rimbaud (*Somebody Else* [1997]) as
a project in narrative that must make visible the "illegible shadows" of
Rimbaud's "lost" years, the ones he spent in Africa working in trade after
abandoning his short but intense and influential career in poetry. There
are few records of these years. Nicholl cannot guarantee that his narrative
is wholly accurate; instead the goal is to recreate the ordinary and exotic
episodes of Rimbaud's African experiences, to "try to make them flicker
into movement like a scene from a film" (p. 5).

Why write a narrative with so little data? Imagining Rimbaud's arrival
in Africa, Nicholl puts himself in his subject's story as someone whose
curiosity is aroused by this strange new arrival at Aden, an Arabian port
that was very difficult to reach. "It is the wonderful anonymity of it which
catches my fancy. Rimbaud is at this moment a complete unknown" (p.
10). Of course, he is not unknown now in the history of modern literature,
but Nicholl initiates his biography in the context of Rimbaud's own efforts
to cancel his previous public identity. The life of the "new" Rimbaud differs
considerably from the one he wished to leave behind. But Nicholl knows
that what he concealed about his past was precisely what made his last
years often so satisfying to Rimbaud himself. His relations with Arabs and
black Africans, for example, reflect his strong sense of himself as an outsider
even in French society.

Nicholl rejects standard narrative intentions. "I wish to restore
Rimbaud's African years not just by piecing them together, by telling their
story. . . . but by seeing them as a sort of doomed existential adventure
which is perhaps the true summation of his curtailed life as a poet" (p. 13).
Rimbaud's life as he himself experienced it directs the form in which it is
represented. Thus, the narrative is shaped by events but also by moods, by
Rimbaud's poetic response to experience even if he was no longer writing
poetry. He moved around the region as his changeable temperament and
business opportunities demanded. "His whole life is a story of departures
and flights, of disappearances and reappearances" (p. 12).

However exotic Nicholl's subject, many writers of narrative will recognize his problem. "It is hard to reconstruct Rimbaud because he was himself

so unconstructed, so much in flux" (p. 35). Can a narrative have form but be "unconstructed?" The key for Nicholl is conveying a sense of restlessness and constant movement. As Rimbaud moves about in the text, Nicholl appears to be at his side. The paradox of this narrative is that even though the evidence is scanty, the story is told with great concreteness. And Nicholl presents his readers with another problem of narrative: "This is a human story, but there is also an archetypal or legendary aspect to Rimbaud, which radiates out of his poetry, which magnifies his gestures and loads his curtest utterances, and which gives to his African travels the sense of epic trek through the outer reaches of discontent" (p. 13). As was the case among his earliest French companions, Rimbaud attracts and repels. Thus does the intimacy of the narrative also reveal the ambiguities of biographical judgment of a subject, for in the end Nicholl acknowledges Rimbaud's reputation as a "radiant sinner and hardbitten pioneer." These are human qualities, but Nicholl gives us a biographical narrative at the edge of ordinary experience.

## The Twist of the Thread

In *The Unredeemed Captive* (1994) John Demos shows how an historian seeks a narrative form in accord with the original drama of events in the past, and reflecting the conditions and resources of his discipline. With narrative history in "deep eclipse" until recently, Demos presents himself in terms of his past as a reader of stories and now as a scholar determined in midlife to reassert "old loyalties, old pleasures." He tells the story of an attack on a village in western Massachusetts by a band of French and Native American allies from Quebec. Many villagers were killed, and many were taken back to Canada. All of the captives eventually returned except for Eunice Williams, the daughter of John Williams, a well-known minister and theologian. Demos makes of this "family story" an unusual captivity narrative, based on the available facts but depending also on reconstructions, at times in the manner of a novelist, of events and of the thoughts and feelings of the primary participants.

A report by a Colonel Partridge on the massacre and its aftermath is an artifact of history and an anticipation of Demos's own role as an historian, in particular the modern author's hope of producing a text that has, in its way, the authority of the first-hand source. Demos was not there of course but he wants in his narrative a sense of his presence in the events.

Inevitably, a scholar who holds (Partridge's report) in his hands sees more than the words on the page: The scholar sees the rough (but remarkably strong) qualities of the paper, the occasional blurriness of the ink, the clear and steady penmanship of the writer (clear and steady in spite of the horror). The scholar sees also, behind the pen and paper, the figure of the colonel moving among the survivors, comforting and questioning (and writing) by turns (p. 23).

Demos too, "moves among the survivors," and his narrative is constructed around his understanding of how their relations changed to reflect the different ways that their lives were altered by the encounter with the Native Americans.

But the past is made part of the present not only because of the vividness of the narrative. There is too its intention to make an example of the experience of the Williams family. In a later account of what he learned as a reader of fiction, Demos (1998) reports becoming in mid-career "an all out convert to historical novels" but without the resources as yet to express such a preference in his scholarly work. First, he needed to learn, as an author, how to make a narrative reflecting historical experience in all its details. "Only thus can we do justice to all the textural (as opposed to structural) qualities of the life of the past" (p. 1529).

A second lesson, crucial to the current debate about the "scientific" uses of narrative and implicit too in Nicholl's interest in the "archetypal" in Rimbaud's story, was in the ways that historical narratives can "engage more directly the foundations of the human condition." It was now "generic themes" that Demos believed should be the primary subject of narrative, and the materials of history are thus made wholly contemporary. Now, as he looks at Colonel Partridge's report, "The pastness of history briefly dissolves—or, rather, re-forms as the succession of present moments it was (and is). The scholar feels that bygone present simultaneously with his own. 1704, 1990; Deerfield then, Boston now; the snowy street of a shattered village, the genteel appointments of a modern library; juxtaposed—no, joined—by the document, at once theirs and ours" (p. 23).

In recounting the experience of John Williams as a chronicler of the events, Demos reveals what is common to narrative of many kinds: Private themes mix uneasily with public ones and the text originates in the wish to learn from the activity of writing it. "The words on the page would be part of his struggle to accept, to adjust, to understand. In the long run, his audience would be all New England—all America—but at first there was only himself" (pp. 66–67). Demos represents how a researcher understands the hierarchy of narrative possibilities available in the data. He acknowledges that most of the Deerfield captives are "beyond reach" by historians. A few cases might yield enough bits of material so that the "thread of a connected life" may be discerned. "[O]nly in one case," he says, "is it possible to go further—to feel the twist of the thread, to catch the meaning of the experience. To know the thoughts and feelings behind the events" (p. 55).

Demos's narrative takes him beyond what he can know within the conventions of historical discourse toward what he wants to understand about the "unredeemed captive." The family history has to be completed with the story of Eunice, whose decision to make a life for herself with her Native American captors represents the most fascinating "captivity" story of all because it cannot be told from the inside (as can her fathers'). She came in and out of view of those who kept records. The story can only end uncertainly in the text, as we are invited to contemplate three possible "conclusions," each representing a different way of seeing how "ties of blood and interest" became permanent historical and psychological pressures on life in the new nation.

## The Darkened Room

Israeli psychologist Amia Lieblich's work has made her increasingly self-conscious about the nature of "psychological truth" and about its place in the methods most likely to gain access to and represent the life course. In *Conversations with Dvora* (1997) Lieblich offers a text as remote from the conventions of academic psychology as her subject—the reclusive writer Dvora Baron—was from the intellectual mainstream. Turning more and more inward in midlife as she became preoccupied with her past and her unexpected and demanding fate as an Israeli pioneer in the first decades of the 20th century, Baron established a pattern of living in which she never left her Tel Aviv apartment. She died in 1956.

Lieblich was in midlife herself as she began work on her unusual biography and facing a personal and professional crisis, in part reflecting her deepening displeasure with the limits of academic psychology and its insistence on an objectifying distance between scholars and their research subjects. She was taught but now rejects the idea that it is "essential to distinguish between fact and interpretation, data and theory, as if the borders between them were etched in stone" (p. x). By ignoring such canons of research, Lieblich believed that Baron's unusual behavior might have something to teach her and her readers. She knew Baron's stories but not her personal "story," at least in the form that would yield to psychological inquiry. Baron had already been dead for more than three decades and there was no first-hand account of her life that provided the psychological insight Lieblich thought it might hold.

The scholar's narrative solution was a radical one. The text is organized into 24 imagined "encounters" Lieblich has with Baron in the last year of her life. Lieblich must abandon the empirical dogma of her discipline and experiment in narrative as she reconstructs Baron's life in her own voice (there are two "hers" in this text). "For a woman artist, one who strives to make her life her art—as a man might—something must occur, even if she invents it, unconsciously of course, to make her life swerve from the ordinary feminine course, the traditional one, to another plot completely, a special eccentric story" (p. 286). She uses material from Baron's stories and relies on interviews with people who knew the writer and her period to make her account as authentic as possible. Despite their differences, Lieblich came to identify strongly with Baron's personality, and "this empathy helped me construct her character until I saw her before my eyes as if she were alive, and heard her voice speaking to me" (p. x).

As her textual relationship with Dvora develops, Lieblich gradually gives up her professional vocabulary in favor of a more natural psychology expressed in a literary voice. In a particularly telling passage Lieblich has Baron urged to make her academic psychology resemble fictional narratives. "One should not work one's material too much; explanation only further obscures things. One must learn to direct one's vision so things become visible in their own light. The intelligent reader can sense what is there in the darkened room, in the spaces around the page" (p. 206). A "darkened room" with its deeply suggestive surrounding spaces, is hardly an image for a text likely to appeal to mainstream scholars. But it suitably represents what the narrative writer expects of the narrative reader.

## CONCLUSION

Our expectations are exactly what are at stake in the matter of teaching narrative. For Robert Madigan (1996), an ardent proponent of APA style and an opponent of more invention in the discourse of psychology, there are professional risks: "To encourage students to adopt a style other than the dominant language of the discipline is, to some extent, to make them pawns in the ideological contests engaging those who are already insiders. . . . Such a pedagogy does not empower students, but keeps them at the margins of a discourse community in which they cannot fully participate" (p. 654). With such complacency, and underestimation of the ability of students to choose for themselves, we consign young scholars—having the freedom from habit that more experienced writers can only envy—to the reproduction of stylistic "domination."

What role can inventive biographies play in teaching narrative, or in learning to be a scholar? As this essay suggests at the outset, there is the opportunity (or even the necessity) to overcome disciplinary parochialism. Another answer lies in what narratives generally do. Demos, echoing Josselson, asks a question on behalf of social and behavioral scientists: "Must we rest content with . . . self imposed limitations? Should we continue to leave the most basic, universal, and personally significant parts of all our lives to novelists, poets, philosophers, religious leaders, and their like? (1998, p. 1529). When I offer biography in my research methods courses it is precisely to move beyond such limits in scholarly convention. Thus, a student who took up *Conversations with Dvora* demonstrated how unexpected the results of committed reading can be. She wrote a narrative reflecting her relationship with Lieblich, imagining her as a dialogical partner in the same way the psychologist had imagined Dvora Baron. Students reading other biographies have learned from them how a well-constructed narrative uses incident, characterization, time, location, and dialogue not only to develop a story (representing the data) but to represent an author's sense of the powers and limits of the form, including its artistic and moral dimensions. In this sense "learning by doing" means activating consciousness of the operations and consequences of writing beyond what studying "methods" implies.

Focusing on reading in teaching narrative also addresses the conditions for learning. There is a jazz pianist who when asked about what he would want to know about a potential pupil responded: "I'd ask right away how much listening time that person had." He urges aspiring pianists to make themselves the students of artists they like, listening to them often, not for purposes of imitation but because "hearing great piano keeps you going as a beginner" (Adams, 1996, p. 247).

I have proposed here a version of this approach to the pedagogy of narrative, focusing on "reading" as a resource to "keep going." Every writer is also a reader. When we teach narrative, we tend to think about our students' writing as solely products of their research—even if it is text-based—rather than also as a form of practical criticism of their reading, in their field and others. A writer's preferences in narrative can come from the nature of problems he or she is investigating and also from a variety of compelling examples of scholarly storytelling, including lessons from biography.

When the novelist Lynn Sharon Schwartz (1996) proposes that "There may be as many kinds of reading as there are books, each one demanding its own form and degree of participation," she invites the multiplication of scholarly relativism even as she highlights more opportunities for subjectivity. If she has perhaps overstated the extent of textual invention, it is still the case that it is readers who give meaning to books, including making them part of their experience as apprentice writers. Because they have no existence apart from being read, so too do they call up in us, Schwartz says, something that is otherwise unavailable: "If we make books happen, they make us happen as well" (p. 118).

## REFERENCES

Adams, N. (1996). *Piano lessons: Music, love and true adventures*. New York: Delacorte.

Behar, R. (1993). *Translated woman: Crossing the border with Esperanza's story.* Boston, MA: Beacon Press.

Behar, R. (1996). *The vulnerable observer: Anthropology that breaks your heart.* Boston, MA: Beacon Press.

Behar, R. (1999). Ethnography: Cherishing our second-fiddle genre. *Journal of Contemporary Ethnography, 28*(5), 472–484.

Bruner, J. (1990). *Acts of meaning.* Cambridge, MA: Harvard University Press.

Clandinin, D. J., & Connelly, M. (2000). *Narrative inquiry: Experience and story in qualitative research.* San Francisco, CA: Jossey-Bass.

Demos, J. (1994). *The unredeemed captive: A family story from early America.* New York: Knopf.

Demos, J. (1998). In search of reasons for historians to read novels. AHR Forum on Histories and Historical Fictions. *American Historical Review, 103*(5), 1526–1529.

Denzin, N. K. (1997). *Interpretive ethnography: Ethnographic practices for the 21st century.* Thousand Oaks, CA: Sage.

Denzin, N. K., & Lincoln, Y. (Eds.). (2000). *Handbook of qualitative research* (2nd ed.). Thousand Oaks, CA: Sage.

Fulford, R. (2000). *The triumph of narrative: Storytelling in the age of mass culture.* New York: Broadway Books.

Geertz, C. (1988). *Works and lives: The anthropologist as author.* Stanford, CA: Stanford University Press.

Gergen, K. (1991). *The saturated self: Dilemmas of identity in contemporary life.* New York: Basic Books.

Goodman, J. (1998). For the love of stories. *Reviews in American History, 26*(1), 255–274.

Gubrium, J., & Sankar, A. (1997). *Qualitative methods in aging research.* Thousand Oaks, CA: Sage.

Josselson, R. (1999). Introduction. Ruthellen Josselson and Amia Lieblich (Eds.), *Making meaning of narratives* (pp. ix–xiii). Thousand Oaks, CA: Sage.

Josselson, R., & Lieblich, A. (1996). Fettering the mind in the name of "science." *American Psychologist, 51*(6), 651–652.

Lieblich, A. (1997). *Conversations with Dvora: An experimental biography of the first modern Hebrew woman writer* (N. Seidman, trans.). Berkeley: University of California Press.

Lieblich, A., Tuval-Mashiach, R., & Zilber, T. (1998). *Narrative research: Reading, analysis, and interpretation.* Thousand Oaks, CA: Sage.

McAdams, D. P. (1999). Personal narratives and the life story. In L. A. Pervin & O. P. John (Eds.), *Handbook of personality: Theory and research* (2nd ed., pp. 478–500). New York: Guilford Press.

Madigan, R. (1996). APA style: Quo vadis? *American Psychologist, 51*(6), 653–655.

Madigan, R., Johnson, S., & Linton, P. (1995). The language of psychology: APA style as epistemology. *American Psychologist, 50*(6), 428–436.

Marcus, G. (1994). On ideologies of reflexivity in contemporary efforts to remake the human sciences. *Poetics Today, 15,* 383–404.

Marcus, G., & Fisher, M. M. J. (1986). A crisis of representation in the human sciences. In G. Marcus & M. M. J. Fisher, *Anthropology as cultural criticism: An experimental moment in the human sciences* (2nd ed.). Chicago: University of Chicago Press.

Nelson, J. S., Megill, A., & McCloskey, D. (Eds.). (1987). *The rhetoric of the human sciences: Language and argument in scholarship and public affairs.* Madison: University of Wisconsin Press.

Nicholl, C. (1997). *Somebody else: Arthur Rimbaud in Africa, 1880–91.* Chicago: University of Chicago Press.

Price, J. (1999). In acknowledgment: A review and critique of qualitative research texts. In R. Josselson & A. Lieblich, (Eds.), *Making meaning of narratives* (pp. 1–24). Thousand Oaks, CA: Sage.

Schama, S. (1991). *Dead certainties: (Unwarranted Speculations).* New York: Knopf.

Schwartz, L. S. (1996). *Ruined by reading: A life in books.* Boston: Beacon Press.

Smith, M. B. (1994). Selfhood at risk: Postmodern perils and the perils of postmodernism. *American Psychologist, 49*(5), 405–411.

# 12

## BRAIDING ESSENCE: LEARNING WHAT I THOUGHT I ALREADY KNEW ABOUT TEACHING QUALITATIVE RESEARCH

MARGOT ELY

### PROLOGUE I

Once upon a time, some five years ago, the administrators of an urban school system requested of a university department chair that several of his professors and students take over a number of that system's elementary, junior, and high school classes. This would be for four days during which the regular teachers were involved in a professional development seminar. I volunteered.

My professional life was rooted in elementary education as a teacher of all grades and then as a professor. For the past 15 years or so, I have been deeply involved as a teacher of qualitative research, qualitative researcher, and writer about these. I teach a one-year course about qualitative field research in an interdisciplinary department. Most of the students enrolled in this class are earning their doctorates. Each year they represent a broad spectrum of majors—nursing, art, physical-occupational-music and dance therapy, higher education, English, early-childhood and elementary education, math and science education, and many others. I love the mix for their insights, experiences, talents, and passion. What's more, most go on to do fine qualitative research and complete fascinating dissertations. I am writing about this course.

This chapter is my attempt to weave what I learned—or perhaps relearned—from the short stint in fifth grade about the teaching of qualitative research in higher education.

# PROLOGUE II

This piece did not want to get written in the worst way.

I did not know the extent of my own conflict until one night, when at 3 A.M. I shook myself awake to my emphatic pronouncement, "Oh, tell them you just can't do it. Offer to write an chapter on A and R instead!" Now A and R is my shorthand for a phenomenon that invariably hits my university qualitative research students around the middle of our second semester. At that time, we are deep into considering alternate forms of analysis and presentation from field logs produced in the first semester. We create poems, pastiche, dramas, first-person narratives, layered stories, pictorial representations, and more (Ely, Vinz, Downing, & Anzul, 1997). At that point, *Avoidance* and *Resistance* become exquisitely complex but somewhat predictable art forms for many:

> I am not creative. How can I create now?
> This takes too much time.
> This is not acceptable research writing to my mentor/department/ profession.
> I can't speak in first person for someone else.
> I wasn't told I'd have to return to my log this way.
> I forgot.
> I'll do it next week.

Usually, I feel some fear in these forms of A and R—perhaps some anger, some frustration. I know. I am wonderful at A and R myself. And so, as instructor I spend some time in class facing the issues and attempting to help people look at and surmount A and R—especially in their support groups. By this time in our year, these groups are paramount to the process of qualitative research learning and teaching.

After all this, why do I introduce this piece with thoughts on A and R when, clearly, I am writing about something else? Or am I? Certainly, I was doing an A and R of epic proportion in trying to circumvent the airing of an experience that was at best bittersweet: My return to elementary school teaching for but a few days while at the same time carrying on with my university work. On reflection, however, this introduction does not seem all that specious. It points to A and R as instructive mechanisms that can alert us to some vital concerns as these weave their way through our doing qualitative research. In this case, I was a different sort of doer from how I carry out my usual qualitative research and teaching. I believe I experienced in heightened and slightly shifted perspectives how some of my university students must feel. And I relearned in a more concentrated personal manner what I thought I already knew: some crucial insights about teaching/doing qualitative research.

## MY RESEARCH PLAN—OF SORTS

I knew these days would be daunting in themselves, especially because I would do double duty in elementary school and at the university from 3 P.M. until late evening for three of the four days. I also knew that I must reflect on what was happening. I had no grandiose ideas about "doing a study" and in no way did I consider what we did an ethnography—blitzkrieg (Rist, 1980) or otherwise.

To document our experiences, we collected as much evidence as possible—videotapes, children's work, parents' notes, pictures. At night—often deep night—I wrote my impressions, observations, and thoughts in my field log during that and the following week. And I thought I was through. However, for the next four years the log took on a life of its own as I dreamed about the experience, reflected on it repeatedly, and discussed it. It was a force—a disquieting one—not to be subdued. Thus, the data we collected became the foundation of this chapter—a chapter not foreseen at the start but one that called to be written.

My path from research to writing about it had been—and is now—far more direct and consciously orchestrated. Never before had I been caught in a process that forced me to do such a double take. I believe that the change had to do with two issues. There was my emerging understanding of the insights I might clarify and communicate about how the elementary school experiences provided lenses on the teaching of qualitative research in higher education. Then there was the impact of my four days in fifth grade on what I had believed in and worked for all these 30-plus years, first as an elementary school teacher and then as a professor. That was a bit more sticky and surely the reason it took so many years for me to shift gears. I write to both of these issues throughout these pages.

The analysis of data for this chapter followed my usual pattern of acquaintance and reacquaintance of the narrative data, categorizing, lifting, searching for themes, megathemes, as well as unique cases, applying a variety of specific analytical tools—in this case, analyses of metaphors and what was not said or done (Ely et al., 1997). I shared my insights with two qualitative research colleagues in order to get their view of things.

On the following pages are some thoughts about what I consider to be crucial to the teaching of qualitative research in higher education and how it tied into the elementary school experience. In each instance, I introduce the topic briefly, present a topical picture of fifth-grade happenings, and then discuss more fully how I see that topic working with graduate students. Now for a bit of context.

# PAINTING THE SCENE: ENTRÉE ACTS

What am I doing here anyhow? Listening to the all familiar drone of school system officials telling us about their ways, their rules, our parameters, the children? "Our major problem is lateness and absenteeism." I wonder.

Here we are. A group of about 30 professors, graduate assistants, and teacher-education students invited to take over a number of classrooms in one public elementary school and one junior–senior high for four days. Four days! In a strange school with yet-to-meet students and other faculty, in the middle of the school year! Am I mad? Perhaps it is the passion for engaging children and their families that I honed as an elementary school teacher years before I entered the halls of "higher learning"? Perhaps the fire to face and overcome impossible odds? Perhaps to counter what I have heard and sensed so often: "These university people! They talk but they don't do." Whatever the reasons, I, fearful and awe-stricken, overplanned and underconfident, take the bus bleary-eyed at 7 A.M. for a ride to a community described by its representatives as blue-collar. My team of three stagger under the load of heavy boxes of books we might or might not need—rolls of construction paper, crayons, scissors, glue, videotape record-ers, audiotapes—as many accoutrements that we can wedge on our laps and under our feet in that yellow school bus without being bodily evicted by the rest of the people. Yes, three of us. John Maynard, my colleague, video and teaching support, and friend, who had staunchly seen me through any number of field projects; Sherrille Sheppard, an undergraduate senior in the program of special education, whose acquaintance I make that same day; and me. Note please that in this chapter I have changed and masked all names of persons, places, institutions—except for three. John Maynard, Sherrille Sheppard, and I have given ourselves permission to be identified.

Even before I meet the children of the fifth grade assigned to us, I am infused with the desire to see what might happen in this situation in such short time and with such tight restrictions. How could we build community if it needed building, empower learning, know children as individuals and in groups, develop trust, create ongoing curriculum, reach out to parents and caregivers, and have some fun? All this while being accepted or at least tolerated by the staff, faculty, and administration of the school we are about to enter? It does not bode well that in the first hour of my first day I am summoned imperiously and loudly on the P.A. to "come to the principal's office immediately." I had forgotten to sign in!

This gaffe and others I perpetrated during the four days would make a chapter of its own. If my colleague Neil Postman had not already thought up the title (1969), I would call it "Teaching as a Subversive Activity." However, none of this deters me from my dual aims: to see what can happen and to study the process qualitatively.

## SNAPSHOT: FIRST DAY

*Setting*: It is 8:10 A.M. John and Sherrille are rearranging the rows of desks into an oblong.

I am writing a hello on the board. Students may enter their classrooms after 8:10 A.M. Or so I think.

*Action*: I see a head peek into the classroom and, as I turn, the head pulls back in a flash. This head appears and disappears in a rhythm that I understand.

**Margot:** (singing) Come in! Come in! Whoever you are.
[No response. No head. No boy.]

**Margot:** Come in! Come in! This is your classroom. We'd love to see you.

**Jorge:** [craning his head in only to reply and to vanish again] No. We can't. We can't until the other bell.

**Margot:** But we're here. The room is ready. You can really come in. This is your room.

[No response. No head. No boy. No other children either, although I see them in a tight, shuffling line behind Jorge.]

*Note*: By the end of the week, the children enter easily as they arrive, all within the allotted time for entry.

At 3 P.M. of our first day, Sherrille, John, and I are sitting on the bus ready to return to the university for our various teaching and learning stints. We hold our heads in dismay and try to boost each other with hope. What we have found is a group of children so outer-directed and routinized that many make fun of, tattle, and stereotype each other. At first, they were bland if not suspicious of people who work with them in ways that communicate they have a stake in their school lives. In addition, it did not sit well with most of them that they must contribute and make some decisions, that mistakes are valuable for learning, that they can think creatively and deeply. Often, these children were self-deprecating when we asked something new of them ("*You* tell me what book to choose," "I don't have any thoughts about how today went and what we should do tomorrow") and automatic ("Let's vote"). It all makes perfect sense of course, but what a deeply depressing blow to my sense of what is owed children, to my sense of professional efficacy.

What we also found is a group who took quickly to our strange ways without too much hostility, children who were often funny and nice, and children we believed had an immense store of intelligence and possibilities. We liked them.

## MY AGENDA: THE "CURRICULUM"

I had pondered long about what we three would/could aim for in these days. The classroom teacher had left copious plans for almost every minute. One look told me that we could not go through that dry, test-driven stuff. My feeble excuse for not following along was that I saw the plans too late in the process.

How to carry on with interesting, real activities so that we could work within the aegis of our philosophical hearts while at the same time leaving evidence that the children learned? Indeed, that they learned many "skills and facts" and that they "behaved," because these were mentioned so often in our orientations. I knew we had to work within the confines of the school culture. I knew I had some latitude. (After all, what were they going to do? Fire me?) I also knew I was determined that the children bear no negative brunt for my curriculum choices. That was prime.

With the intuitive and rather wild confidence to take risks that I have developed as a teacher over the years, I presented a possible solution to the team. Why not engage the children in qualitative research strategies. It works for most doctoral students. Why not fifth graders? Maybe this could be the four-day tie that binds?

We set out to do just that.

## THE HEART OF THE WORK

Usually, huge appendices and long quotations put me off, so I hope that you, the reader, take kindly to my sharing three assignments we created. Implicit in each is what we were working toward, how we involved the children and their families, and, very important, a view of how we spent large chunks of time during our four classroom days to make it possible for the children to carry out the assignments, to own them.

---

**ASSIGNMENT #1**

Tuesday

Work for tonight:

1. Please find one person at home to talk with for about 10 minutes.
2. Explain that we are studying what people remember about growing up. This is called oral history. The people we are most interested in are the ones who are close to us, like our families, and ourselves, and our friends.

---

3. Ask "Tell me a little bit about how you grew up." Listen to what your person tells you. Ask other questions as you listen, but try not to interrupt too much.

4. Don't write while you are listening and talking.

5. Take about 10 minutes after your interview to make notes about what you learned from your person. We'll use our notes tomorrow to continue, so be sure to bring them in in writing.

6. Share this note with your family, please:

Dear Parents, Friends, Caregivers,
Thank you so much for being good sports and helping us to learn a bit about your story.

Sincerely,

Margot Ely with John Maynard and Sherrille Sheppard

---

**ASSIGNMENT #2**

Work at Home—Wednesday
Today please do an "oral history check."

1. Share your story about the interview with the person you interviewed. Give the person time to read it and to think.

2. Ask your person to tell you how she or he feels about your story. Did you tell it the way your person lived it?

3. Ask your person to tell you about 5 minutes more of information about how she or he grew up to make your story more: colorful—dramatic—complete. Take notes after the 5 minutes.

4. Bring notes to school so we can work on Thursday.

A note to the people at home: (please share)

Dear People:
We are having a wonderful time getting to know and work with your child. If you have something to tell us, we'd love to hear from you.

Thank you again.

John Maynard Margot Ely Sherrille Sheppard

## LINKS: INSIGHTS ABOUT TEACHING QUALITATIVE RESEARCH

### A Case for Interest and Involvement

We give much lip service to interest and involvement. Like apple pie à la mode, how can they be bad? It was not until this elementary school experience, however, that I gave voice to their tremendous power and, furthermore, finally crystallized why I strive so in teaching qualitative research at a university to support people's interest and its partner, involvement. It is true that interesting work interests me. But there is more to it.

*Fifth Grade*

Our tripartite team discussed often how quickly and happily the children took the choices we offered and made them their own. Whether we asked them to make seat arrangements, to learn to interview each other and us, to create personal time lines, to reflect orally and in writing, to run the video equipment and to study the ensuing video projects, to interview family members, to collect survey information, to write stories in first-person, and to create a variety of other narrative projects—poems, pastiche, drama—by and large, they jumped right in. They were interested. In addition, by the end of Day 1, they began to offer their own ideas for planning the next days. Subtly, planning changed from rote to something entirely different. Our team learned to accept most of their ideas even if at times we bit our lips: "Let's invite the 6th graders to come dance with us during lunch time now that we decided to stay in the classroom for lunch." As long as their suggestions made some sense and we could accommodate them, we went along. It was their world.

### Higher Education

At the beginning of our year together, I stand on my head in an effort to make the case that each person choose a field experience of high personal interest. As I see it, this field experience is not predetermined by what that person plans as dissertation research. Many doctoral students understand in a flash. They go off to study life in a bar, a hospital emergency waiting room, an AIDS support group, a church committee.

It is an understatement that some students have a very hard time with this. They "know" what they wish to study and feel that our research class should get them right into collecting data and, oftentimes, collecting data in specific ways: "I am going to interview. That is what I want to do here." Often, it makes little impact to explain that the purpose of our qualitative field research course is to learn a variety of ways of thinking about this research and many ways to collect and analyze data. Such a base can then help a researcher to make informed choices. With these people, I try to suggest fieldwork related to but of different scope than the intended study. So, if a person wished to do a dissertation about the interactions of a hospital hospice team, I might suggest she consider a study of hospice patients in a ward or at home, or a class of nursing students, or a patient group not in a hospice program, or a family support group. Many such students see the point and go to it. Some do not. Some attempt to hide their intentions and proceed to do "their" field project anyhow even though they know I would not agree happily.

A second group of dissidents are people who, in desperation to "get into the field" and to find a doable but not what they consider to be an all-consuming project, forego my urging of interest and select the nearest if not the most fascinating project. After giving it my best shot, I support them—albeit with a sinking sensation. In retrospect, I have been more right than wrong.

Overall, the people who select fieldwork of interest to them fly! It is amazing the kind of work they do and the depth of their commitment and involvement. In our ensuing year together, they find the time—often much more than I request—they feel they need in order to move their work and learning further. What is more, they do so gladly, generously, with off-beat humor—even if I suspect that their loved ones would throttle me cheerfully. Sometimes what they learn with their fieldwork is that they need to—want to—change what they first thought would be their dissertation focus to shape their research in ways they had not imagined before. Some even find new research topics. Mostly, that move—feared before—is made with élan and courage.

I have found that students who stick too closely to their prequalitative research course-determined project tend to have tunnel vision. Many find it difficult to see what the data are offering and do not move flexibly into the recursive cycles of qualitative work. There is too much at stake for these people. They have put down their markers and will not move them for a variety of reasons, among which may be a good dollop of fear. In our year, some of these students do, however, open up to other possibilities and often shed their too rigid limits. They may later return to their preplanned route, but usually wiser.

The people who select fieldwork that bores them—in which they find no path to interest even after having lived it for a while—are generally uneasy for the rest of the year. Sometimes, the second semester, with its emphasis on writing strategies and presentation devices, inspires them. However, I have found that mostly their work is thin and their spirits are low. Many of these people are the volunteers who ask to come speak to the next year's group about selecting a project of interest. They do a good job and, I hope, convince some students not to follow their footsteps. But I sit there and look at the new crew and think, "Here we go again."

Helping students catch on to their own interest takes time, patience, humor, and careful communication in class and out. Some professors of qualitative research give their own blanket field assignment: "This year we will study community school boards." Certainly, this is more direct, and some or many students do get interested. But it is not for me. I am after self-direction and fascination, if at all possible.

## And Then There Is Learning

All people learn. Some learn to kill. Some learn to ennoble their own lives and those of others! Still and all, Rogers and Hammerstein's "You've Got to Be Taught" speaks volumes. There is something about teaching—any sort of teaching—by self, others, environment, music—that helps us internalize, learn something.

What is that? How can learning be other than rote in a society that seems to love rote? What ingredients can make a difference? The fifth-grade experience cast a particular light on that issue for me as I considered teaching qualitative research at university.

## Fifth Grade

After taking the risk to enter what we offered, I can say that all children learned. Most learned voraciously the new strategies and routines each day. They practiced until they felt they "got it right," and when they did not, we and they worked out alternative solutions. Take a look at the following pastiche (Ely et al., 1997) by bringing to bear on it your own lens of learning. The pastiche was created from the fifth graders' reflections written at the end of each day.

In the doing, these children learned facts. That was obvious. They learned how to find facts, how to think about them, how to winnow, and how to put them together in ways that spoke to the rest of us. They learned about their families and themselves. And while the class did not always hum along peacefully and productively, we had lots more time when the buzz was about work, where the quiet was calm and supportive.

This is not to say that all children learned equally or as well. A few, three or four, never got too high off the ground. Their strategy, in the main, was to repeat what they already knew, what gave them security. I thought at times I would go ballistic if Orson did just one more of his comic strips! The three team members could sense these children's dis-ease, their nervousness, their putting on false fronts. These were the children who had been the butts of jokes and derision the first day, and they were usually at center stage when we had trouble spots in the ensuing three days. It seemed to the team that possibly their styles, needs, had been so highlighted, so accepted by all in that class that they had become pariahs, and there had been little or no effort to ameliorate this. We knew that, with all of our support and strategies, it would take more than four days to help these children turn around and, of course, the others with them. But we worked at it.

Two children also suffered from being stereotyped—in a different way, but, to us, just as destructive. They were highly verbal and described by other children as "the intelligent ones." These two boys knew it and let others know it, too:

> "This is easy. It's baby stuff."
> "This is a waste of my time."
> "I'm bored."

Previously, the way to handle this situation was to send the boys out several times a day to other classes considered more advanced or to the library. It came as a distinct shock to them—and probably to the others—

The most thing that I liked today was that you showed us how to work in a community

I liked when we had time for feedback on oral history. Tomorrow we should do different seating arrangements.

Tomorrow we can watch the video if we use it and have a good time interviewing and move our seats anyhow

and we got to dance in our own way

I liked it when we had Scholar Reading time. It was very fun to learn much more things than doing work

Today was very nice because we got to sit next to our friends and did not get into trouble once

I think we should interview and get more time to poloroid. John told us about his life and tomorrow Lana and I will interview John again

The time line worked for me because I was able to find things and remember

I would like to play chess tomorrow. I would like to play chess with Margot because she knows how to play. And I want to be camera person

# PASTICHE:
# PLANNING AND REFLECTION SNIPPETS

We learned to say good questions and what is a committee.
We did timeline this morning. Sherrille told a story about a boy who lived on a train track. Margot gave us books from the library.
I SUGGEST TOMORROW WE READ OUR WEEKLY READER BEFORE THE TEACHER COMES BECAUSE SHE' LL GET MAD IF WE DON'T

I want to ask you a question. What is your greatest desire (besides being a teacher) ?

It was good to watch ourselves on TV

think we should put our seats in groups of two- and we will help each other

I liked the oral history because we ask parents, friends to tell about how they grew up. We rewrote the notes today.

I liked personal choice time because I get to know more about things and people

She taught us that we shouldn't ask narrow questions. But ask good questions that I flatly refused this "solution." I bore the brunt of glaring looks for a day before they decided to surrender. There were plenty of challenging things for them to do and, while it seems like a Hollywood ending, they became creative and helpful class members for the rest of the time. I do not fool myself that this continued after we left.

## Higher Education

Qualitative research is founded on the creed that people have both similar and different attitudes, skills, temperaments, feelings. And while I might expect the adults who opt for doctoral work as well as for the qualitative research sequence to be more similar than not, I do not believe it for a moment. Who my students are, how they see life, their ways of learning, how they feel about themselves create a million-hued, ever-shifting rainbow. So, to involve them productively in two and a half hours once a week for two semesters becomes a mighty challenge.

To be sure, I believe we must have a set of core activities to use as springboards for amalgamation. That said, the core activities must contain opportunities for choice. Thus, while we all do a field project, the selection is centered on the individual. While we all write field logs, students are encouraged to create their own presentations within the guidelines for logs we have established together. While I insist that they take no notes during observations and interviews, the devices they use to recall—the audiotaped interviews, the maps, the word graphs, the scribbles in the hall or on the bus home, the "remembered quotes," the audiotape made in the car after the event—are their own creations—often taken up eagerly by others as these are shared. Individual style, it seems to me, must be honored as far as possible. In addition, in such a class, this is not a choice but a demand on the professor because, all else considered, qualitative research is learned by living it—by doing it—by honoring the precepts we write and talk about.

This is by no means easy. It takes a lot for me to insist that everyone practice a particular skill. Consider, for example, the not taking of notes in front of their participants while observing and interviewing. Here I am asking some students—perhaps many—to go against their very note-taking-centered professional and academic lives. So, while not taking notes is an immediate relief for some, for others it is frightening. I am asking people to act on faith because I know from experience how much they will learn from this, how much they will remember, how much the audiotapes will trigger their recall, and how this will support their semesters to come and their research after that. I also know it is of little use to tell some how they will open up to seeing more, to feeling more in tune with their participants, to being more trusted by them, to writing richer field logs, *if they would only drop their pencils*. So after a few tries, I insist. Most will do it. Some will not. They will continue to take notes in process, but they will not tell. This group usually "slips" in time, often when they share field logs and interact with their support groups. Their writing and speaking give them away. By this time, their slips are often grounds for supportive amusement. At that point, many will be ready to take the risk.

The issue is when, how, and why to insist and when, how, and why not to.

Many examples of the insisting dynamic come to bear because in my teaching I am so utterly convinced that people abstract and learn deeply as and after they engage in some action. Not a new idea. But it works itself out in many ways:

> Why do we have to write this ongoing field log? Why not only a few entries?
>
> (Wait a few weeks more when we begin to analyze, and next semester we'll analyze in even more complex ways.)
>
> Why do I have to choose my own field project?
>
> (Wait until you've "been in" for 5 weeks and then let's discuss it again.)
>
> Why must I mask names and places? After all, my participants want their real names in.
>
> (Why not read what others have to say about this? Source—Source—Source.)

And so it goes.

The trouble is that some qualitative literature is of no help at all in that it counters several of the strong stances I have developed as a researcher, teacher of research, and dissertation member. There are plenty of researchers and authors who take notes in full view of their participants and not after each data collection. Plenty who always construct detailed, predetermined interview guides for what they call "ethnographic interviewing." Plenty of people who identify by name and place. Plenty of qualitative researchers who still do not provide a personal stance. Plenty who still try to fit qualitative into quantitative thinking instead of honoring both in their place. At times, students use these sources to reason against the "believing game" I ask of them. Here I have to be strong in both my view of the work and in being open to revise that view when someone makes a good case. Generally, I rest on the fact that how I see qualitative work is honed by my experience and that my understandings about this have rarely led me or my students astray.

I must say that while the continuum of insisting on collegial decision making in learning clearly reared its head in elementary school, these children were very quick to trust and to play the game with very few naysayers. Maybe it was the shorter time and dramatic impact of three quirky, rather different people. Maybe it was relief in comparison. For many—not all—university students, there may be more at stake. "Is this scholarly?" "How do I learn what I believe I need?" "How can having fun be serious study?" "What is happening to my dissertation plans with all this new stuff?" "How will I use what I'm learning here?" "I love it, but will my department love it?"

Overall, and over two semesters, people learn an amazing amount. Far more than they envisioned. When the facilitators (to be described next) and I read their final logs, we gulp at the power of what we have set in motion and of how the students have made it their own. There are now literally scores of dissertations that attest to the success of our qualitative research students.

## Life Lines

I, who write about, espouse, create, and generally attempt to live by support systems in my university work, could not have imagined the importance of being part of such a system during my four days in fifth grade. Trite as it sounds, I could not have done it without my team. I am still reflecting on why I had not "known" this and why it shook me so. The closest I can come is that this was one intense, unique, frightening experience of such mesh and quality that it was essentially different from other teaching and qualitative research projects in which I had been involved. I needed a particular web of support.

### Elementary School

Without too much preplanning and to-do about how we would work, our team functioned as an integrated whole. Now there was a piece of luck! All I needed was to see the lift of Sherrille's left eyebrow to understand that I was being too pushy or had overlooked a child who wanted to talk. John's videotapes, while important, were not as important as John himself gently saying, "You know, Margot, why don't we get Juan and Annie to take charge of scholarly free reading time tomorrow?" I read his real meaning. We three rarely went into the purely congratulatory mode but, instead, celebrated some of our small victories by describing them and, often as not, having a good laugh. One result of this was that we pulled off from the other university people because we needed every shard of time and because even our lunch period was now spent in class. We talked and planned on the run—in the bus—and, quickly, before the class entered. Deeply exhausted at night, I faced my renewed respect for the teachers of this school, who surely carried an amazingly heavy burden of work each day, while at the same time thinking that I would never fit in such a context.

More than anything, our team of three trusted each other deeply— without a word being said. I knew I could make terrible blunders and it would be all right. I never felt put down, even though John and Sherrille faced me with some extraordinarily painful insights about me as teacher—and I am sure I returned the favor. We, who were such different people—age, gender, place in profession, religion, race, culture, life experience, disposition, style—were in tune at the start and in symphony at the end. I knew again that affect and cognition are unerringly and unbreakably united, no matter how much some of us try to tease them apart.

In a cycle, we felt good and often we felt we did good, and we did not know or care which came first.

Perhaps the children caught our spirit early on. They, who had not done so before, worked increasingly and productively in small groups, usually self-selected. But this succeeded only when group tasks were meaningful. Fortunately, our qualitative research curriculum provided more than enough stuff of interest, involvement, and self-direction to most. As the days went by, the children did appreciably less tattling and bad mouthing, and we laughed together more.

Not perfect, but a lot closer to what we wanted.


*Higher Education*

By now, almost all who know and work with me understand my dedication to helping qualitative research students form and maintain support groups. This is not an extra, even though away from class it is a noncredit extra contribution many students make to their own education. Support groups are essential to the process as I see it. They are the amalgam to help students own their development as researchers—the instrument whereby they can shift the classroom power balance from teacher-centered to collegial. My view is that more than most researchers, qualitative people need to be both deeply independent and collegial. So in their university courses, they need to relearn, reexperience, and hone the stances many of them left behind in infancy or childhood.

In this section, I center on some aspects of support-group formation and ensuing work that I have found particularly helpful, with the proviso that every teacher has unique ways and may well shape these suggestions or throw them out entirely.


**Some Suggestions About Support Groups**

- Help students form support groups early on in the first semester. Provide a flexible group experience in the second session. We usually chart and discuss some readings in groups we have made by counting off. Ask these "accidental" groups to assess how they worked. Share in large groups.

- Plan one or two other group experiences during third and fourth sessions. By that time, students will have worked with people they know and with those they are meeting for the first time. They will have had an opportunity to be members of different groups from their first, although some love their first group and stay together.
- Complete the process by end of fourth session. Emphasize that people will be asked to reconsider this grouping after the next few sessions.
- Emphasize—insist—that a support group may not consist entirely or in majority of people from the same program. Further emphasize that the more varied the programs of the group members, the more varied the group members themselves—for example, they need not all be at the same place in doctoral work—the better the support groups have functioned and served each other. (Horrors!)
- Ask people to rely on their intuition to create a support group. Ask them to take a leap of faith.
- Request that each support group create an agenda of how members will share pieces of their work and how they will allot time to each member for discussion and feedback of work read. We constitute groups of four to five members, request all members to give chunks of logs to each other every week for reading and responding over that week, and to select two people for particular feedback the next week. At times, every member shares a piece of writing by reading aloud.
- Build in time for support group meetings in ensuing class sessions. At times, weave in opportunities for groups to consider other work being done in class and via readings as well as to meet their own agenda. For us, groups work well as they consider entrée, their ideas for useful field logs, and a host of issues that spring up from their ongoing work.
- Explain that field logs must be begun *before* each student enters the field to catch feelings and plans and questions—and continued every week thereafter. These budding field logs provide a wonderful sharing and working core.
- After about three meetings, ask support groups to consider how their group is functioning, what might be needed for it to function better, and what, for individuals, cannot be worked out in this group.
- Be ready to maintain a supportive, flexible stance if some people opt to move to other groups.

- During the year, ask groups to assess their process several times.

Now comes the place when I write more deeply of people I have been hinting about at the edges: the facilitators. Facilitators—one per group—are a magnificent help. In my case, often these have been students from the past year's sequence who want to continue noncredit and/or to take on other roles in the teaching/learning of qualitative research, some faculty colleagues who wish to take part in the year-long process, some people who are writing their dissertations and who feel they would like a shot of vitamins. The bulk of these people volunteer their time—which is substantial. They attend and take part in every class for the year and, when groups are formed, they read one group's work as well as carry out particularly important roles in facilitating the group process. Often, the university comes up with a small honorarium and a few facilitators sign up for independent study, which I then mentor. It is extremely fortunate that these people are, thus, integral to the teaching team.

Before they select their groups and vice versa, facilitators spend a session with several groups. After selection, facilitators usually stay with the same group for the semester and often for both. This choice is flexible for them, as it is for the students.

I spell out the roles of facilitators as clearly as I can to them and to the class, but what I know is that understanding comes from the experience itself. What we aim for is facilitation, often indirect, that supports group members increasingly to take on their own responsibilities and direction. What we do not aim for is a facilitator—boss—star—lecturer—answerer of all questions, who makes people increasingly more dependent in the process. This is essential. And it is subtle. And it is hard, especially for people who may love to "parent" in particular ways. So ongoing teaching team communication and feedback are key. We go to dinner after class! And, yes, I, too, am a facilitator for one group, and often I read the work of other groups on a rotating basis.

Now that facilitators have been introduced, I can return to the list:

- Plan that support group meetings take on increasing importance and time per class session so that by the second semester support-group work constitutes almost the entire session and the roles of facilitator shift in the main to observer and listener.
- Help groups practice increasingly sophisticated feedback techniques for each other's work. We use a variety of ways to help them do that (Ely et al., 1997, pp. 320–328). For example, one response scheme we have found useful was suggested by Chris Anson (1989). This highlights responses that range from those about surface features and discourse conventions to responses

that solely express pleasure or lack thereof about the writing, to more multilayered reflective responses that offer the writer some options in rethinking the work.

A few sticking points in the support group process emerge each year with striking similarity. Some students are determined to work only with their program mates—usually preselected—and have the most detailed rationales for this:

"We've already begun."
"We have a lot of good history together."
"We work supremely well with each other."
"We won't let program issues get in the way."

When I have gone along with this, it has not worked well most often. The group so constituted is in danger of acting like an "in-group" and of being seen that way. They are too close, too familiar, too ready to talk of other things such as their classes, their professors, their other projects. They pay less attention to the work at hand and are not as ready to provide consecutive, meaningful, written feedback to each other. Often, they do not face each other with difficult but vital insights. I am always surprised that they also do the most griping about our qualitative research activities. Some very brave of these students break the line and change groups along the way. This has worked well for them.

Of course, there are exceptions to this phenomenon, especially where there is no choice but to constitute support groups of people from same or similar programs and professional contexts. There is also the matter of people from the same program who play the qualitative research support game superbly well and do not fall into the traps I described above. I have been blessed to work with some of these.

There are groups with other problems from the start. The membership is too disparate. Some faithfully read and comment on what others hand them. Some are "too busy." Some are not smooth group members; they may be scathing or pull off from group action. Some are generous in work and interaction; some are miserly. At times, the other group members' readings differ so drastically from what the writer set out to do that they create doubt, confusion, or defensiveness instead of support. Sometimes, indeed, the very amiability and support a group provides mask the fact that they are giving poor advice that is then accepted by the writer. Sometimes, the group climate is such that a person opts quickly to join another group. We have found that lots of these jagged edges are smoothed out in the first few weeks as people see each other's serious intent and work, and as facilitators extend sensitive and knowledgeable input about group process during group meetings. Often, the very person about whom we tear our collective hair turns out to be a strong member and a group favorite on settling down and experiencing others' real attempts to understand and support a particular style. Humor helps. At times, the facilitators work individually with a person when this seems called for. At times, a person has a private talk with me.

Some, very few, groups never make it. The groupiness, the dynamic, turns them off or they find other sources of support—human, literature, Internet. After our year, some prefer to go it alone.

That all said and done, the great majority of support groups work beautifully (Ely et al., 1991, 1997). Often, the groups hold together after our course year and even past the time each member has earned a doctorate. Some go on to network together as they continue their publications.

It is a particular joy to see the support groups huddled in some offbeat university corners, avidly at work, and to see them attend—en masse— each other's final dissertation orals. That's my real pay.


## WHAT I DID NOT SAY

In the mid-1980s, my friend and colleague Ruth Vinz stunned and elated me by writing a chapter in her dissertation—and later in her book (1996)—about what she did not say. This was long before the risen star of studying the unsayable and silence (Rogers et al., 1999; Taylor, Gilligan, & Sullivan, 1995)—at least in present research days. The sensibility of what Ruth did bowled me over because I saw in a flash that, of course, what we do not say is often important—nay critical. It tells us something.

I now want to ponder on what I did not say in this chapter. This is another product of narrative analysis. To carry it out, I studied the preceding pages in several rounds in order to consider and face what was not there that might be or should have been. I will next highlight what I consider the most telling skipped areas. "Aha!" you say. "And thereby talking about what you didn't say in the first place." Exactly. That is the intent of this analysis. But brief.

### Linking the Introduction

I did not discuss my reasons for creating such a multifaceted introduction with its various narrative devices, my feelings on writing this chapter, the two prologues, entrée, the "curriculum," the research plan, and, in all of these, my stance as a person and as a person who is a researcher and teacher.

Actually, I felt the reader would understand that I was working to build a collage a person could walk into, something palpable. Something consonant with qualitative presentation forms that send messages above and beyond their words (Atkinson, 1990, 1992; Ely et al., 1997). It is the only way I choose to write this.

## Going Native

I did not describe and discuss the phenomenon of going native, although John, Sherrille, and I did this with amazing frequency. We were so much "with" the children that we bridled at the seemingly hundreds of routines and rules that may have been understandable in this school but that functioned to mold them and their days. Toilet at the same time for everyone, permission slip to bring a sister in another class her forgotten lunchbox, parent signature for a 5-minute lateness. For me, the apogee came when I took on a gym teacher who was yelling at one of "my" children and giving him homework: "Write 100 times: I will not be rude in gym."

We did not forget that we had to fit in. We did not lose track of making creative solutions where we could. We were not sent packing. But in our heads, we had lost it. Our perspective was with the children and their families. And we chafed.

It seems to me that there is a clear tie to teaching qualitative research. I will never again find it amusing when a student goes native, or get annoyed that this person obviously does not see what needs to be seen. Going native itself needs to be explored more deeply. The trick, I think, is keeping the passions inherent in it, while at the same time working to build a fair vista, a balance.

## Ripples on Self; Ripples on Participants

I did not discuss the heartwarming ties created by the children with members of their families by involving them in qualitative strategies, how generous the adults were with their time and comments, how proud and excited the children were to know new things about a grandmother, mother, or uncle, and to write their stories. Here is a sampling of three first-person accounts:

*My Grandmother Speekes: My Story*
I was born in 1943. I lost my father in Cuba. I went to school up to sixth grade and I worked when I was 7 or 8. I got married at 14. I was sad. I had my first child. Had my second child. Had my third child. All in Cuba. It hurt a lot. I went to America in 1972 because my husband said it would be good there. I cried a lot. I had my forth child in America and had stress because I was haveing a baby.
Javier

*My Mother Speaks: My Life*
I am Nora Lopez. I was born in New York, Manhattan. I lived in a 5 room apartment. My sister was Mari Vega now she is Mari Blanco. We both had different fathers. My father left me yrs. ago. I stayed with my mother and cook, cleaned and did luandry. I went to Cathlik school.

When I went to college that is were I met my first boyfriend. When I was 16 I married him. I had to get out 6 weeks before grauchain. My husband stayed in school to get a job. I would go to school next but he left me 5 years later. And now I work in a supermarket. Before that I had 3 jobs but now it is back to normal.

Lydia

*My Life (Mom speaks)*

I lived in a different house in Puerto Rico because that my parents separated. I had to live with my aunt. They kicked us out of the house because we didn't pay the rent. I had to clean house because my mother didn't want to work—but only me. I was 10 years old and I had to cook dinner, iron the cloth, wash the floor and the cloth.

My friend showed me Bill. I dated him. We got married and had a great party in my house. I have three daughters, Janet, Tatiana and Duvi and two sons, Norman and Eugenio. I used to work in a factory and a grocery store. I am 42 years old.

Tatiana

During our time, a number of family members would find the opportunity just to peek in the room. None would come in when invited.

The link to teaching qualitative research underscores again how often our participants tell us they feel enriched, listened to, respected and not judged by us and our research. While many university students fear that a participant check will turn sour, that an interview will be too long, that they will lose their participants, actually the opposite happens. We are in a powerful, integrating, supportive human process.

## Full Circle

I hinted at but did not discuss fully why the four-day teaching experience was so bittersweet. Certainly, wonderful things happened. The children came through in amazing ways. Why then did I leave so depressed? Why could I not write of it until five years had passed?

On reflection-writing, I know now that these four days stand as a critical incident in my life. What is more, my grasp of and work about both education and qualitative research has been invigorated all out of proportion to the limited time spent with that fifth grade. Somehow, and without foreknowledge, there was a lot on the line for me. It seemed that my entire professional life, my passion for children, my credo for what education might be, my fear that in all these years I had busily done nothing at all to move the situation forward—all this and more shone like a laser beam on these four days.

I did not want to face some of my dismal feelings. And I certainly did not want to write about them.

I know some of the ingredients of this brew. We had our starting doubts about a four-day shot. How fair was it to the children when even during the last day we could see our victories washing away? What would we be doing to the children's views of themselves, of schooling? I have always decried the practice of a consultant or visitor coming in to do a splendid thing—and then leaving. Too easy. Yet that is what I did.

Then there was the shock and anger at how we found the children and the sinking feeling about their chances after we left.

Very important, essential, there was also the weighty knowledge that we were privileged. We could do things not allowed classroom teachers in such a school. We changed the "curriculum," we changed the seating, we changed the rules, we changed student–teacher relationships, we changed the books and materials. We never tested. We never punished. And there were three of us! It was quite understandable, as a student wrote me later, that the teacher went back to her arrangements and ways with great determination now that we had gone.

Teaching must be seen in its context. In some fashion, we were not of that context. I cannot say I would do it differently, but I do know that the culture and the press on teachers must be better understood and acknowledged if they are to be involved in their own development. Qualitative research can help us in that quest both by providing complex description of school-community life and by serving as one instrument for self-study.

## REFERENCES

Anson, C. M. (1989). Response styles and ways of knowing. In C. Anson (Ed.), *Writing and response: Theory, practice and research* (pp. 332–366). Urbana, IL: National Council of Teachers of English.

Atkinson, P. (1990). *The ethnographic imagination: Textual constructions of reality*. London: Routledge.

Atkinson, P. (1992). *Understanding ethnographic texts*. Newbury Park, CA: Sage.

Ely, M., Anzul, M., Friedman, T., Garner, D., & Steinmetz, A. (1991). *Doing qualitative research: Circles within circles*. London: Falmer Press.

Ely, M., Vinz, R., Downing, M., & Anzul, M. (1997). *On writing qualitative research: Living by words*. London: Falmer Press.

Postman, N., & Weingarten, C. (1969). *Teaching as a subversive activity*. New York: Dell.

Rist, R. (1980). Blitzkrieg ethnography: On the transformation of a method into a movement. *Educational Researcher, 9*(2), 8–10.

Rogers, A., Casey, M., Ekert, J., Holland, J., Nakkula, V., & Steinberg, N. (1999). An interpretive poetics of languages of the unsayable. In R. Josselson & A.

Lieblich (Eds.), *The narrative study of lives* (Vol. 6, pp. 77–106). Newbury Park, CA: Sage.

Taylor, J. M., Gilligan, C., & Sullivan, A. G. (1995). *Between voice and silence: Women and girls, race and relationship*. Cambridge, MA: Harvard University Press.

Vinz, R. (1996). *Composing a teaching life*. Portsmouth, NH: Boynton/Cook.

# 13

# DIALOGIC PEDAGOGY: DEVELOPING NARRATIVE RESEARCH PERSPECTIVES THROUGH CONVERSATION

MARY GERGEN AND SARA N. DAVIS

In this chapter we have two major goals: To illustrate how a continuing conversation between us over a prolonged period led to the development of a research project in narrative studies and to explore several significant issues related to this project. Our chapter is formed in a manner that is designed to fulfill the mandate of this volume, that is to address issues of pedagogy in the teaching of narrative methods. Through a reconstruction of five "conversational moments" in which we represent how we develop a narrative research project, we try to demonstrate how a class might be structured as a dialogic encounter among teachers and students.

Our approach is born out of a commitment to social constructionist viewpoints, which encourage the co-creation of knowledge among interlocutors (Gergen, 1999). We hope that our dialogic experiences can serve as encouragement to teachers and students in all educational milieus. Because of the pedagogical aims of this chapter, we have been selective in how we have presented our encounters. The text suggests a coherence that exceeds that which we normally achieve in our everyday talk. After each conversation we have created a section designed to raise questions that we believe have particular pedagogical significance.

We wish to thank the editors and the anonymous reviewers of our chapter, who through their kind and helpful comments helped to improve the richness and coherence of our text.

## CONVERSATION 1: FRESH SLATES AND FANCY IDEAS. AT MARY'S BREAKFAST ROOM TABLE

We meet to discuss the possibility of doing a research project to explore midlife transition narratives of women. The impetus for this is the call for papers from Ruthellen Josselson and Amia Lieblich, who are engaged in creating a new volume in their series, *The Narrative Study of Lives*. We are particularly drawn to the issue of life transitions for women who have reached a mature age and are often confronted by debilitating narratives, especially disphoric menopausal ones (M. Gergen, 1990, 2001; Martin, 1987). We are interested in investigating stories of women's lives that may be more satisfying than what is currently available on the "dry goods" shelves of developmental psychology. As we talk, we begin to imagine the diversity of stories we might expect from our inquiries. We talk about the terms of our investigation, especially the meanings of *midlife* and of *transition*. The terms that seemed clear at the outset of our conversation become murky and complex. We wonder whether or not all midlife women have stories to tell of transition. Perhaps there are individual differences to be found, with some women telling very disjunctive or transformative stories and others, stories that are seamlessly smooth. Perhaps some have no stories to tell at all.

With concern for the nature of the interviewing questions themselves, we ask: To what extent will we be framing a woman's life story for her if we ask her to tell a story of transition? What if we were to ask for stories of continuity instead? Further inquiry leads us to consider the possibility of a situation in which certain areas of a woman's life might be framed as transitional narratives—the departure of children from the home, a divorce, or a death in the family, and others as continuity narratives—staying in the same occupation, neighborhood, religion, or friendship circle. In addition, what is viewed as transitional by an outsider in a person's life might not take on that status for the narrator. A story of being promoted may seem to be a transitional narrative to an interviewer, but not to the storyteller. The rate of the transition may also vary. While one woman might tell of the departure of her children as a story of dramatic change, another might view their leaving as having occurred gradually and without disruption, perhaps even with mild relief. We conclude that the stories generated in interviews would depend very strongly on how the questions are posed. If we assume transitional narratives are normative, we might encourage these stories. If we are more open-ended in our questions, we might be surprised by a greater diversity of responses.

We also talk further about social science theories of women at midlife. It seems clear to us that much of psychology has little to say that is positive about the lives of maturing women and much to say about negative transitions, especially around the time of menopause (Bart, 1971; Chrisler, John-ston, Champagne, & Preston, 1994; Dalton, 1972, 1983; Gannon, 1985; Lock, 1993).[1] Also, in clinically oriented theories, especially within psycho-dynamic traditions, the loss of fertility has been taken as a significant marker of a woman's changing personality and motivational structures (Deutsch, 1945). Menopause-related changes around age 50 serve as the symbol for transition in the popular literature and are deeply symbolic in the culture in general (Agee, 2000; Formanek, 1990; Greer, 1993; Jacobowitz, 1996; Landau, Cyr, & Moulton, 1995; Sheehey, 1998; Wulf, 1980).

We discuss how our culture is becoming increasingly interested in menopause as a "market issue" as demonstrated by the growing attention to health-care products designed to counteract the symptoms of this so-called medical condition. We ask ourselves: Can we find ways of escaping the powerful central tales of the culture today, or are we trapped within them? If people *can* tell multiple stories, which ones are more influential in shaping women's lives? Must some not inevitably be more powerful than others? Acknowledging the "ageist" assumptions about women's lives, we discuss the importance of finding (and expanding) the range of stories for women. If we are to interview a number of women will they tell what we feel have been identified as tales of loss or will they surprise us with stories of strength? Will our presence as interviewers, with our own possibly more positive outlooks on midlife, have an impact on those who we interview? What would the consequences of such an approach be? Would not the function of our research become more than simply providing our version of what narratives are prevalent in the culture? Would it not also provide some generative possibilities for our respondents? The research might become a critical wedge creating a cleavage between the certainty of aging as a process of decline and more positive possibilities. This option opens the function of research to new definitional dimensions, as well as new dangers.

The last topic on this fruitful day relates to a concern Sara voices: So often when narratives are collected, researchers in their zeal to support theoretical positions or hypotheses strip the storyteller of the story. Very special stories are combined for analytical purposes so that the details of the particular are crushed and molded into an overarching thematic form, one that supports the rhetorical power of the argument most strongly. We recall Margery Franklin's concerns about how she will deal with these and other similar issues when interviewing a group of artists who were also her

---

[1] Although we wish to argue that the mainstream of developmental psychology has a disphoric view of women in midlife and later, we also wish to acknowledge that many new avenues for more optimistic futures for mature women have been created in the last decade, especially in narrative psychology (Datan, 1986; Gergen, 2001; Komesaroff, Rothfield, & Daly, 1997; Stewart & Ostrove, 1998).

friends (1997). We remember Ruthellen Josselson's sensitivity to the nuances of individual stories in *Revising Herself* (1996). Mary realizes that she has not thought enough about the liberties researchers typically take with individual stories. She ponders whether her own zeal for abstractions has made her too willing to disrupt the unity of individual stories. As much as possible, we agree to keep the integrity of any individual's story intact.

## Issues of Pedagogical Potential: Conversation 1

1. What does it mean to say that "research is a process of socially constructing the world?" What are the consequences of declaring that there are no "objective" narrative methods?
2. In what ways can our questions and responses to interviewees regulate the research conversation and its outcomes?
3. How can narrative research take on a critical function, one that closely evaluates the current cultural repertoire of stories and themes?
4. How can research serve a generative or creative function, one that introduces new narratives into the culture and individual lives? How might this function create new definitions for research?
5. How can one respect the integrity of single stories, even though research work, by definition, requires selection, compression, and interpretation? What does it mean to say: "The average of everything may not be a description of anything."

## CONVERSATION 2: TEXTUAL FRIENDS AND MOUNTING COMPLEXITIES: AT SARA'S KITCHEN TABLE

We bring to the table the books, articles, journals, and other literary resources we have collected over the past year on narrative research.[2] We know that it is important to consider theoretical as well as practical interests when embarking on a research endeavor. We look to other narrative scholars for their guidance and examples. We share and exchange readings that seem to each of us important resources to expand our potentials for research. We are both excited and wary of our enjoyment of this stage of the process and our proclivity for proliferating ideas far beyond what is useful for the day. Our conversation stimulates even more puzzlements and caveats. In particular we

---

[2] Some of the more significant resources that guided our path, in addition to the references cited, include Fonow & Cook, 1991; Personal Narrative Group, 1989; Reinharz, 1992; Ribbens & Edwards, 1998; Rosenwald & Ochberg, 1992; Sarbin, 1986; Sarbin & Kitsuse, 1994; and Vaz, 1997.

are absorbed by ethnographic research in which researchers have written their work in such a way as to represent their research respondents and themselves as multivocal, that is, speaking/writing themselves as having more than one subject position (Denzin & Lincoln, 2000; Ellis & Bochner, 1996; as well as many of the articles published in *Qualitative Inquiry*.)

We explore the assumption that people are composed of multiple selves and what it means for narrative research if people harbor many different voices and different stories. If it is the case that people can become different selves as they move through life and, as a consequence, tell different stories of their lives, must they settle on any single one, even in a particular situation? More precisely, what factors in the interview situation inhibit certain selves, and certain versions of a life story and activate others? We know that the interviewer is one important factor in this choice.

We do think there is much to ponder here. It is almost overwhelmingly complex. Sara brings forth two examples in which people have told life stories with multiple voices. It is clear from her examples how important being able to tell multiple stories has been in shaping each of their lives. In the first, Gail Landsman (1998) wrote about how she constructed a story about her daughter who was born with physical problems so severe that she was in a coma near death; on the tenth day of life, she began to breathe on her own. Rather than telling a story of the baby along the ominous story lines projected by the doctors, she described a miracle baby who has "fought back from the very brink of death" (p. 69). Landsman emphasizes the marvelous, even miraculous, aspects of this feat. "It is a story I now tell often. . . . The way I usually tell it, DJ's is a story of triumph over adversity, of a victory of the human spirit against the odds. It is a true story. But it is only one of many I could choose to tell" (p. 70). Landsman also has other less positive stories in her repertoire, such as how this is a disabled child who may never walk or talk, how drained and exhausted she is much of the time, and how doctors were guilty of malpractice in their treatment of her child. For her, the multiple versions co-exist to be told to herself and others as circumstances invite.

The second of Sara's examples is of Lisa Scottoline, well-known mystery writer, who also was able to restory her life to better support her risk-taking activities during a critical juncture.[3] At one time she was a single mother, with very little income, who had relinquished her law practice in order to become a novelist. She used the last of her savings to make a copy of her first book manuscript; she felt very guilty for doing this, as she saw herself putting her desire to publish her novel ahead of her child's daily needs. Scottoline made a conscious decision to reconsider the story she was telling

---

[3] Scottoline told this story in a talk at Rosemont College, April 2000.

herself and to find a way to shape it differently. She told herself a story of finding a publisher, sending off the manuscript, having the book published and becoming a great success. This new story enabled her to keep the novel-writing enterprise alive and altered her perspective on what it was she was doing, including taking good care of her daughter. As it turned out, her story was well-received; the book was published to critical acclaim and she is now a successful author. For her, the ability to imagine an alternative story probably changed the course of her life.

We talk together about what these examples help us to understand. In both of these instances there was a conscious use of stories—and changing one's story held the key to a more creative and promising lifestyle. Both were aware that there were benefits to being able to retell one's story. They were also comfortable with the ambiguity that resulted from abandoning the seeming surety of a single story and accepting the condition of shifting from one story to another. Each discovered that there was more than one story that could form their experiences. There were several possible stories that they imagined and played with; the capacity to do this enhanced their options. Sara and I agree that what is striking about these examples is that not only are they examples of restorying in service of justifying one's past actions, they involve a conscious alteration of the story lines to expand possibilities in the ongoing lives of the tellers. These stories serve to create new identities for the tellers.

We talk again about the various conditions that might lead people to recast their stories, either consciously, as in the stories above, or without being aware that they are doing so. Although people might do this easily in their lives, how could we conduct interviews that would mirror the process so that we could study it more closely? And if we did succeed, what then? Would we create something that would never otherwise exist? Would we risk missing styles of talk in their "natural" state? And how could we gauge the impact our own presences might have on the process? We wonder particularly about the relationship of interviewer and interviewee, as it might change over time. Franklin (1997) has shown how different styles of interviewing have the potential of either freezing content or enabling fresh perspectives to flow at the time of the interview. Shulamit Reinharz (1992) has written about examining her field notes taken during the course of a year at one of her ethnographic sites. She noted that as her involvements with her research participants lengthened and friendships developed, the nature of the materials she collected became more revealing and at the same time more in conflict with the original stories that had been told. This is to say that the identities of the interviewer and the interviewed were destabilized as an outcome of their relational conjoining in space/time. The notion that a person might be "known" through the narrative is less and less believable.

At this point our energies flag and the mood at the table becomes somewhat depressed. What is there left in the shifting sands of narrative instabilities on which to launch our research? Surely the notions that research is the discovery of objective facts or firmly based on grounded theory does not stand. We cannot even take much comfort in a postmodernist position, which accepts the mutable, the transient, and the relational nature of the true. We must take our satisfaction in research endeavors that only give us glimmers of temporary truths. There must be more.

### Issues of Pedagogical Potential: Conversation 2

1. How should one balance the desire to do research that develops from issues of everyday life with that which is spurred by theoretical or empirical interests derived from the research literature? Why is it important to be aware of the ongoing "conversations" in one's field?
2. What are the consequences of the capacity of people to tell multiple stories of themselves? What does it mean that stories are not necessarily told consistently over time or place?
3. If stories are co-created in social settings by individuals whose identities are formed within that relationship, is it possible to understand who the storyteller is?
4. If each story is embedded in specific space/time coordinates, what are the consequences for doing narrative research?
5. How should a researcher work with multiple, fragmented stories? Of what value is this type of research?

## CONVERSATION 3: TELLING MULTIPLE STORIES: AT THE COFFEE KLATCH, MEDIA, PA

Today as we are chatting, two of our acquaintances stop by the table, and we spend some time talking with them about our project. We are eager to try out some of our ideas with them. They join us for a time to chat about midlife stories. During the discussion, Anne volunteers a narrative about her life, which has the theme that the "fifties" for her are a time of feeling useless and uncertain about her future. As the conversation moves on, however, she begins to describe multiple interests and involvements that make her life seem much fuller than what she had originally suggested. Her tone of voice becomes more vibrant as she describes a spiritually oriented quest she has embarked upon with her partner. She states that she is very satisfied with her everyday life. Before our very eyes we find support for the ideas that people can quite easily move within the same conversational space from one kind of story to another. Later, alone, we again ask ourselves: What variety of stories could people tell? When and where are different stories told? What functions do these diverse tellings serve?

After Anne and Sue departed, the conversation between us takes a dramatic turn. We basically give up our project of studying the midlife stories of women and decide to direct our efforts precisely to questions related to the context and conditions that facilitate particular narrative expressions, as well as the conditions for changing them. We are turning over a new leaf in our research history together.

If we ask people about their own potentials for polyvocality, would we find that they could tell multiple stories about different stages of their lives? Would our interviews reveal this to them even if they were previously unaware of it? Could people accept their own multiple perspectives and react in such a way as to begin again within the same space/time coordinates to retell their lives? Or is this too difficult an adjustment for most people? This would be a fascinating research endeavor in itself; moreover, it would endanger some of the sureties of narrative researchers who usually presume that the raw material of narratives with which they deal are stable enough to draw conclusions about the tellers.

We also consider the relationships that are developed between researchers and those who produce narratives in terms of sharing theoretical perspectives. Narrative researchers often do not involve their interviewees with the details of their theoretical investments. We wonder if most researchers, no matter how well-intentioned, do not tend to approach their participants with a "need to know" orientation, that is, to tell them a sufficient amount such that they agree to enter into the research and no more. We consider doing otherwise—opening up the purposes of our research as much as possible to our respondents—letting them see totally through the research veil—encouraging them to join us on our quest for how meaning making is done—listening attentively to their ideas. We are eager to continue this conversation.

### Issues of Pedagogical Potential: Conversation 3

1. Is it possible that a research interview can assist a narrator to become more aware of the ways in which narratives are used to create meaning?
2. How can one explore the conditions that bring about certain narrative expressions and those that may transform them?
3. What are the consequences of sharing or not sharing one's theoretical positions with participants? To what extent might researchers be advantaged by taking respondents into their confidences? (Stewart, 1994)

## CONVERSATION 4: TAKING ACTION AND SHARING DISCOVERIES; AT SARA'S KITCHEN TABLE

We decide it is time to stop drinking tea and talking about the immense challenges of doing narrative research and act. We have abandoned our original idea to ask midlife women about their stories of transition and focus directly on the question of polyvocality in narrative research. We plan to proceed by conducting a limited number of interviews in order to explore the types of responses we will get when we encourage people to consider their polyvocal potential in telling stories of life transitions. We will be open with our respondents about what it is we hope to achieve and provide examples of ways in which people construe their lives in multiple ways.

Specifically, our plan is to ask people to tell us a story of a life transition of their choice. We will stress that the story may be about any topic they choose, and that it need not be deeply significant, if they so wish.[4] Following their telling of the story, we will inform them of our view that people are able to tell more than one version of a life story. We will then ask them to retell the story in a different way or to tell us what other versions they have told in the past. In this instruction we hope to bring to awareness our theoretical orientation and our research involvement, as well as set the groundwork for their own responses. We want to encourage them to view the story told as one possible construction among many. In this sense we hope to offer the research experience as a liberating one, in which people can expand their potential for retelling their lives.

We are also interested in whether people will conform to our requests. We realize that our design places us at a considerable disadvantage. We wish to document new, almost instantaneous, retellings despite being within the same researcher–researched relationship and in an almost identical spatial/temporal context. If we can elicit such retellings, what might we learn from our respondents about the manner in which it is accomplished? This is a delicious question to ponder.

Despite careful advanced preparation, we each approach our interview work in different ways. Although the lengths of interviews are the same, on average, about 45 minutes, and although the original question is the same, we diverge from one another in our extended probings for polyvocality. For Sara the thrust is less on immediate changes in the narrative obtained in the interview and more on probing to find out whether the interviewee had ever altered this story during the course of her life. Mary, on the other hand, stresses the present; can the respondent retell the story in such a way

---

[4]Despite our instructions, all of our respondents told us stories from their lives we judged to be highly significant to them.

as to make it obviously different from what was originally told within the same context? Our results reflect these differences in the nuance of the questioning, and also expand ways of addressing the central question of polyvocal narrative production. The difference in emphasis allows us to see the results of these two foci as well as to suggest fruitful avenues for future research.

In selecting our interviewees, we decide to expand the base of the interviews beyond the "usual suspects"—that is, middle-class, well-educated, White, native English-speaking, respondents, usually female. To this end, of our ten respondents, six had postgraduate educations and the remaining four had not pursued a college education. Three non-Americans were represented in the group, including two Asians and one European. We interviewed seven women and three men.

As we talk over the interviews we have taperecorded, we confront some important questions. We ask ourselves, how do we determine if there is a difference in repeated tellings of a story? How much difference is a difference? In the stories by Scottoline and Landsman that launched our study, differences were clear. They consciously described ways in which they constructed multiple stories and how they used these. For our respondents, there were more subtle shades of difference (if, in fact, they were to be considered differences at all.) For example, some storytellers manipulated the content by including and excluding information. One woman, in recounting the experience of her parents' deaths said that she could tell this same story over and over again, but that certain details were difficult to share. So, for her, different versions meant the inclusion or exclusion of different details. The story she told in the interview included details that she rarely mentions, especially those related to the particular circumstances of her father's death. "I never like people to know that my father died on Thanksgiving. In fact, I choose to work on that day." Do we conclude that she has varied her story? Does the significance of such details constitute a new story or simply a fleshing out of the more ordinary version? Does distance from an event, for example, from childhood to adulthood, and the enhanced perspectives that accompany this story, constitute polyvocality or not?

Another respondent described being rendered mute by her mother's death when she was a young child. Her feelings were not verbalized even with close relatives. As she became a teenager she could express the pain of the event, which continued to remain a tragic occurrence in her life. Now, as an adult, she can talk about the ways in which she was advantaged by her mother's death in terms of promoting her maturational process, despite the intense grief she has suffered. This embellishment of the story over time represents a development but would it be considered as an example of polyvocality? She can currently see the more limited versions of her previous renderings. She notes her growth over the evolution of the story.

However, she was unable to consciously adopt different perspectives on the story during the interview itself. We discuss the possibility that a distinction should be made between the development of a more nuanced story that grows slowly as a result of distance and continuing diverse life experiences (for example, the telling and retelling of a parents' divorce between the ages of 5 and 15), and one in which a kaledioscopic shift occurs, much as it might in a therapy session, in which the whole world is turned topsy-turvy in a single moment. For example, a man "discovers" his homosexual longings through narrating his sexual history.[5]

During the process of another interview, a change in the valence of the basic lifetime story became clear. This was a woman who was interviewed at the time that she was about to make a career move. She told a story of feeling very excited and positive about the changes she was making. However, in the past she reported telling stories in which change was an undesirable outcome. What became clear to both interviewer and interviewee during the course of their conversation was that she had always told negative stories about change and had never sought it. Despite this, changes had occurred in her life. The results had been leading her to alter her basic story in a positive direction. The reflexive dimension of the interview, in which Sara and she discussed this shift, also made this transition much more vivid to her. In this sense the interview process itself was a change agent in the storied aspect of this woman's life.

Another important issue that emerged from our analyses of our narrative materials was a question of what degree of flexibility can exist within an interview situation? Does a person feel constrained to present a unified story in a particular setting or not? Even if there is normally fluidity in the ways that individuals talk about themselves, do they feel that this is not legitimate with the same listener? We could not determine how strongly each person felt constrained by Western notions of self-consistency to stick to the same story, but certainly this tendency to be consistent also mitigated against our finding changes in story lines.

We also note that a story can be so habitual, and so central to one's identity formation, that it cannot be relinquished. In one interview a young woman told a story of a dysfunctional family history, one that was saturated with alcoholism, drugs, forms of parental abuse, abandonment, and even murder. Her entire life history until she was in her early twenties was influenced by the consequences of these diverse strands of events, and she

---

[5] There is a strong resonance between the concerns we have with people's capacities and motivations to tell multiple stories of their lives and narrative therapy. Although we are more interested in the naturally occurring modifications and shifts in narratives, these therapists design their processes so as to enhance the capacities of their clients to restory their lives in order to live more fully and satisfyingly. A fuller discussion of narrative therapy can be found in Hoyt, 2000.

is not entirely free of the relational connections with these family members even now. She has not had the opportunity to relinquish any of the tragic tale that she has developed, and which has been encouraged by various therapy groups, including those she was required to attend during her high school days. When asked to retell her story in some other fashion, she was speechless. She indicated that she could only tell a "made up" story about the perfect family, the one she always had dreamed of having herself, but she could not connect that story to her past life. She seemed embarrassed to have failed in her efforts to reconstruct her life story, but she was not able to re-image it. Her sense of who she is and how she must guard against past influences of family members makes reevaluating any aspect of her life story highly threatening. It also would require her to challenge normative stories of what a good and bad family upbringing might be. As it is she clings to conventional notions of normalcy in order to have some guidelines for her life choices. On a more positive note, her tragic story also gives her some pride in all that she has accomplished in her life, despite negative influences.

Another respondent told a very harsh story about the biggest mistake of his life, which centered on walking off the job one day over some minor insult and never again being able to get another job in this lucrative field. Thus, he was sentenced to a life of a laborer, earning half the wages of his former job. His story was seemingly indestructible and tragic. However, because Mary continued to see him occasionally following the interview, she was able to note that he had begun a process of reframing his story. He would approach her periodically to make a new statement about his life, such as, "Well, my girlfriend stuck by me through the whole thing, so I guess that was a good thing." He also began to make sense of his departure in a broader fashion by declaring, "I think I was also afraid that the computer was taking over my job, and one day, I'd be out of there . . . you know, like an elevator operator. The young guys were all using the computer, and I just didn't think I could master it. I didn't have the education. Well, maybe I could have, but I didn't think so then." Here, as in a previous example, the interview process itself served to create the opportunity for a new story to form. In this sense the research process itself becomes a generative tool for individuals to recreate their lives in more promising ways.

Perhaps because the narrative is co-constructed in a very essential way, it requires some form of cooperation or collusion between researcher and researched to revise a story to any large degree. One of our respondents seemed to enjoy the freedom of playing with versions of her story. Her revisions are diverse and compelling, although much shorter than the original narrative. However, it does not seem that her "heart" is in all of the versions equally. She understands the request to tell the story differently as in the nature of an intellectual game, and she complies in retelling her story about a transition in her adolescence.

> **J:** You could say I had a great time when I was 19 running around, partying, madly in love, didn't really care about the future. Didn't really think about that. Typical normal growing up. Everybody goes through some type of rebellion.

> **J:** Or I could say, I had a pretty good life. I never got arrested, and I never had a car accident. I never broke a bone. Some people go through terrible things in their rebellions. What happened to me was a natural progression . . . nothing too dramatic.

> **J:** It could be a dark and dreary story. During that time . . . seven of our friends died in car accidents, drunk driving, somebody drunk hitting them. We lived for the day for tomorrow we may be gone.

This respondent demonstrates the capacity to envision a wide range of perspectives. She grasps the fact that she could frame her story in a variety of ways, each of which would capture some of the elements, but not all. She can move the story through different emotional valences. It appears that she produced these versions in the spirit of the interview, but does it go much beyond a game for her? It is not clear if she has made use of this capacity in her life, or if she is more able to do so as a result of her interview experiences.

Overall, although we wrestle with the issue of what constitutes difference, we generally conclude that individual narratives tend to remain fairly stable in the same shared setting with the interviewer. Personal integrity seems to be bound up with a single story. We realize that an anchor for creating a stable narrative is the presence of the interviewer, who is co-constructing the narrative with the interviewee through attention, questions, probes, and other forms of active listening. At the same time, the tenor of the relationship between the interviewer and the interviewee can create the possibility of new stories never before envisioned through the enhancement of latent themes, novel metaphors, and unusual transitions and expositions arising. People can recall changing their stories, as well as generalize about their capacities to do so when motivated by desires for a positive self-image and for enhanced interpersonal rapport.

### Issues of Pedagogical Potential: Conversation 4

1. What are the consequences of having a research design that is highly participatory, open, and nonhierarchical? Might researchers learn more about narrative theory and its relationship to the broader cultural context when sharing ideas with respondents?

2. How should a researcher balance an interest in what stories have been told in the past and a focus on the possibility of telling a new story in the present and in the future?
3. Is it useful to differentiate narratives as to whether they are developmentally altered (in the manner of a growing onion), or kaleidoscopically (as in a sudden patterned shift) or might they be described as on some continuum of slow to sudden change? What difference might this difference make to under-standing narratives more adequately?
4. What are some of the social constraints on storytelling, such that people may prefer to tell one story over many? What are the factors that will lead people to change?
5. To what extent does searching for alternative narratives en-hance the capacities of people to give them, even in the same setting? To what extent are people able to change their stories, but remain emotionally fixated on one in particular?

CONVERSATION 5: PRESENTING NARRATIVE RESEARCH:
ON MARY'S PATIO

Having amassed lengthy interviews, we now turn our attention to issues of how to best present what we have learned. A new opportunity to view our work through the lens of teaching and learning has arisen with a challenge from *The Narrative Study of Lives* series editors, Ruthellen Josselson, Amia Lieblich, and now Dan McAdams, who are planning an American Psychological Association symposium on pedagogy. We have shared and participated with our informants, and their stories are important and alive to us. But how best should we represent them? Because the social constructionist position asserts that words and worlds are not intrinsically related, it follows that there is no optimal way to present research (Gergen & Gergen, 2000). There are no transparent forms that allow an audience to apprehend the research experience and interpretations as the researcher and participants have. This problematic situation is also a liberating one, one that allows for openings for multiple forms to be created and allowed. Our discussions reveal several overall factors.

We are cognizant of the strict forms that regulate how research findings should be presented. Each journal publishes a specific set of criteria that is to be followed. This disciplinary strategy has the advantage of allowing efficient sharing from one set of researchers to another, but it also suggests that the delivery of findings to audiences is undistorted as long as the proper forms are obeyed. It also places many constraints on how the material can be both understood and organized. The forms in which narrative research are delivered often do not reflect the co-constructed and temporally fixed nature of the tellings; they do not give the audience indication of the instability of the research endeavor. Rather, researchers, as writers, often pretend that the results of their inquiry are firm and objective. We resolve that the evolving relational nature of our interviews should be represented in the final narratives that we produce.

Our discussions center on the forms that will allow us to have a theoretical stance while at the same time preserving the human quality of the interviews. As mentioned initially, narrative researchers often generalize from diverse stories of particular individuals gathered from interviews to create universal themes. In so doing the individual narrative loses much of its uniqueness. Special connections between various events are disregarded in the effort to make an overview that can encompass many lives. Although there is much that may be unfortunate about this tendency to create generalized life courses, there is also the opposite difficulty of evading the mission to draw some conclusions from one's work. If there is no interpretive activity on the part of the researcher, what is the value of having collected the specific case materials at all? It is also problematic to imagine that stories can somehow speak for themselves, and it is also incorrect to suggest in one's presentations that there has been no editing, selecting, or reordering of the materials to give them some semblance of order. How could it be otherwise? Thus, the researcher in making a presentation of interpretations or outcomes is caught between the tendency to be overly cavalier in disregarding the storylines of single individuals and to misplace that individual in a lifestream that would be difficult for that person to claim, and on the other side, to be lax in relating the narratives to theoretical, historical, and critical materials that would help to organize and interpret the information. The researcher may oscillate between the process of differentiation and that of generalization. The content and emotional urgency of our interviews are present with us, and we contemplate the richness of the lives that have been revealed during the course of the interviews. We discuss ways of achieving balance between the power of individual stories and a more abstracted conception of the ability to tell versions of life events.

How are we to think of the interviewees as we move their stories into the public domain? What is the relationship of our presentation to the participants who have openly shared critical aspects of their lives in a closed setting? Even though our interviewees were informed of the purposes and uses of their stories, how will they feel if they were to see them in print? Here divided loyalties and expectations can clash over the way in which research outcomes are interpreted and transmitted (Gergen & Gergen, 2000.) Aside from the obvious issues of protecting the confidentiality, privacy, and the dignity of one's participants, a researcher also is caught in a difficult position if one distorts one's interpretations to avoid confronting "bad reviews" from one's participants. What is the responsibility of the researcher to one's academic colleagues, to one's professional group, and to the public, as well as to one's participants?

Also in terms of presentational styles, what if one's participants cannot read a text that has been written or can make little sense of it. Is that relevant? Is one obligated to share one's writings with one's participants? Should one write two versions of a text, for different audiences with different levels of sophistication about a topic? Should one allow the participants to edit the writings, to suppress the writings, to rewrite the material in different ways? (See Lather & Smithies, 1997, who labor with these issues in their text.) Should one's obligations be fairly clear from the beginning of a project in terms of one's relationships to all the parties concerned? Is it possible that the exchange between the interviewees and the interviewer is settled at the exit door of the interview? Or does it extend beyond and, if so, in what fashion?

One of the outgrowths of the research and the considerations of a social constructionist position is that presentations of research need not be in formal scientific writing only. There are other ways of presenting research that are categorized as performative, including forms of autoethnographies, biographies, short stories, poems, collages, "happenings," and visual imagery (Denzin & Lincoln, 2000; Ellis & Bochner, 1996). We consider the impact of each of these on our material and whether they might enable us to maintain the life force of the interviews and the power of our conclusions.

As we talk, we confront our own long course to these endings. Although there is never a neutral place in which to stand in order to reflect, we search for other perspectives from which to judge the adequacy of our work. We resolve to include these reflections in our representations. We celebrate a conclusion to a long, complex, yet rewarding process.

### Issues of Pedagogical Potential: Conversation 5

1. How can the researcher retain the personal and evolving nature of the interviews while interpreting and bringing new meaning to the materials?
2. How can researchers maintain the integrity of their relationships with the people interviewed as their stories are moved from the private to the public domain? How active a role should/could respondents have in the interpretation process? How do we maintain the confidence that they have placed in us? How do we honor the relationships we have with colleagues and the standards of one's field?
3. What advantages and disadvantages are there in following traditional forms of reporting research as opposed to experi-

menting with new and more adequate or complete forms of expression?

4. Why is it important that researchers always maintain a reflexive stance toward their work?

5. What are the benefits of accepting that there are no final answers to the questions posed?

## REFERENCES

Agee, E. (2000). Menopause and the transmission of women's knowledge: African American and White women's perspectives. *Medical Anthropology Quarterly, 14*, 73–95.

Bart, P. (1971). Depression in middle-aged women. In V. Gornick & B. K. Moran (Eds.), *Women in sexist society* (pp. 23–35). New York: Basic Books.

Chrisler, J. C., Johnston, I. K., Champagne, N. H., & Preston, K. E. (1994). Menstrual joys: The construct and its consequences. *Psychology of Women Quarterly, 18*, 375–387.

Dalton, K. (1972). *The premenstrual syndrome*. London: William Heinemann Medical Books.

Dalton, K. (1983). *Once a month*. Claremont, CA: Hunter House.

Datan, N. (1986). Corpses, lepers, and menstruating women: Tradition, transition, and the sociology of knowledge. *Sex Roles, 14*, 693–703.

Denzin, N. K., & Lincoln, Y. S. (2000). *Handbook of qualitative research* (2nd ed.). Thousand Oaks, CA: Sage.

Deutsch, H. (1945). *The psychology of women*. New York: Grune & Stratton.

Ellis, C., & Bochner, A. P. (Eds.). (1996). *Composing ethnography: Alternative forms of qualitative writing*. Walnut Creek, CA: AltaMira Press.

Fonow, M. M., & Cook, J. (1991). *Beyond methodology: Feminist scholarship as lived research*. Bloomington: Indiana University Press.

Formanek, R. (Ed.). (1990). *The meanings of menopause: Historical, medical and clinical perspectives*. Hillsdale, NJ: Erlbaum.

Franklin, M. (1997). Making sense: Interviewing and narrative representation. In M. M. Gergen & S. N. Davis (Eds.), *Toward a new psychology of gender* (pp. 99–116). New York: Routledge Press.

Gannon, L., (1985). *Menstrual disorders and menopause: Biological, psychological, cultural research*. New York: Praeger.

Gergen, K. J. (1999). *An invitation to social constructionism*. Thousand Oaks, CA: Sage.

Gergen, M. (1990). Finished at forty: Women's development within the patriarchy. *Psychology of Women Quarterly, 14*, 451–470.

Gergen, M. (2001). *Feminist reconstructions of psychology: Narrative, gender and performance*. Thousand Oaks, CA: Sage.

Gergen, M., & Gergen, K. J. (2000). Qualitative Inquiry: Tensions and transformations. In N. Denzin & Y. Lincoln (Eds.), *Handbook of qualitative research* (2nd ed., pp. 1025–1046). Thousand Oaks, CA: Sage.

Greer, G. (1993). *The change: Women, aging and the menopause*. New York: Fawcett Books.

Hoyt, M. F. (2000). *Some stories are better than others: Doing what works in brief therapy and managed care*. Philadelphia: Bruner/Mazel.

Jacobowitz, R. S. (1996). *150 Most-asked questions about menopause: What women really want to know*. New York: William Morrow.

Josselson, R. (1996). *Revising herself: The story of women's identity from college to midlife*. New York: Oxford University Press.

Komesaroff, P., Rothfield, P., & Daly, J. (Eds.). (1997). *Reinterpreting menopause: Cultural and philosophical issues*. New York: Routledge.

Landau, C., Cyr, M. G., & Moulton, A. W. (1995). *The complete book of menopause*. New York: Perigee.

Landsman, G. H. (1998, Autumn). Reconstructing motherhood in the age of "perfect babies": Mothers of infants and toddlers with disabilities. *Signs, 24*, 69–101.

Lather, P., & Smithies, C. (1997). *Troubling with angels: Women living with HIV/AIDS*. Boulder, CO: Westview Press.

Lock, M. (1993). The politics of mid-life and menopause: Ideologies for the second sex in North America and Japan. In S. Lindenbaum & M. Lock (Eds.), *Knowledge, power, and practice: The anthropology of medicine and everyday life* (pp. 330–363). Berkeley: University of California Press.

Martin, E. (1987). *Woman in the body: A cultural analysis of reproduction*. Boston: Beacon Press.

Personal Narrative Group. (1989). *Interpreting women's lives: Feminist theory and personal narratives*. Bloomington: Indiana University Press.

Reinharz, S. (1992). *Feminist methods in social science research*. Oxford: Oxford University Press.

Ribbens, J., & Edwards, R. (Eds.). (1998). *Feminist dilemmas in qualitative research: Public knowledge and private lives*. Thousand Oaks, CA: Sage.

Rosenwald, G., & Ochberg, R. (Eds.). (1992). *Storied lives*. New Haven, CT: Yale University Press.

Sarbin, T. R. (Ed.). (1986). *Narrative psychology: The storied nature of human conduct*. New York: Praeger.

Sarbin, T. R., & Kitsuse, J. I. (Eds.). (1994). *Constructing the social*. London: Sage.

Sheehy, G. (1998). *The silent passage: Menopause*. New York: Pocket Books.

Stewart, A. (1994). Toward a feminist strategy for studying women's lives. In C. E. Franz & A. J. Stewart (Eds.), *Women creating lives: Identities, resilience and resistance*. Boulder, CO: Westview Press.

Stewart, A. J., & Ostrove, J. M. (1998). Women's personality in middle age: Gender, history and midcourse corrections. *American Psychologist, 53,* 1185–1194.

Vaz, K. M. (Ed.). (1997). *Oral narrative research with Black women.* Thousand Oaks, CA: Sage.

Wulf, H. (1980). *Menopause in modern perspectives.* New York: Appleton-Century-Crofts.

# 14

# A FRAMEWORK FOR NARRATIVE
# RESEARCH PROPOSALS
# IN PSYCHOLOGY

RUTHELLEN JOSSELSON AND AMIA LIEBLICH

"The most promising words ever written on the maps of human knowledge are *terra incognita*—unknown territory."
—Daniel J. Boorstin, *The Discoverers* (1985, p. xvi)

For the last 10 years we have been teaching narrative studies in various frameworks in academia. As more and more students wished to write master's and doctoral theses using narrative approaches, we became aware that the old patterns of writing research proposals were unsuitable for this purpose and often created havoc with their research plans.[1] The present chapter attempts to clarify our position in confronting these problems.

In narrative, as opposed to paradigmatic, modes of thought (Bruner, 1985), the aim is to create interpreted description of the rich and multi-layered meanings of historical and personal events. The search is for truths unique in their particularity, grounded in firsthand experience, in order to extend and enhance conceptualization and/or to sensitize practitioners to

The authors wish to thank the following people for their reactions to and helpful comments on earlier drafts of this paper—and for indicating that they would make use of this guide with their students: Michael Bamberg, Clark University; Eyal Ben-Ari, Hebrew University of Jerusalem; Ardra Cole, University of Toronto; Hanoch Flum, Ben Gurion University; Hal Grotevant, University of Minnesota; Katherine Randazzo, Fielding Graduate Institute; George Rosenwald, University of Michigan; Paul C. Rosenblatt, University of Minnesota.

[1] Another problem we encounter is that students who have never taken a class in qualitative research in their academic program (because there are not too many of those in academic programs!), believe that they can qualify to do such research for a master's or doctoral program, because it seems to be so intuitive, or—according to their perception—close to their clinical psychology background.

their occurrence. The emphasis is on content and its meanings, which are sometimes revealed in structural forms. There is no prescribed infallible means for unearthing and creating meanings. The qualitative/narrative[2] researcher eschews methodolatry in favor of doing what is necessary to capture the lived experience of people in terms of their own meaning-making. The pursuit of interesting and interpretable content takes precedence over rigid adherence to prescribed rules of procedure. Without detailed stories drawn in some way from participants, stories that reveal the way in which people view and understand their lives, narrative study is impossible. But the fact that this is research and not journalism means that some scholarly or conceptual context either frames or will frame the final report.

In that narrative research is a voyage of discovery—a discovery of meanings that both constitute the individual participant and are co-constructed in the research process—researchers cannot know at the outset what they will find. How, therefore, does one write a proposal about the research one intends to do?

In most psychology graduate programs, the structure of thesis or dissertation proposals is dictated by the paradigm of quantitative, positivistic research. Hypotheses to be tested are set out and located within the research tradition or theory from which they emerge. Methods are employed to test the defined hypotheses. Statistical analyses that will be conducted are specified. Faculty committees authorized to supervise the research then argue among themselves and with the students about whether the hypotheses are intelligent, whether the methods are appropriate, whether the statistical procedures are apt. They also seek to evaluate what is innovative about the study, relative to the knowledge in the area. On a structural level, these traditional proposals are built like regular research papers, using the chapters of Introduction, Method, Results, and Discussion.

Students who wish to work with qualitative or narrative methods, though, find themselves trying to fit themselves into a Procrustean bed. They have no hypotheses—only questions or interesting people to explore. They have some idea whom they hope to interview and how they intend to begin their inquiry, usually with a rough interview format. But, trying to work within the standard proposal format, they get stuck—stuck at many points, but most formidably when they try to specify how many people they will study and how they will analyze their data. In place of the traditional methods section, which they cannot quite reshape their initally envisioned procedure to fit, they usually retreat to presenting some exegesis on the philosophy of hermeneutic or phenomenological research or writing a com-

---

[2] Although some scholars distinguish qualitative from narrative research, we find this unnecessary for the present chapter. Suffice it to say that "qualitative" includes a wider scope of research approaches, e.g., observations, whereas "narrative" usually refers to work done with verbal accounts or stories.

pendium on grounded theory. And the supervising faculty committee still has little idea of what they really intend to try to find out, if they are capable of undertaking the work, finishing it, or whether the final project is likely to be an embarrassment to all. In our experience, committee meetings often then degenerate into battles about "how many" participants the student needs to have, whether all the research terms are well-specified in advance, or why a particular subgroup has been chosen as an object of study and not another. Or students are taken to task for not being clear enough on the conceptual framework within which they will try to understand their data, how they are going to conduct their "analysis"—or for being too wedded to a particular theory such that they may "force" their data into a preexisting shape.

Nor can we adopt forms from the humanities. Although the thinking and analytic processes in the humanities are closer to those of narrative research, students in literature and history already have the materials they will work with and know at the outset the themes that are present that they plan to highlight, explore, and discuss.

We offer this chapter, then, as an effort to design a format for qualitative/narrative research proposals in psychology, one that will better suit the nature of this work.[3] We hope, in doing this, to make life a bit smoother for both students and supervising committees. What are the components that students must offer at the outset to satisfy their supervisors that they are competent to carry out the work, to describe what the work will be, and to argue that the work is potentially significant?

Qualitative research based on analysis of narrative material is inherently inductive. The work takes place in hermeneutic circles, where new learnings are built as background knowledge expands. Thus, a researcher may begin at a certain point only to learn, as a result of the research, that the question she or he had so carefully framed loses meaning in the context of the experience of the participants and has to be reshaped to fit the local circumstances. To this extent, qualitative analysis can be considered a craft, because "methods that are successful are of necessity innovative and are not usually "off-the-shelf'" (Liberman, 1999, p. 47). In our work, we have dropped the term "methodology," which carries deep connotations of the traditional research paradigm, and prefer to speak in terms of modes of inquiry.

As with any voyage of discovery to an unknown place, a narrative research plan must argue for the importance of the journey in the context

---

[3] In preparation for this chapter, we consulted works that discuss the preparation of dissertations in other fields that use qualitative methods such as fieldwork or naturalistic inquiry (Ely, personal communication; Munhall & Boyd, 1993; Sandelowski, Davis, & Harris, 1989). But we have chosen to focus this chapter on the use of interview materials since these are most often used for qualitative studies in psychology.

of prior knowledge, must state clearly what sort of knowledge is sought, and must chart a plan for how one hopes to carry out the exploration, including the tools that will be carried to aid the work, how the voyage will be documented, and how it will later be understood and discussed. In addition, discoverers must offer some discussion of their position with regard to the voyage—how they intend to undertake it and to understand it. Finally, would-be discoverers must state what they hope this new knowledge will contribute in a scientific, theoretical, scholarly, or programmatic context. In more formal language, these requirements would be expressed as statements about the

1. Background of the study
2. Research question and its significance
3. Plan of inquiry
4. Approach to analysis
5. Significance of the findings
6. Reflexive statement about the position of the researcher in relation to the work.

Because narrative studies encourage creativity and flexibility, we do not expect exactly that the above subsections in the proposal will appear with these titles, or in that particular order. Moreover, we encourage students to experiment with new modes of writing and problematizing representation (see Gergen & Gergen, 2000), but these are not likely yet to have fully germinated at the proposal stage.

1. **Background of the Study** (Here is the state of knowledge so far and the contexts within which the work will proceed.)

Many, perhaps most, questions students propose for narrative research derive from their own experiences—with particular problems, issues, or subgroup identities. They seek to give voice to what is not well-represented in the science of human experience, which is a commendable goal. Often, such students are trying to shape a long-held protest that emerges from years of studying psychology and not finding some deeply etched personal knowledge anywhere discussed. These students are "connected," often "passionate" knowers (Belenky, Clinchy, Goldberger, & Tarule, 1986) who aim to bring together their personal and scientific knowledge and are willing to put unusual amounts of energy and efforts into their studies. Our attitude is to respect personal knowledge and self-study as well as scientific sources. (For additional discussion of this issue, see the chapter by Ellis & Bochner on autoethnography in Denzin & Lincoln, 2000).

Together with this personal curiosity, every good research question flows from a thoughtful reading of the existing state of knowledge. But the issue of the relationship between theory and phenomena in qualitative research is a thorny one. Grounded theory, as it was first understood, was to be a method in search of theory, and many advocated that qualitative research be undertaken with a blank slate on which emerging theoretical constructs would later be inscribed. More recently, Strauss and Corbin (1994) have made a strong statement that this was never the intent of grounded theory—that there was always the supposition of theoretical sensitivity, that is, a body of theoretical knowledge that the researcher held loosely in mind, not providing hypotheses to test, but conceptual fields within which to understand the observed phenomena. Still, there is enormous disagreement across the social sciences about the role of theory in narrative inquiry (Clandinin & Connelly, 2000).

The aim of the background section, then, is to hold the tension between personal and theoretical knowledge, to straddle the line between a necessary openness to phenomena that are as-yet-unknown and theoretical sophistication that, loosely held but firmly integrated intellectually, stands in the wings to illuminate the interviewees' words, readings of the texts, and understandings of the narrative that will emerge.

The theoretical part of the background section of the proposal must open the inquiry, not narrow and focus it. By stating the boundaries of the theoretical/conceptual field within which the student intends to work, it outlines in a general way the student's erudition and frame of mind. It provides orienting (but not operational) definitions of key terms (Sandelowski et al., 1989) that enclose the investigation. In what theoretical language does the student think, with what concepts, what lenses? To which theorists is the student likely to turn to move phenomenological description to more abstract, conceptual ground? Or perhaps the student intends to challenge or extend a particular theoretical position by analyzing cases that question or enlarge theoretical assumptions, or to try to enrich a theory by parsing in more detail than is customary particular instances that the theory addresses.

In the final narrative of their study, students will have to return to a conversation with the theoretical literature in order to place their findings and understandings. The theoretical overview section of the proposal, therefore, outlines the possibilities of ongoing discussions that the student's work might join while not foreclosing the possibility that other conceptual frameworks will, in the end, prove to be more useful.

A theoretical background section written too tightly begins to read either like a hypothesis-testing enterprise or a confining framework that may preclude the discovery of new knowledge. On the other hand, a sparse theoretical background section may suggest that the work is purely descriptive and is likely to invite criticisms of not being scholarship. This section primarily serves the function of demonstrating the students' sophistication in the literature, their ability to read integratively and to leave space for alternative voices in psychological theory and practice. It sets out what the students have read and what they have made of it, what seem to be the important issues and debates, what is necessary to advance theoretical knowledge in this sphere. At the same time, this section should demonstrate that students are open to the complexity of the phenomena rather than rooted in a particular a priori conceptualization.

The theoretical background section also must include an empirical literature review—that is, a summary of relevant and related studies that bear on the subject of the proposed research. In order to establish the merits of doing the study, the student must demonstrate that what we know collectively is not enough. But this is often a problematic section as the student struggles with the level of detail to include and how far to range in considering what is relevant. Narrative research is more complicated to summarize and present—as well as to find—than are the more quantitative and positivistic studies. Quantitative studies are organized around method; studies build on each other using similar or related methods or they contradict one another by showing that changes in method change results. Qualitative studies, by contrast, are focused on processes—and some of the most interesting findings of a study are often buried among the narrative quotations or in discussion sections of papers or books that, in terms of their content, may seem unrelated. Thus, a student who wishes to study the processes incurred by a certain immigrant subgroup in Finland may find much that is relevant in a study of immigrants to Israel. But the points of similarity cannot be known at the outset. What counts at the proposal stage is that the student is aware that such related literatures exist and is prepared to study them as data analysis proceeds.

One major difference between the processes of doing quantitative and qualitative research is the notion of sequence. Students trained in a quantitative tradition learn that first you create your hypotheses, then you collect your data, analyze it, and then write it up. There are no comparable phases in qualitative research. Teachers of qualitative methods try to teach their students to begin writing (their thoughts, suppositions, expectations, reflections on the research process, etc.) before they even collect data (Janesick, 2000; Woolcott, 1990; also chapter 12, this volume). Reading the literature of related work should be continuous—and most intense as data collection is underway. (I always find that when I am actively collecting data, everyone whose work I read seems to be talking about my data—even novelists—and when I tell my students this, they find it true for them as well but felt embarrassed about it before I legitimized it for them.) Some professors in anthropology encourage their students to delay most of their reading until after the empirical stage, so that their approach to the "field" might be as pure as possible. Our position is that the literature summary does not have to be complete before the proposal is approved—just that the student demonstrates an awareness of the works he or she needs to interact with throughout the life of the study. In the finished work, most of the discussion of related empirical literature ought to be in the discussion section, integrated or compared with the student's findings. In the proposal, though, the literature review must launch the study in such a way that the research question evolves naturally from it.

The format for the theoretical background section, then, should be: Here is a phenomenon that interests me. Here is a theory (or theories) that was created to organize and understand the phenomenon of X, but it falls short in some important way. Here are some empirical ways that people have tried to understand X and this is what they seem to have discovered so far. And this is what I (possibly with some statement at this point about who "I" is)—provisionally, tentatively, critically, inquiringly, and with great curiosity—think is important here.

2. **The Focus of Inquiry and Its Significance** (Here is what I want to know and why I think it is important.)

The theoretical background section is always written somewhat teleologically in that it must lead inevitably to a statement of the student's research purpose. This always takes the form of: "After reviewing the available theoretical and empirical literature and considering the intersection between them, and after reflecting on what I have learned from my own personal experience about that (if it is relevant) . . . I find the following problem or lacuna in the relationship between theory and phenomena; or I think that Y group has been omitted from consideration and might have a unique experience; or maybe if we look at the processes in X with narrative modes of inquiry we might find that X takes a different shape"—or some variant of these. The research question must be clearly stated, not as one that can be answered, but as one that calls for exploration. In narrative/ qualitative projects, the question usually has a "how" either explicit or embedded in it because "how" points to dynamic processes that can be thickly described. "How" or "what kinds of" also imply that the exploration will involve multiple descriptions at varied levels of analysis. In some ways, the word "question" here may mislead the student. The "question" is a focus of inquiry, broadly conceived, and is more likely to be a paragraph than a single phrase with a question mark following. It is more likely a statement of a problem that needs investigation, a set of meanings that call for articulation and elucidation or a space that has not been sufficiently filled in. Still, the student must clearly state what he or she hopes to discover. Proposals often fail because the research problem appears too vague, too general, too unfocused—"How do women adapt to midlife?" "How do people choose their careers?" "How do people decide who to marry?" These are all from early drafts in our files.

Most good "questions" for narrative research are open-ended but focused on specific experiences or societal subgroups, bounded by conceptual frameworks. For example: How do battered women, now living in a shelter with their children, experience themselves as mothers; in what areas or when are they pleased with versus critical of their mothering? To what do they attribute these phenomena? How are they related to their memories of being mothered?

Or, in another area: How do adults who had been educated in a special program for the underprivileged construct the story of their schooling and its results in their lives as adults? How do these experiences illuminate the role of environment in educational attainment?

3. **Plan of Inquiry** (How I intend to find out something about all of this.)

As we stated above, we have dropped the word "method" from our teaching and writing because it has become shrouded, in our reading, with a kind of mystical reverence, as though the procedure, rather than the thinking, produces knowledge. The proposal has already stated what is known, in what terms it has been understood in this and other research traditions, and what the student wants to know or develop about the topic. The aims of narrative inquiry are to turn to some relatively unexplored or unknown phenomena and to reexamine them naively (Sandelowski et al., 1989)—this is foundational.

Simply put, this section must address the question "How are you going to begin to try to find out?"—recognizing that as the investigation proceeds, the form of "finding out" may change. A long exegesis on qualitative methods is superfluous here. People do not usually write a treatise on the philosophy of science underlying logical positivism. With the advent of acceptance of phenomenological, hermeneutic and constructivist inquiry in the social sciences (Denzin & Lincoln, 2000) it is not necessary to justify the epistemology in a proposal. It may, however, be necessary to explain why the research question necessitates a qualitative or narrative approach (e.g., because it deals with subjective experiences of a phenomenon rather than its causes or correlates, or because it deals with the personal construction of past experiences).

This section should focus on how data will be generated: which participants the students intend to study and why; how students will present themselves and their goals to the participants; how participants will be selected; what they will be asked to tell about their experiences, in what setting, in what way, with what approach, and with which ethical cautions. This design is understood to be a starting point and is not intended to limit its evolution. Here, a supervising committee will want to know exactly how the student intends to recruit participants (and if the student has thought through how the way in which participants are recruited will affect the data produced), by whom and under what conditions they will be interviewed, and exactly what they will be told about the study. Many students simply say they will use an open-ended interview, but it is also necessary to show what the opening interview question will be and what follow-up questions the student has in mind to maximize having the participant talk about what the student wants to study. We found much to be commended in Chase's suggestion (chapter 5, this volume) to have students write a very detailed sequence of questions that they would like to have answered by the interviewee. These questions will not be presented during the interview, though, but rather serve as a guideline for the researcher's listening. In a proposal, these detailed questions may give the committee a better understanding of the student's goals and directions in the study.

Ethics are an important part of this section—not just in knee-jerk informed consent terms, but a thoughtful presentation of what participation in the study is likely to mean in the life of the participant (Fine, 1994; Janesick, 2000; Josselson, 1996; Stacey, 1988). Ethical issues are embedded in every aspect of a narrative study and the student should demonstrate awareness of the manifold dilemmas of researching the personal.[4]

The question of number of participants is one of the thorniest we have run into in committee meetings. Received wisdom in narrative research is that the work continues until "saturation"—meaning that in the opinion of the researcher, additional interviews (or data instances) will only provide redundant results. Therefore, most students simply state that they will interview until they reach saturation. We go along with this but at the same time recognize that this is a kind of dodge. Neither of us have ever reached any kind of saturation in our work—every person has a unique story and there is always something new to be learned. Rather, we stop interviewing when we "feel" saturated—that is, we already have learned more than we will ever be able to contain and communicate and we feel we have enough of interest to write about. But we have been at this work for a long time

---

[4] A discussion of the relationship between ethics and the sociopolitical implications of narrative research is beyond the scope of this article. For excellent treatment of these important matters, see Fine, Weis, Weesen, & Wong, 2000; Lincoln, 1995; Rosenwald & Ochberg, 1992.

d this is not a guideline students can feel comfortable with. What if, after e or two interviews (as often happens), they already feel overwhelmed and feel they have enough for two dissertations? So we end up pulling a number out of a hat—do 10 interviews—or 12, we tell them—and they usually accept it because having a numerical target is better than not having one, even if there is no particular rationale for choosing it. It is simply not possible at the outset to know "how many" interviews or participants will be necessary. The number necessary is inversely proportional to the intensiveness of the study. Relatively few deep, long intensive interviews observed in highly detailed, multilayered ways will yield about as much material as many shorter, less intensive texts. What is necessary depends on what the researcher intends to find out, and at what level(s) of analysis she or he intends to treat the material. We are mindful of the fact that there is as much danger in having too much data as having too little. It is important to have enough material to represent the richness and diversity of the phenomena, but not so much as to be overwhelmed (see Kvale, 1996). Generally, we advise students to specify a range—at least 5, no more than 30, seem like reasonable boundaries for most interview-based projects. The supervisor can discuss this issue with the student as the work proceeds. (Do I have enough? What other kinds of interviewees do I still need?) It is rarely a good topic for a proposal meeting. Often such discussions just serve to enact everyone's discomfort with the unfamiliarity of working in narrative modes. A more productive issue for discussion relates to the subgroups of participants to be sought: Should they be homogenous, or "represent" various classes? (For example, in a study of single mothers, should they include widowed, divorced, as well as never wed—or just one such subgroup—and how is such a decision related to the research aim and background theory, and what is its meaning for possible conclusions from the study?)

**4. Approach to Analysis** (How I'm going to figure out and demonstrate what I've learned.)

This is perhaps the most difficult part of the proposal to write. The primary task of the analytic process is to decipher the meanings inherent in the material and to render them in a form consistent with the research question. *How* this is done is the art of this kind of work and the process cannot be specified a priori. Doing a thematic (and/or discourse) analysis of narrative material always involves multiple readings and rereadings—and that, in effect, goes without saying. Thus, it may strengthen the students' position if they state that another reader (usually a peer, or a peer group) of the empirical data (or part of it) will be used to open up multiple perspectives and provide additional viewpoints and interpretations (see chapter 12, this volume).

Stating in the proposal that one will conduct a reading which is primarily content versus form-oriented, or holistic versus categorical (Lieblich, Tuval-Mashiach, & Zilber, 1998), or any combination of these foci of analysis, may demonstrate some of the notions the student has at this stage about the way the research project will unfold. However, there should be enough freedom for the researcher to change perspectives if better modes of reading emerge from the actual collected data. Stating in the proposal that one will use computer-based analytic programs neither strenghtens nor weakens the proposal, nor does saying that one will use one or the other reading guides or tabulation guides that are available (e.g., Brown et al., 1988; Miles & Huberman, 1984)—although either of these might prove very useful as an aid in thinking through the material.

We have found that the best way for committee members to get a sense of how students plan to treat their material is to ask the students to present a demonstration interview and analysis as part of their proposal. This gives research supervisors an up-close look at what kind of data the student will be working with and the student's capacity to interpret the material in an interesting and meaningful, as well as accurate, manner. We have found no abstract description of what the student intends to do to be as revealing and illuminating as seeing a segment of what a finished product might resemble. The demonstration submitted, however, is intended to demonstrate what the student *can* do, not necessarily what *will* be done in the final report. Themes that seem predominant at the outset might well recede in importance or their role in the overall scheme might change as the work proceeds. This preliminary work, then, is a demonstration, and a tool to make the student think about the difficulties of analysis and how to cope with them, rather than a constraint or a sample of the final product.

One important skill the demonstration interview makes apparent is the student's capacity to reflect on a mind other than his or her own. Can they construct and work with experience told by another? Can they hold in mind *simultaneously* their personal reflections and intuitions, the others' words and meanings as well as some conceptual ground that makes it of interest to scholars? Is the student apperceptively complex and attuned to nuance of expression and language? Thus, one important function of the analysis section is not so much to say how they will analyze but to demonstrate that they can.

The demonstration work also indicates the student's skills as an interviewer. Narrative research interviewing is different both from traditional research interviews and clinical interviews, with which most graduate students of psychology are more familiar. It requires that the interviewer keep her research aims and personal interests in mind, while leaving enough space for the conversation to develop into a meaningful narrative. It has to procure "stories," namely concrete examples, episodes or memories from the teller's life. Is the interview presented in the proposal conducted appropriately, with empathic listening, without undue direction, intervention, or emotional reaction born of anxiety? It was at this stage that we once found a student whose idea of interviewing was to challenge and argue with her interviewee about the morality of her behavior. Students who fail to satisfy criteria of good narrative research interviewing should either be dissuaded from this kind of research or referred for additional training in the process.

The requirement of the demonstration interview or interviews thus brings the narrative dissertation proposal process closer to what is usually required in the humanities. There, materials that will be the subject of the work are already available (e.g., certain literary texts the student intends to interpret in an innovative manner), and students are, therefore, able to demonstrate the kind of analysis they plan to undertake.

In this analysis section, students should also address questions of authenticity, trustworthiness, and credibility (Lincoln, 1995; Lincoln & Guba, 1985, 2000). How do they intend to check their reading of the material? Will they work with a reading group or a second reader? Will participants be invited into the analysis process—to check the transcripts? to comment on the interpretations?

Issues of reflexivity are also relevant here. How does the student view him- or herself as a constructor of knowledge? What effect does his or her experience in the relevant area—and positioning with regard to gender, age, race, nationality, or other sociocultural factors—have on their presentation of themselves as interviewers and how do these factors influence the ways in which they will read the data? This cannot, of course, be a final statement, because much will be learned about the self as a researcher in the course of the study and the statement in the proposal should in no way limit this learning process. Rather, it should indicate that the student is aware of the issue.

## 5. Significance of the Findings (So what?)

In narrative research, there are no "negative results." A good research question means that the absence of anticipated connections within the material is as interesting as what might have been expected. No proposal, however, no matter how well-crafted, can guarantee in advance that something of significance will emerge from the work. Taking into account that one does not know what will be discovered and discussed in the final product, the summary of the proposal must address the ways in which the findings, whatever they may turn out to be, will have meaning both to the academic world and to the community or grouping of individuals who have been researched.

6. **Reflexive Statement of Research and Personal Stance** (Who I am and what I already think about all this.)

A personal statement about the researcher's personal characteristics that have impact on the research must be included somewhere in the proposal. It might make most sense in the background section or in the plan of inquiry section, but if it fits nowhere else, it can come last. Because narrative research does not assume "objectivity," it is important to state what is already known about the subjectivity and context of the researcher and how that intersects with the research project. "To orient oneself to a phenomenon always implies a particular interest, station or vantage point in life" (Van Manen, 1990, p. 40). Here, a summary of journal notes that have led to the proposal might be put to use. Already-conscious philosophical, professional, or personal assumptions and biases that influence their stance as researchers should be explored here. Personal circumstances that orient the research to more than a superficial, passing interest in the topic might be expressed, as these are of value in motivating the endeavor. Personal experiences and agendas in regard to the topic are better expressed here; airing them and making them explicit decreases the possibility that they will be projected into the participants. The student might also state how they envision using autobiographical material or personal narrative (autoethnography, as the ethnographers call it; see Ellis & Bochner, 2000) in the finished work. If nothing else, this section strives to be consistent with what the student has been taught in qualitative research courses about the use of the self in this form of research—and stands to encourage the student to continue reflecting about the role of the self throughout the project and into the final product.

This section should, however, be of reasonable length and not a complete autobiography of the researcher.

## GENERAL ISSUES IN EVALUATION OF RESEARCH PROPOSALS

Unlike quantitative research, in which proposals can be evaluated largely on the merits of the hypotheses and methods derived from a thorough grounding in a well-defined conceptual and research tradition, the final quality of narrative/qualitative research is largely a function of the skill and creativity of the researcher. Narrative data may speak for themselves, but transcripts do not make a thesis. Meanings in terms of larger questions must be inductively created through a process of insight, attunement, and calibrated movement between concept and voice. The successful narrative research report persuasively guides the reader to embedded meanings and their larger significance. Thus, a supervising committee must assess the capacity of the student to carry out the work—not just the research plan as it is stated in the proposal.

We are forceful in telling our students that narrative research is the far more difficult road and usually takes longer to complete—it is for the hardy, the passionate, the student who can bear enormous anxiety and ambiguity and persevere. It is for those who are comfortable knowing certainly but without certainty who can recognize that all knowledge is tentative and provisional but can still have confidence in what they know. It is for mature students, people with certain life experiences in their selected area of study and with interpersonal skills, and for students with a humanistic bent. Students who need a lot of structure, who tend toward the concrete and definite, students without a broad intellectual background and wide-ranging reading habits—these we steer toward more hypothesis-testing designs.

In the end, we find, we approve the student for the work as much as the work itself. It falls upon the student who wants to follow this road, then, to demonstrate to us his or her capacity for inductive thinking, for creative interaction with narrative data. For doctoral dissertations, we ask that students have taken narrative research courses where they produce projects they can use to demonstrate their skills. At the very least, students must show that they have systematically studied the philosophical foundations of hermeneutics and postmodern inquiry, that they have had supervised experience in research interviewing and can demonstrate competence in textual analysis and interpretation. Students must have a firm mastery of theory as well as a capacity to suspend their theoretical knowledge in order to approach narrative material naively, openly.

The ideal student—and therefore, the ideal proposal—offers this fine-tuned balance between academic maturity and investigatory naivete—a flexible, informed mind that is open to encountering a *terra incognita* and emerging from it with an interesting and valuable story to tell.

## REFERENCES

Belenky, M. F., Clinchy, B. M., Goldberger, N. R., & Tarule, J. M. (1986). *Women's ways of knowing.* New York: Basic Books.

Boorstin, D. J. (1985). *The discoverers.* New York: Vintage.

Brown, L. M., Argyris, D., Atanucci, J., Bardige, B., Gilligan, C., et al. (1988). *A guide to reading narratives of conflict and choice for self and relational voice* (Monograph no. 1) Cambridge, MA: Project on the Psychology of Woman and the Development of Girls, Harvard Graduate School of Education.

Bruner, J. (1985). *Acts of meaning.* Cambridge, MA: Harvard University Press.

Clandinin, D. J., & Connelly, F. M. (2000). *Narrative Inquiry: Experience and story in qualitative research.* San Francisco: Jossey-Bass.

Denzin, N. K., & Lincoln, Y. S. (2000). *Handbook of qualitative research* (2nd ed.). Thousand Oaks, CA: Sage.

Ellis, C., & Bochner, A. P. (2000). Autoethnography, personal narrative, reflexivity: Researcher as subject. In N. K. Denzin & Y. S. Lincoln (Eds.), *Handbook of qualitative research* (2nd ed., pp. 733–768). Thousand Oaks, CA: Sage,.

Fine, M. (1994). Working the hyphens: Reinventing self and other in qualitative research. In N. K. Denzin & Y. S. Lincoln (Eds.), *Handbook of qualitative research* (pp. 70–82). Thousand Oaks, CA: Sage.

Fine, M., Weis, L., Weseen, S., & Wong, L. (2000). For whom? Qualitative research, representations and social responsibilities. In N. K. Denzin & Y. S. Lincoln (Eds.), *Handbook of qualitative research* (2nd ed., pp. 107–131). Thousand Oaks, CA: Sage.

Gergen, M., & Gergen, K. (2000). In N. K. Denzin & Y. S. Lincoln (Eds.), *Handbook of qualitative research* (2nd ed., pp. 1025–1046). Thousand Oaks, CA: Sage.

Janesick, V. J. (2000). The choreography of qualitative research design: Minuets, improvisations and crystallization. In N. K. Denzin & Y. S. Lincoln (Eds.), *Handbook of qualitative research* (2nd ed., pp. 379–400). Thousand Oaks, CA: Sage.

Josselson, R. (1996). On writing other people's lives. In R. Josselson (Ed.), *Ethics and process in the narrative study of lives: The narrative study of lives* (Vol. 4, pp. 60–71). Thousand Oaks, CA: Sage.

Kvale, S. (1996.) *Interviews.* Thousand Oaks, CA: Sage.

Liberman, K. (1999). From walkabout to meditation: Craft and ethics in field inquiry. *Qualitative Inquiry, 5*(1), 47–63.

Lieblich, A., Tuval-Mashiach, R., & Zilber, T. (1998). *Narrative research: Reading, analysis and interpretation.* Thousand Oaks, CA: Sage.

Lincoln, Y. S. (1995). Emerging criteria for quality in qualitative research. *Qualitative Inquiry, 1,* 275–289.

Lincoln, Y. S., & Guba, E. G. (1985). *Naturalistic inquiry.* Beverly Hills, CA: Sage.

Lincoln, Y. S., & Guba, E. G. (2000). Paradigmatic controversies, contradictions, and emerging confluences. In N. K. Denzin & Y. S. Lincoln, *Handbook of qualitative research* (2nd ed., pp. 163–188). Thousand Oaks, CA: Sage.

Miles, M. B., & Huberman, A. M. (1984). *Qualitative data analysis: A sourcebook of new methods.* Thousand Oaks, CA: Sage.

Munhall, P. L., & Boyd, C. O. (1993). Qualitative research proposals and reports. In C. O. Boyd & P. L. Munhall (Eds.), *Nursing research: A qualitative perspective* (2nd ed., pp. 3–36). New York: National League for Nursing Press.

Rosenwald, G. C. (1992). Reflections on narrative self-understanding. In G. C. Rosenwald & R. L. Ochberg (Eds.), *Storied lives* (pp. 265–289). New Haven, CT: Yale University Press.

Rosenwald, G. C., & Ochberg, R. L. (Eds.). (1992). *Storied lives.* New Haven, CT: Yale University Press.

Sandelowski, M., Davis, D. H., & Harris, B. G. (1989). Artful design: Writing the proposal for research in the naturalist paradigm. *Research in Nursing & Health, 12,* 77–84.

Stacey, J. (1988). Can there be a feminist ethnography? *Womens' Studies International Forum, 11,* 21–27.

Strauss, A., & Corbin, J. (1994). Grounded theory ethodology: An overview. In N. K. Denzin & Y. S. Lincoln (Eds.), *Handbook of qualitative research* (pp. 273–285). Thousand Oaks, CA: Sage.

Van Manen, M. (1990). *Researching lived experience: Human science for an action-sensitive pedagogy.* New York: SUNY Press.

Woolcott, H. (1990). *Writing up qualitative data.* Newbury Park, CA: Sage.

# AUTHOR INDEX

*Numbers in italics refer to listings in reference sections.*

# SUBJECT INDEX

Harvard Project on Women's Psychology
and Girls' Development, 51
Higher education. *See also* Students, narrative research
compared to elementary education,
215–237
Holocaust survivors, listening to, 8,
101–111
fragility of communication, 110
Leon's story, 102–107, 111
lessons of, 107–111
Mala's story, 108
remembering names, 104
significance of story, 105–107
understanding atrocity, 105–107
Homelessness
interviewing the homeless, 82,
90–91
Homosexuality, 80, 82, 94, 249

Identity, 201
Inspiration
in painting, 26
Interpretation, 8, 70
casual hypothesis error, 147
Interpretation, teaching of, 8, 49–59,
113–131, 135–149, 200–202
clusters, 118–121
counter-evidence, 123–127
difficulty with rulebook for, 8, 114
life-historical, 143–144, 147
psychobiography and, 140–142
psychodynamic conflict, 121–123
reading for images, 116–118
as a separate course, 128
Interpretive poetics, 49, 52–53
Interview guides, 83–84, 86, 228
Hays's, 85
Martin's, 86
Interviewing, 8, 70, 247. *See also* Questions
coding of, 39–41, 91–94
connected, 38
ethnographic, 228, 243
intrusive questioning, 89, 90n
life stories and, 87–91
narrative research and, 8, 81
practice, 37–38
problems with, 90–91, 129
reading of, 51

student fears of, 88–89
summary of, 92
taking no notes during, 227–228
taperecoerding, 89, 90, 91–92, 94, 248
technique of Perry, 30
writing questions for, 83–87

*Jackroller* (Shaw), 128–129
James, Henry, 9
childhood of, 181–182
eating disorder of, 191–192, 193
grief over brother's death, 193, 194
nervous breakdown of, 190–192, 193
photo with William, 183–184
relationship with brother, 180–181,
182–184, 189, 191–192, 194
"third manner" writing style of, 186–
190, 193
James, William, 9, 144
character of, 182
critique of Henry's writing, 186–190
death of, 193
photo with Henry, 183–184
relationship with brother, 180–181,
182–184, 189, 191–192, 194
Juvenile delinquency
*Jackroller* story of, 128–129

Kafka, Franz, 9, 151
absurdity in his fiction, 156
father's grave, 161
isolations in his fiction, 158–159
pavlatche memory of, 156–157, 160
Kerouac, Jack, 9, 151, 161, 162
prototypical life scene, 160, 165–168
relationship with brother Gerard,
165–167
thrownness, 167
*Kiss, The* (Harrison), 163, 164
Knower(s). *See* Knowing
Knowing. *See also* Women's Way of
Knowing
collaborative connected, 42–45
connected, 7, 34–35, 38, 41, 42
constructed, 37, 46
procedural, 31, 37
received, 31, 37, 43
separate, 7, 34–35, 42
subjective, 37

# ABOUT THE EDITORS

**Ruthellen Josselson**, who is professor of psychology at the Hebrew University of Jerusalem and on the faculty of the Fielding Graduate Institute, has offered narrative research seminars at both institutions as well as at the Harvard Graduate School of Education. She has also presented workshops on this topic both nationally and internationally. Her research, presented in her books, has used narratives to investigate the dimensions of human relationships (*The Space Between Us*), women's identity development (*Revising Herself*), and the dynamics of friendship in girls and women (with Terri Apter, *Best Friends*). She received the 1994 Henry A. Murray Award from the American Psychological Association (APA). In addition, she is a practicing psychotherapist.

**Amia Lieblich** is a professor of psychology at the Hebrew University of Jerusalem. Her books have presented an oral history of the Israeli society and deal with war, military service, prisoners of war, and the kibbutz. Her psychobiography of Israeli female author Dvora Baron, *Conversations With Dvora*, was published by University of California Press in 1998. She also published, together with two of her students (Rivka Tuval-Mashiach and Tamar Zilber), *Narrative Research: Reading, Analysis, and Interpretation*, a book that presents her approach to narrative research. She has taught graduate courses on life stories and their use in research.

**Dan P. McAdams** is the Charles Deering McCormick Professor of Teaching Excellence, professor of human development and psychology, and director of the Foley Center for the Study of Lives at Northwestern University. A

Fellow of the APA and recipient of the 1989 Henry A. Murray Award, he has published widely on the topics of identity and the self, intimacy, generativity and adult development, and the role of narrative and life stories in personality and developmental psychology. He is author of *The Stories We Live By* and *The Person: An Integrated Introduction to Personality Psychology* and editor (with Ed de St. Aubin) of *Generativity and Adult Development: How and Why We Care for the Next Generation*.